Reading Places

Reading Places

Literacy, Democracy, and the
Public Library in Cold War America

Christine Pawley

University of Massachusetts Press

AMHERST AND BOSTON

LC 2010008807
ISBN 978-1-55849-822-8 (paper), 821-1 (cloth)

Designed by Sally Nichols
Set in Cochin
Printed and bound by Thomson-Shore, Inc.

Library of Congress Cataloging-in-Publication Data

Pawley, Christine, 1945–
Reading places : literacy, democracy, and the public library in Cold War America /
Christine Pawley.
p. cm.
Includes bibliographical references and index.
ISBN 978-1-55849-821-1 (library cloth : alk. paper) — ISBN 978-1-55849-822-8
(pbk. : alk. paper)
1. Door-Kewaunee Regional Library—History. 2. Public libraries—Wisconsin—
Door County—History—20th century. 3. Public libraries—Wisconsin—Kewaunee
County—History—20th century. 4. Rural libraries—Wisconsin—Door County—
History—20th century. 5. Rural libraries—Wisconsin—Kewaunee County—
History—20th century. 6. Books and reading—Wisconsin—Door County—
History—20th century. 7. Books and reading—Wisconsin—Kewaunee
County—History—20th century. 8. Libraries and community—United States—
Case studies. I. Title.
Z733.D66P39 2010
027.4775'62—dc22
2010008807

British Library Cataloguing in Publication data are available.

For Jim, my partner on many journeys.

Contents

Acknowledgments

❖

This research was supported by a number of institutions. I am very grateful to the University of Iowa for two Old Gold Fellowships and an Arts and Humanities Initiative award; to the Wisconsin Historical Society for an Amy Louise Hunter Fellowship; and to St. Catherine University, St. Paul, Minnesota, for an Abigail Quigley McCarthy Center for Women's Studies Award for Research and Creative Work, and a Faculty Research and Scholarship Award.

Some material has already appeared in print, and I thank the publishers for agreeing to my incorporating it into this larger work. Parts of Chapters 1 and 9 appeared in "Beyond Market Models and Resistance: Organizations as a Middle Layer in the History of Reading," *The Library Quarterly* 79, no. 1 (2009): 73–93, and part of Chapter 3 in "Advocate for Access: Lutie Stearns and the Traveling Libraries of the Wisconsin Free Library Commission, 1895–1914," *Libraries and Culture* 35, no. 3 (2000): 434–58. Parts of Chapters 5 and 6 appeared in "A 'Bouncing Babe,' a 'Little Bastard': Women, Print, and the Door-Kewaunee Regional Library, 1950–1952," in *Women in Print: Essays on the Print Culture of American Women from the Nineteenth and Twentieth Centuries*, edited by James P. Danky and Wayne A. Wiegand (Madison: University of Wisconsin Press, 2006). Part of Chapter 8 appeared in "Blood and Thunder on the Bookmobile: American Public Libraries and the Construction of 'the Reader,'" in *Institutions of Reading: The Social Life of Libraries in the United States*, edited by Thomas Augst and Kenneth Carpenter (Amherst: University of Massachusetts Press, 2007), and parts of Chapters 1 and 8 in "Reading *versus* the Red Bull: Cultural Constructions of Democracy and the Public Library in Cold War Wisconsin," *American Studies* 42 no. 3 (2001): 87–103 and "The Wisconsin Idea in Action: Reading, Resistance, and the Door-Kewaunee Regional Library, 1950–52," *The Wisconsin Magazine of History* 91, no. 4 (Summer 2008): 29–39.

Thanks also go to audiences who listened to presentations and offered valuable comments and suggestions at meetings of the Mid-America American Studies Association (MAASA) in Omaha (Nebraska), 1999, Madison (Wisconsin), 2001, St. Louis (Missouri), 2002, and Iowa City (Iowa), 2003; at meetings of the Society for the History of Authorship, Reading, and Publishing (SHARP) in Vancouver, (B. C., Canada), 1998, Mainz (Germany) 2000, Williamsburg (Virginia), 2001, and Claremont (California), 2003; and at New Scholarship in Book History and Print Culture: An Interdisciplinary Conference, University of Toronto, 2002, and the Modern Languages Association, New York, 2002.

Many people have helped to produce this book. I owe especial thanks to the many residents of Door and Kewaunee counties who shared their memories with me, including Al, Anita, Bob, Clarice, Delores, Doris, Dorothy, Eileen, Emily, Gayle, Gerry, Hazel, Janice, Kathy, Lucille, Marlene, Ruth, Shirley, and Sylvia, as well as Virginia Johnson of the Kewaunee County Historical Society, Robert Miller, and Lee Traven. The assistance of local librarians was invaluable, and I particularly thank library directors (some now retired) Rebecca N. Berger, Marcia Carr, Barb Gigot, Susan Grosshuesch, Kaye Maher, and Ann Schmitz, as well as the staffs of the public libraries of Algoma, Bailey's Harbor, Forestville, Kewaunee, Sturgeon Bay, and Washington Island, especially Laura Kayacan, Alyce Sutter, Linda Vogel, and Kathy White. Special thanks are due to Rebecca Berger for permission to use the cover photograph. The person I owe most to, Jane Livingston Greene, died in 2004. I very much regret that I did not finish this project in time for her to see its completion. Without Jane's generous and forthright sharing of her recollections and insights it would not have been possible.

Several people took precious time from their own work to read and comment on earlier versions of the book: Rima Apple, Jane Greer, Cheryl Malone, Erin A. Smith, and Wayne Wiegand. I thank all of them, as well as Thomas Augst and an anonymous reviewer for their invaluable suggestions. It was Wayne Wiegand who pointed out the existence of the Door-Kewaunee Regional Library circulation records. Andrew Wertheimer and Sarah Roberts helped unearth resources at the Wisconsin Historical Society. Particular thanks go to the staff of the Archives Reference Room there, and to students who worked on the database and interview transcriptions, including Stephanie Gowler, Amber Johnson, Heather Stecklein, and Christy Vos. I'm very grateful to Martyn Lyons, who shared techniques for interviewing readers and passed on many helpful tips. Many thanks, too, to Bruce Wilcox, Carol Betsch, and Sally Nichols of the Press and copy editor Kay Scheuer for their expertise and professionalism throughout the publication process, and to Laura Moss Gottlieb for her expert index.

Jim Pawley and Hilary Elliott joined me on some of my research trips. As always, they and other members of my family, Alice, Emily, John, Roger, and Steve, have offered support, encouragement, and advice that encouraged me to persist throughout the more than ten years that it took to complete this book.

Abbreviations

ALA	American Library Association
CPL	Chicago Public Library
DCLA	Door County Library Archives
D-K	Door-Kewaunee
IWA	Iowa Women's Archives
LSA	Library Services Act
LSCA	Library Services and Construction Act
LSTA	Library Services and Technology Act
PLDM	Public Library of Des Moines
PLI	Public Library Inquiry
UWA	University of Wisconsin Archives
WFLC	Wisconsin Free Library Commission
WHS	Wisconsin Historical Society
WLA	Wisconsin Library Association

Reading Places

❖

1
Literacy: Debates and Dangers

It seems to me that education (including librarianship) must
either take a vital part in everyday life, or be dropped overboard
by life as it progresses.

John Chancellor, "Education for Democracy"

The basis of Communism and socialistic influence is education
of the people.

Congressman Harold Velde (R., Illinois, 1950)

One evening in early November 1952, Jane Livingston, director of the
Door-Kewaunee Regional Library, and assistant Andy Kroeger drove
the county bookmobile south from Sturgeon Bay to a meeting at a tav-
ern with some furious inhabitants of the township of Montpelier in
Wisconsin's Kewaunee County. "There were people down there having a royal fit," Livingston later recalled in an interview, "because a
library book had some pretty frank language—an adult book."[1] In
Montpelier, anxieties about reading "bad books" was a symptom of a
more general community opposition to an experiment in providing
public library services in rural Door and Kewaunee Counties. The two
library staff members realized that they were about to encounter some
tough questioning. They little knew, however, that some people in
Montpelier were planning to confront them in more a direct and unambiguous manner.

In the tense atmosphere of the Cold War, complaints about the subversive or immoral nature of some library books were not unusual, but

---

1 Interview with Jane Livingston, 23 October 2000. Interviews with former librarians, teachers, school students, and other past and present members of the Door and Kewaunee County
communities took place between 2000 and 2002. To protect interviewees' privacy, most are
referred to only by first name.

these Montpelier residents were opposed not only to the specific book in question. They also wanted to register their displeasure with the library's very existence. Livingston and Kroeger had convened the town meeting in the hope of carrying out a discussion about the challenged book, but when they arrived, they found the Montpelier residents already primed with other kinds of ammunition. "They tried nailing me to the wall with complaints and criticisms and everything else," Livingston later remembered. Help came from an unexpected quarter. "The Lutheran pastor was there, and he stood up for me," she recalled, still astonished in retrospect, since some local clergy had spoken out against the library project. But even he failed to persuade the crowd, and when the library staff members finally came to leave, they discovered a new problem: the bookmobile failed to start. "It was a matter of spark plugs or something, not permanent damage," Livingston said. "Well, I have not had very kindly feelings about the township of Montpelier." Fortunately, Kroeger's mechanical skill saved the day, and they reached home safely that night. "Andy, dear Andy, figured out just what might have happened to the bookmobile."

Why was the Regional Library such a contentious issue, and what led this group of citizens to express such anger against it that some were prepared to sabotage the bookmobile? *Reading Places* tells the story of this mid-twentieth century experiment that policy-makers around the country carefully watched. Understanding the region's responses, which included both eager support and fierce opposition, involves investigating the contemporary print culture of the area and its history as well as the history of the experiment itself. In part, opposition to the library rested on long-standing antagonisms arising from class, gender, and ethnic differences that contributed to a suspicion of official projects to expand education. Such differences had their roots in a history of tension between different groups of nineteenth-century migrants who created Wisconsin as a site of cultural contest. On the one hand were Yankees (white Americans born in the states of New England and the Mid-Atlantic), who brought with them beliefs about civilization that underpinned efforts at social and educational reform. On the other hand were more recent European immigrants, at least some of whom resented paying taxes for such initiatives as public schools and libraries since they felt that they derived little benefit from them. Descendants of these migrants had inherited these various beliefs, and now reproduced them in the mid-twentieth century context of the Door-Kewaunee Regional Library. Library opponents also drew inspiration from contemporary Cold War rhetoric that rejected such social programs as at best ineffective against the threat of Communism and at worst helping to bolster it.

Support, on the other hand, rested on a vision of print and reading as essential to the exercise of democracy, as well as a desire to widen educational opportunities for local children, especially those growing up on hardscrabble farms where books and magazines were rare. Fluency in reading and writing was essential for successful participation in modern economic, social, and political institutions, library proponents believed. Indeed, for most Americans, print infused daily existence. From the mid-nineteenth century on, free schools and libraries played a crucial part in teaching Americans the skills and habits of reading and writing. Nineteenth-century print culture included not only nationally produced and distributed fiction, but also newspapers and gendered magazines that depended on the advertising of national brands. Such publications emphasized reason, method, professionalism, and the superiority of white middle-class taste. Commercial and noncommercial institutions adopted new managerial techniques associated with bureaucratization and standardization that built heavy use of print technology into their business and administrative practices. Print materials produced by secular organizations adopted the language of efficiency and effectiveness—managerial discourse that stressed the possibility of progress, and encouraged standardized practices at home and at work. By the end of the nineteenth century, officially sanctioned print was playing a central part in the lives, whether at work, school, church, or in the home, not just of educated elites, but also of millions of ordinary Americans—those who lived unremarkable lives in relative anonymity. In many organizational contexts, reading helped promote a forward-looking attitude that gradually accepted as normal the rationalization associated with industrialization.

Access to national print culture varied by region, though. Literacy had been a subject of public policy in America since Colonial times, but in the first half of the twentieth century it was a matter of particular governmental concern, especially in rural areas. In 1938, library researcher Louis Round Wilson published *The Geography of Reading*, a comprehensive overview of library services across the United States that highlighted regional disparities. Southern states made an especially dismal showing. The proportion of the population with library service in Arkansas was only 15 percent, and in Georgia 29 percent. At the bottom of the list was West Virginia, with 12 percent. For African Americans the situation was even worse. In twelve southern states, Wilson reported, just over 10 percent of the black population received library service from a total of only forty-five public libraries.[2] At the other end of the scale, northeastern states and California led the country with over 90 percent of their populations enjoying access to libraries (Delaware and Massachusetts actually scored 100 percent). In general, city dwellers enjoyed better public libraries than those living in the country.

As a group, the still heavily rural midwestern states lagged behind the northeast. According to Wilson, Wisconsin ranked seventeenth (along with Oregon), achieving a 70 percent access rate. Ten years later, little progress had been made. By the late 1940s, a quarter of Wisconsin's population still lacked access to free libraries, and rural literacy rates were especially low. Since 1896, the Wisconsin Free Library Commission (WFLC; the state agency charged with promoting public libraries) had helped Wisconsin cities and villages establish local libraries. The agency had also circulated "traveling libraries"— boxes of books—to rural areas.[3] But in the 1940s, many of Wisconsin's libraries, like those in other rural parts of the United States, were underfunded and provided only mediocre service. A 1948 American Library Association report complained that while some public libraries had excellent resources and provided services to match, many more were small and ineffective. Book collections tended to be outdated, and most library staff lacked a college education. Although combining small libraries into larger county or regional systems was an effective means of improvement, in 1946 fewer than one-third of the counties

---

2 North Dakota also ranked poorly, coming in at forty-sixth place, with 19 percent. See Louis R. Wilson, *The Geography of Reading: A Study of the Distribution and Status of Libraries in the United States* (Chicago: American Library Association and the University of Chicago Press, 1938), 12–13, 32–34.

3 Christine Pawley, "Advocate for Access: Lutie Stearns and the Traveling Libraries of the Wisconsin Free Library Commission, 1895–1914," *Libraries and Culture* 35, no. 3 (2000): 434–58.

in the United States had taken this step. None of these was in Wisconsin.[4]

Drawing on an American tradition that linked the health of the republic with the participation of informed citizens, the WFLC argued that public libraries were an essential vehicle for strengthening democratic values and promoting the exercise of citizenship through the spread of information. To draw rural citizens into the democratic process, in the late 1940s the WFLC planned a "demonstration" of ideal library service in a rural area. Library supporters hoped that once rural residents actually experienced the very best public library service possible, they would be willing to support this level of service on a permanent basis, through local taxes. The plan was to establish a regional library that would provide a much wider range of services and recent materials than any single village or town library could provide on its own. A key element would be bookmobile service that would reach even the most remote country districts. Funding would be shared between the state and the selected region. The WLFC publicized the projected Regional Library Demonstration widely across the state, and was rewarded when a number of districts stepped forward as candidates. In selecting the area for the demonstration, the WFLC used several criteria. Most important, local librarians and citizens must be enthusiastic, and the majority of municipalities in the region must agree to take part. The area should be lacking in good library service, but it should not be so poor that it would be difficult to avoid failure.[5] After all, the whole point of the exercise was to encourage other districts to fund their own library systems, as well as to show legislators that their commitment of state funds was justified. For the demonstration to have a widespread effect, the WFLC needed to be able to point to success.

After reviewing the contenders, the WFLC announced its selection of the adjoining counties of Door and Kewaunee that together form the Door Peninsula, the "thumb" of Wisconsin that juts out into Lake

---

4 Carleton B. Joeckel and Amy Winslow, *A National Plan for Public Library Service* (Chicago: American Library Association, 1948), 19–30. A handful of small "county" libraries existed in Wisconsin prior to 1950 mainly to provide service to schools. See *The Idea in Action: A Report on the Door-Kewaunee Regional Library Demonstration, 1950–1952* (Madison: Wisconsin Free Library Commission, 1953), 6.

5 Anne Farrington, "Wisconsin's First Regional Library." *Minnesota Libraries* 16, no. 7 (1950): 201.

Michigan. With its sandy beaches, cherry orchards, and picturesque villages, the Door Peninsula is known today mainly as a tourist destination easily accessible by fast highways, but in the postwar period it was still a country backwater. Viewed from Wisconsin's state capital of Madison, it must have seemed remote and even cut off. In fact, as WFLC Secretary Walter S. Botsford confessed privately, the Commission had little choice in its selection, since most of the competing districts encountered difficulty in raising the necessary matching funds. "The only area that has appropriated money for the demonstration includes Door and Kewaunee counties," he confided to a commission board member early in 1949. "Fortunately for us, the area qualifies in every respect for the demonstration. It is predominantly rural, has a bit more than the average per capita valuation, and, most important, it is practically 'virgin territory' insofar as library service is concerned."[6]

The other part of the plan, securing state support, was not an easy task at a time when libraries and librarians were under political attack. Against a backdrop of a steadily worsening international situation as the Cold War took shape in Europe and a "hot" war threatened the Korean Peninsula, many saw Communism rather than lack of access to books and information as the principal threat to democracy. Wisconsin stepped into the national limelight when in February 1950, the state's junior senator, Joseph McCarthy, accused the State Department of harboring Communists. Other Republicans pinpointed mobile library service as exposing rural people to moral and political danger. Argued Illinois Congressman Harold Velde in March 1950, "Educating Americans through the means of the library service could bring about a change of their political attitude quicker than any other method. The basis of Communism and socialistic influence is education of the people."[7] In Wisconsin as elsewhere, calls for controversial books to be removed from library shelves multiplied, especially in small towns, and librarians as well as WFLC officials felt themselves under pressure to comply.

Despite the unfavorable political climate, in September 1949 library officials and supporters were rewarded, when, overriding Republican

---

6 Walter Botsford to William J. Deegan, 29 February 1949. WHS Series 1967/205.

7 Congressional Record—House (81st Congress, 2nd session) 6, no. 3 (9 March 1950): 3129.

Governor Oscar Rennebohm's veto, the Wisconsin Legislature passed a law that allowed the WFLC to "establish a single demonstration . . . in a limited, predominantly rural area . . . now lacking an efficient coverage by existing library systems."[8] The project's purpose was to demonstrate the library's value as "an important educational and informational asset . . . [and] to prove and perfect more efficient and economical procedures."[9] For the first time in its history, the state of Wisconsin agreed to provide funds in direct support of community library service, as long as the communities involved matched the state funds. Otherwise, the law only set out the general guidelines for the project. The details were left to the WFLC to work out in conjunction with the areas to be selected. The plan provided for six (later seven) existing library "units" (permanent library buildings), plus two new bookmobiles, each capable of carrying at least a thousand volumes. Recognizing that past studies had shown that children and women tended to be the most frequent users of public libraries, the WFLC hoped that by providing a wide range of reading materials, the Demonstration would attract more men to the library.[10] "We're on our way," the WFLC told Wisconsin's librarians triumphantly in December 1949. "Door and Kewaunee counties make a particularly homogenous combination because of the similarity of educational and nationality backgrounds of the people and comparative valuation of the two counties."[11]

The Demonstration began in 1950, and for the following three years residents of Door and Kewaunee counties experienced a vastly improved library system. Local libraries not only cooperated in selecting, purchasing, and cataloging materials, but also provided public services—including reference, readers' advisory, and children's storytelling—that urban residents might take for granted, but which rural residents rarely, if ever, enjoyed. The regular bookmobile service also offered a range of choice in reading materials that the region's farm families had never previously encountered. Overall, library circula-

---

8 *The Idea in Action*, 16.

9 Walter S. Botsford, "From the Commission," *Wisconsin Library Bulletin* 47, no. 2 (1951): 39.

10 For a comparison of contemporary studies that described library users' demographic characteristics, see Bernard Berelson, *The Library's Public* (New York: Columbia University Press, 1949), 19–50.

11 "We're on Our Way," *Wisconsin Library Bulletin* 4, no. 12 (December 1949): 1.

tion figures soared to two-and-a-half times their previous level. Over 90 percent of grade-school children in the rural schools made use of the bookmobile service, and their reading scores improved beyond expectation.[12]

For teachers and students alike, regular bookmobile visits transformed rural classroom reading opportunities. Staffed by a librarian and a driver, each van carried hundreds of books, arranged by age and subject level. Whether at school or a crossroads near their homes, children eagerly anticipated the bookmobile's arrival. On bookmobile days, "it was like a party," recalled Lucille K., a former teacher. Expert observers also remarked on the children's enthusiastic responses. "To an outsider it seems miraculous that more than nine out of ten farm children of school age within range of the big bookmobiles rolling across Door and Kewaunee counties are regular borrowers," wrote one visitor. "But to some of us who have gone over the route and have seen the youngsters swarm down on the bus when it stops, fill it to bulging, capture the attendants with shrill questions and chatter, and then squeeze through the check-out station and drift home thumbing pages and looking at pictures as they go, it is more believable."[13]

To library officials and others who supported the experiment, the Regional Library proved itself a resounding success. Yet despite what seemed to them like overwhelmingly positive evidence, when at the end of the three-year trial period, voters were asked to pass a referendum authorizing the project's continuation, Door County voted in favor, but Kewaunee County turned it down. Parents complained, teachers protested, and schoolchildren wept, but their entreaties failed to move the local board of county supervisors on whose shoulders the final decision rested. Although the Door County bookmobile rolled on for another forty years, the Kewaunee County bookmobile service came to an abrupt halt.

During its short life, the Regional Library attracted many supporters, but also the opposition of residents whose personal reasons ranged from fear of the influence of "bad" literature to resentment at the prospect of government interference. Some formed themselves into a pow-

---

12   *The Idea in Action*, 33, 5.
13   Baker Brownell, "Foreword," in *The Idea in Action*, 5.

erful and organized group in Kewaunee County who from the beginning of the project mounted a consistent and effective challenge to the
library. The bookmobile itself came to represent the entire library project, while incorporating different meanings for different groups of residents. If to some it stood for an increase in welcome resources for
expanded education, information, and entertainment, to others it exemplified a waste of precious tax dollars and the intrusion of a dangerous
new technology. Librarians and state officials, too, held divergent goals
for the project. Politicians, university professors, and WFLC members
based in the state capital of Madison anticipated that the project would
help stimulate the democratic participation of citizens in community
affairs, but local librarians saw the main benefit as encouraging in rural
children the habits of lifelong reading.

Geography Matters

The story of Wisconsin's Door-Kewaunee Regional Library reveals
details of how, in the middle of the twentieth century, local cultures of
reading and politics interacted with formal institutions through the
implementation of an official literacy policy. Through the use of rare
institutional records, the project's history sheds light on the choices of
ordinary individual readers, whose reading practices can be hard to
recover. *Reading Places* brings insights from the history of print culture to
tell the story of this policy initiative through the eyes of the groups intimately involved in it and pulls together three levels of analysis—societal,
individual, and institutional. The societal-level analysis is informed by
structural dimensions of gender, class, and ethnicity, as well as broad
themes that include concepts of citizenship, postwar economic adjustment, anticommunism, fears of the effects of mass communication and of
consumerism, changing gender expectations, and anxieties about rural
life. Individuals make appearances through such sources of evidence as
interviews, newspapers, and several thousand library records that
miraculously survived in unprocessed boxes at the Wisconsin Historical
Society (WHS). It is at the institutional level, however, that we can most
clearly discern the exercise of individual agency, as well as the constrain-
ing effects of social structure. Prominent in the story were participants

in the state's political structures (including state legislators and county supervisors, the Wisconsin Free Library Commission, and electors themselves) and in the public libraries and rural schools. However, members of many other organizations also played a part, including the county extension agencies, the County Normal School, women's and homemakers' clubs, and professional organizations such as the Wisconsin Library Association. Through their participation in these institutions, politicians, WFLC officials, librarians, and teachers encountered the rural farmers, homemakers, and school students who were the main targets of the state's efforts to improve literacy, as they struggled to interpret and implement the enabling legislation.

An important step to recovering the reading history of less well documented readers such as those living in rural areas like the postwar Door Peninsula is to recognize that literacy practices of the past were tightly interwoven with everyday community routines and experiences. From the Great Books projects of the mid-twentieth century to present-day One Book, One City projects that consciously promote reading within geographic communities, many policy initiatives have tried to build on the interconnectedness of reading and locality. Print culture historians recognize the social nature of reading that renders place significant. Elizabeth Long refers to the social infrastructure of reading, while Roger Chartier reminds us that the practice of reading takes place as a "specific act and habit, and in specific places." One of our tasks as historians, Chartier says, is to "identify the . . . distinctive traits of communities of readers, reading traditions and ways of reading."[14] Ronald J. Zboray and Mary Saracino Zboray describe what they call "socioliterary experience" in antebellum New England as unfolding in "often dense networks of kin, friends, and neighbors, deeply imbuing it with social relations and implicating it in them." James A. Secord calls attention to the importance of the geography of reading and comments that "the history of reading can best begin as local history."[15]

14 Elizabeth Long, "Textual Interpretation as Collective Action," in *The Ethnography of Reading*, ed. Jonathan Boyarin (Berkeley: University of California Press, 1993), 190–92; Guglielmo Cavallo and Roger Chartier, "Introduction," in *A History of Reading in the West*, ed. Cavallo and Chartier (Amherst: University of Massachusetts Press, 1999), 2.

15 Ronald J. Zboray and Mary Saracino Zboray, *Everyday Ideas: Socioliterary Experience among Antebellum New Englanders* (Knoxville: University of Tennessee Press, 2006), xviii; James A.

Indeed, stories of localities may be easier to recover than the stories of individual readers who lived in them. In the spatially dispersed, virtual world in which most middle-class professionals now live, it is easy to forget how relevant and all-embracing face-to-face communities were for many Americans in the relatively recent past, and in many areas still are, even today. Perhaps because it was print technology and capitalism that facilitated the development of imagined communities, print culture historians have tended to focus on dispersed communities of readers, rather than localized geographical communities.[16] Some have used relatively amorphous, large-scale categories, like Jonathan Rose's study of the British working class, a work that encompasses three countries and two centuries.[17] Rose comments that the experiences of "common" or "ordinary" readers, are especially "hard to find" since records that enable the historian to "enter the mind" of such readers are themselves hard to find.[18] Rose's general prescription for an empirically grounded history of audiences that seeks to analyze the experiences of real readers is to "ask the reader," and in *The Intellectual Life of the British Working Classes* he draws on a bibliography of nearly two thousand published and unpublished working-class autobiographies to explore the reading choices of individuals often hitherto considered unreachable, as well as some of their most popular texts and the group settings in which they read. Still, Rose's readers are by definition not the anonymous individuals whose experiences are most elusive.

Others, like Anne Ruggles Gere, Elizabeth Long, and Elizabeth McHenry have studied clubs, book groups, and literary societies as

---

Secord, *Victorian Sensation: The Extraordinary Publication, Reception, and Secret Authorship of* Vestiges of the Natural History of Creation (Chicago: University of Chicago Press, 2001), 157.

16 Benedict Anderson, *Imagined Communities: Reflections on the Origin and Spread of Nationalism* (London: Verso, 1991); Trish Loughran argues, however, that local print culture practices of the early Republic were more important than historians have sometimes depicted. See *The Republic in Print: Print Culture in the Age of U.S. Nation Building, 1770–1870* (New York: Columbia University Press, 2007).

17 Jonathan Rose, *The Intellectual Life of the British Working Classes* (New Haven: Yale University Press, 2001).

18 Jonathan Rose, "How Historians Study Reader Response: or, What Did Jo Think of Bleak House?" in *Literature in the Market-Place: Nineteenth-Century British Publishing and Reading Practices,* ed. John O. Jordan and Robert L. Patten (Cambridge: Cambridge University Press, 1995), 195. "Common readers" is Richard Altick's term (Richard D. Altick, *The English Common Reader: A Social History of the Mass Reading Public, 1800–1900* [Chicago: University of Chicago Press, 1957]).

reading communities, but have generally not contextualized these small-scale groups as part of a specifically geographical context.[19] Deborah Brandt's study of contemporary American literacy practices relies on interviews with eighty south-central Wisconsin residents, and yet avoids exploiting this common setting, preferring to characterize the participants in her study as representative of America as a whole in terms of their incomes, ethnicities, education, religion, occupation, and experience.[20] The ethnographic turn in book history emphasizes using a variety of sources and methods to build up a thick, multi-layered description of local communities that include not only individual readers and writers, but also the institutions that sponsored these literacy practices.[21] Among the sponsors of literacy, Brandt includes schools, libraries, churches, and the military, as well as commercially provided mass media sources that included radio and television, fan clubs, magazines, and newspapers. Yet the otherwise useful term "sponsorship," with its clear top-down implications, may fail to recognize the ways in which geographically specific institutions of reading and writing were, and are, deeply intertwined in the lives of their participants, reinforcing or resisting each other's effects, and sometimes blurring the implied lines between those who sponsor and those who are sponsored.

As other works have shown, people's experiences of reading and writing often overlapped across a variety of dimensions, and the face-to-face local settings in which they lived their daily lives shaped their literacies in significant ways. Studies that are firmly grounded in localities include William Gilmore's study of literacy in the Upper Connecticut Valley of Vermont in the early nineteenth century, Harvey Graff's research into literacy in nineteenth-century Ontario, Canada, David Henkin's study of reading in the public spaces of antebellum New York, Charlotte Hogg on the work of older women as sponsors of lit-

---

19 Anne Ruggles Gere, *Intimate Practices: Literacy and Cultural Work in U.S. Women's Clubs, 1880–1920* (Urbana: University of Illinois Press, 1997); Elizabeth Long, *Book Clubs: Women and the Uses of Reading in Everyday Life* (Chicago: University of Chicago Press, 2003); Elizabeth McHenry, *Forgotten Readers: Recovering the Lost History of African American Literary Societies* (Durham, N.C.: Duke University Press, 2002).

20 Deborah Brandt, *Literacy in American Lives* (Cambridge: Cambridge University Press, 2001), 15.

21 According to Brandt, "Sponsors . . . are any agents, local or distant, concrete or abstract, who enable, support, teach, and model, as well as recruit, regulate, suppress, or withhold, literacy—and gain advantage in some way" (*ibid.*, 19).

eracy in the tiny community of Paxton, Nebraska, David Paul Nord's work on "communities of journalism," and my own research into the print culture of a late nineteenth-century town, Osage, Iowa.[22] A thorough investigation of the social and cultural circumstances of the lives of readers and writers living in a particular geographical community carries insights into print culture that have a special value. "Life circumstances, material and cultural, helped to direct people's interests, experience, and public engagement in complicated ways," wrote Gilmore. His book, he went on, was a "history of infrastructure, a term which we will understand broadly as containing both cultural and material factors."[23] Gilmore's study of eleven townships in Windsor County, Vermont, included a range of general community dimensions, including family structure, rhythms of work, and the distribution of wealth and property, as well as print culture–related factors like the extent of family libraries, in understanding the print culture of this geographical region. Moving forward in time, Charlotte Hogg's study of contemporary Paxton illuminates the ways in which older women bring a stability and richness to their community life that depends on the cultural work of telling stories, maintaining memories, and enhancing the literacy opportunities of its members. The scenes of Paxton life that Hogg describes are instantly recognizable to anyone familiar with small-town America, particularly across the broad swath of the Midwest.

Institutions—a form of organized sociability—constituted the building blocks of the towns and villages that American settlers (mostly white and of European origin) established in the heartland during the nineteenth century. Some were commercial, like banks and insurance companies, while others were cultural and cooperative, like churches, schools, and public libraries. All made use of print, a technology that

---

22 William Gilmore, *Reading Becomes a Necessity of Life: Material and Cultural Life in Rural New England, 1780–1835* (Knoxville: University of Tennessee Press, 1989); Harvey Graff, *The Literacy Myth: Literacy and Social Structure in the Nineteenth Century City* (New York: Academic Press, 1979); David M. Henkin, *City Reading: Written Words and Public Spaces in Antebellum New York* (New York: Columbia University Press, 1998); Charlotte Hogg, *From the Garden Club: Rural Women Writing Community* (Lincoln: University of Nebraska Press, 2006); David Paul Nord, *Communities of Journalism: A History of American Newspapers and Their Readers* (Urbana: University of Illinois Press, 2001); Christine Pawley, *Reading on the Middle Border: The Culture of Print in Late Nineteenth-Century Osage, Iowa* (Amherst: University of Massachusetts Press, 2001).

23 Gilmore, *Reading Becomes a Necessity of Life*, 7.

settlers employed to establish their communities as permanent features of the landscape, and that depended on other technologies like the railroads (and later the highways), to knit communities together in increasingly interdependent relationships. Along with the common school, the public library took on the role of literacy sponsor. Out of a social library movement through which readers banded together to share books on a subscription basis emerged the earliest tax-supported libraries, beginning in New Hampshire in 1849. Gradually the idea of tax-supported free public libraries spread west and south with the migration of Yankee ideas of what constituted a successfully settled community.[24]

As the century progressed and the commercial production of books skyrocketed, librarians debated about what they should include in their collections. All agreed that libraries should only offer "wholesome" reading, but what exactly fell into that category? Novels and stories—"fiction"—came under particular scrutiny among members of the expanding occupation of librarianship.[25] Professional literature of the late nineteenth century expressed opinions on all sides of the fiction debate, ranging from recommending an outright ban on novels to grudging and qualified acceptance. When in 1879, the American Library Association adopted the motto "The best reading for the largest number at the least cost," librarians entertained little doubt about what the "best" reading consisted of. Reading for pleasure, they felt, should take second place to reading for "self culture." Nonfiction was preferable to fiction, and in the latter category a hierarchy privileged "classics" over "trash" and the writings of male writers like Walter Scott, Charles Dickens, Nathaniel Hawthorne, and Herman Melville over the writings of women writers like E.D.E.N. Southworth and even the Brontë sisters. However, librarians found access to fiction easier to demonize than to curb. Contrary to their recommendations, library patrons persistently expressed an overwhelming desire for novels, and by the middle of the twentieth century many librarians were acquiescing at the notion that reading "harmless" fiction could at least

24 Jesse Shera, *Foundations of the Public Library: The Origins of the Public Library Movement in New England, 1629–1855* (Chicago: University of Chicago Press, 1949).

25 Esther Jane Carrier, *Fiction in Public Libraries, 1876–1900* (New York: Scarecrow Press, 1965).

encourage the habit of reading, hoping that patrons' taste would naturally progress, with encouragement, to literature of a more elevated
quality.

By the beginning of the twentieth century the inhabitants of many
states were investing in public libraries on a large scale. Donations
from philanthropists, particularly Andrew Carnegie, provided one
impetus, and the founding of state library commissions another. In the
meantime, librarians had formed themselves into an organized profession through the activities of American Library Association (ALA),
founded in 1876. The Midwest was gaining new significance in these
processes. Midwestern states were the chief beneficiaries of Carnegie's
donations, and in the first decade of the twentieth century the heartland's new state library commissions were beginning to flex their mus-
cles within the profession. The rapid development of the public library
movement at the turn of the century was shifting the balance of influence in the ALA toward the Midwest, and librarians from Wisconsin
were among those agitating for a reorientation of the organization's
attention away from centralized library services in large cities and
toward the many small public libraries springing up all over rural
America. In 1909 the ALA transferred its headquarters from Boston to
Chicago in a move that was symbolic as well as practical.

The Institutional Middle Layer

Using often overlooked primary sources, including institutional
records, analysis of circulation data, and interviews with about twenty-
five local residents, this book sets Wisconsin's experiment in social
policy within a history of reading and of libraries that stresses the
importance of a middle layer of analysis—organizational context—in
making the link between individual library users and the wider social
and cultural conditions within which they lived, read, and sought information. This middle layer is one that print culture historians have
tended to overlook. Classical economic—or "market"—models in the
history of reading that separate the structural functions of textual production and consumption (the best articulated and most influential is
Robert Darnton's "communications circuit") tend to depict readers as

at the final, receiving stage of a production process, only tenuously connected to the writers at the beginning.[26] Thus they set up a dichotomy between authoritative print producers (writers and publishers) and relatively passive consumers (readers). By contrast, other scholars, anxious to emphasize readerly agency, focus on reading "resistance," sometimes employing a poaching metaphor, especially for "ordinary" readers of popular materials, who may have left no personal record of their encounters with texts.[27] However, I suggest that since the first focuses primarily on structural factors in the commercial circulation of books, and the second primarily looks at individual readers, neither can make a theoretical link between structural accounts involving, say, gender, race, and class, and the agency of individual readers. Both also marginalize or even ignore the many noncommercial sites — including libraries — in which nineteenth- and twentieth-century readers encountered texts.

Situating institutions of print as a middle layer of analysis can bridge the gap between structure and agency and between societal (or "macro") and individual or ("micro") levels of analysis. These sites (noncommercial as well as commercial) are spaces where activities of reading and writing may intersect, since they provide opportunities for individuals to both produce and consume texts. By adopting an institutional view, researchers can also incorporate thick description in a way that adds richness and nuance to their understanding of the acts of reading and writing by those non-elite groups for whom individual records are scant. Clifford Geertz originally appropriated the idea of thick description from the philosopher Gilbert Ryle, who likened it to

---

26 Robert Darnton, "What Is the History of Books?" in *Reading in America: Literature and Social History*, ed. Cathy N. Davidson (Baltimore: Johns Hopkins University Press, 1989), 31. See also Christine Pawley, "Beyond Market Models and Resistance: Organizations as a Middle Layer in the History of Reading," *Library Quarterly* 79, no. 1 (2009): 73–93.

27 Highly influential is Michel de Certeau, *The Practice of Everyday Life* (Berkeley: University of California Press, 1984). See especially pages xxi and 174. For examples of works on the history of books and reading that make use of de Certeau's poaching metaphor, see the following: S. Elizabeth Bird. *For Enquiring Minds: A Cultural Study of Supermarket Tabloids (Knoxville: University of Tennessee Press, 1992)*; Priya Joshi "Culture and Consumption: Fiction, the Reading Public, and the British Novel in Colonial India," *Book History* 1 (1998); Martyn Lyons, *Readers and Society in Nineteenth-Century France: Workers, Women, Peasants* (Houndmills, UK: Palgrave, 2001). Writers on popular culture include John Fiske, *Understanding Popular Culture* (London: Routledge, 1989), and Henry Jenkin, *Textual Poachers: Television Fans and Participatory Culture* (New York: Routledge, 1992).

"a many-layered sandwich."[28] What Ryle thought of as layers in a sandwich, Geertz called the "sort of piled-up structures of inference and implication through which an ethnographer is continually trying to pick his way."

The public library is an institution that can shed light on what "ordinary" Americans read by exposing these layers to view. Although more common in certain parts of the country than in others, and more frequently used by some categories of readers than others, public libraries can be found in all fifty states. Since they are public institutions, their records are in principle openly available to researchers. Given how widespread public libraries are and their central place in the lives of many Americans, reading researchers might expect public library records to be thoroughly analyzed not only by print culture historians, but by historians of American social life in general. And indeed in recent years, print culture scholars have begun to exploit libraries as a rich and widely available source of data. Particularly useful library documents are those that record circulation. The term "circulation records" is ambiguous, though. One usage refers to library practices a century ago of tracking the circulation of individual titles. Another usage refers to aggregated data that indicate how many items circulated during a given period. Sometimes these aggregates are subdivided, for instance, into fiction and nonfiction, which makes them marginally more useful to historians of reading, but on the whole these are the least helpful category. In *Reading Places*, however, the term refers to records of borrowers' names and the book titles they checked out. Records of borrowings by named individuals represent a historical gold mine, because they allow researchers to link specific texts with real readers, especially valuable for ordinary readers, who may have left no other records of their reading experiences. By linking the library records with manuscripts of federal and state census population schedules (available up to 1920), researchers of earlier periods can go an important step further, by linking the reading of specific texts to demo

---

28 Clifford Geertz argues, "The whole point of a semiotic approach to culture is . . . to aid us in gaining access to the conceptual world in which our subjects live so that we can, in some extended sense of the term, converse with them" (*The Interpretations of Cultures* [New York: Basic Books, 1973], 24); Gilbert Ryle, "The Thinking of Thoughts: What Is 'Le Penseur' Doing?" in *Collected Papers*, vol. 2 (New York: Barnes and Noble, 1971), 482.

graphic variables such as age, sex, marital status, occupation, race, and sometimes even religion.[29]

Given their scholarly potential, one might expect circulation records to be carefully preserved in libraries and readily available for inspection by researchers. Some thoughtful librarians and archivists have indeed seen the value of such records, and provide researchers with access to them. More commonly, however, circulation records have gone the way of too many other records of library operations: to the dump. Public libraries are notoriously short of space, and librarians often lack training in the history of their own institution. What could be easier, then, than for library directors to discard the apparently worthless notebooks and slips of paper in which previous generations of library clerks carefully recorded the movements of texts and the choices of patrons? In recent times, two interconnected trends have accelerated this process. Automated library record-keeping techniques need leave no paper trail, and an increased value for patrons' privacy (combined with fear of government snooping) has encouraged librarians to deliberately ensure that circulation records do not survive beyond the very short period required to ensure that books are properly returned.[30]

For these various reasons, circulation records have unfortunately rarely survived, and even more rarely have archivists processed them for ready retrieval. Even when located, library records can present a variety of challenges. In addition to the usual problems with manuscript sources (including legibility and completeness), their use may be hedged about by legal and institutional restrictions. Although researchers may make unfettered use of library records of the distant past, confidentiality laws are likely to protect more recent library circulation

---

29 See the following for examples of analyses of library circulation records; Gilmore, *Reading Becomes a Necessity of Life*; Pawley, *Reading on the Middle Border*; Emily B. Todd, "Walter Scott and the Nineteenth-Century American Literary Marketplace: Antebellum Richmond Readers and the Collected Editions of the Waverley Novels," *Papers of the Bibliographical Society of America* 93, no. 4 (1999); Ronald Zboray, *A Fictive People: Antebellum Economic Development and the American Reading Public* (New York: Oxford University Press, 1993). An especially exciting "find" is that of the Carnegie Library, Muncie, Indiana (the site of the famous Middletown studies by Robert and Helen Lynd). In 2004 approximately 350,000 individual records turned up during renovations to the library. Under the title *What Middletown Read*, a group of researchers from nearby Ball State University has launched a major initiative to exploit this discovery (see https://bsu.edu/middletown/wmr/).

30 Leigh S. Estabrook, "Sacred Trust or Competitive Opportunity: Using Patron Records," *Library Journal* 121 (1 February 1996): 48–49.

records. These vary among states, but the effect is to confine researchers to treating the data as an aggregate and to prevent any follow-up of
the information about individuals. Moreover, researchers lacking
familiarity with library operations may find the records dauntingly
opaque. The reality facing print culture historians, then, is that library
circulation records, although very widely produced, are not very widely
available, and may be located and interpreted only with ingenuity,
luck, and assistance from knowledgeable archivists and librarians.

Unearthing Records, Locating Interviewees

The records that form the basis of this book were a lucky find. In 1998,
I was teaching at the University of Wisconsin–Madison and writing up
a study that made extensive use of library circulation records.[31] I was
eager to start a new project. Aware of my search for a new set of circulation records (any circulation records, as long as they included the
crucial details of readers' names and book titles), my colleague, the
historian Wayne Wiegand, mentioned the existence of some records
that he believed existed in the archives of the Wisconsin Historical
Society.[32] He was vague about the details, and nothing in the online
catalog appeared to be related to library circulation records. Then he
remembered a key piece of information; the records, he said, had something to do with a special library project in Wisconsin. I had already
been researching the archived records of the Wisconsin Free Library
Commission (merged since 1965 with the Department of Public
Instruction) for a project on Wisconsin's traveling libraries, and now
on a hunch I started to pick more carefully and systematically through
the entire WFLC listing. Before long, this search yielded a promising
possibility when I found that the WHS Archives catalog listed three
unprocessed boxes titled the "Door-Kewaunee Regional Library
Demonstration, 1950–1952." The term "unprocessed" indicated that

---

31 Wayne Wiegand generously drew my attention to the records that form the key data set in
Reading on the Middle Border. He had discovered them with the help of librarian Cindi Youngblut,
an enthusiastic and knowledgeable library historian.

32 The Wisconsin Historical Society was then titled the State Historical Society of
Wisconsin.

archivists had not written detailed description of their contents or evaluated them for their usefulness. While this unprocessed state might seem to be a disadvantage, in fact the opposite was the case and, as we shall see, would eventually be crucial to the feasibility of this research project.

The catalog yielded no clue as to what the three boxes might contain. When they were wheeled on a cart to my table in the wood-paneled reading room, they turned out to be cardboard boxes roughly similar in size to those that moving companies provide for transporting books. My notes, taken on April 2, 1998, provide a brief indication of what I found inside. The first box contained "time sheets, time cards showing distribution of hours among different personnel." These might be interesting to a historian of professional practice, perhaps, but not what I was looking for. The second, however, contained not only more time sheets, but also something more exciting: hundreds, if not thousands of yellow paper forms about two inches by four inches. The slips were preprinted with the following: name, address, city, author, title, copy, and, most important, filled out (usually in pencil). Box number three held yet more yellow slips, along with some photos and graphs. I recognized immediately that the thousands of slips represented an important find; they were indeed original circulation records, and they did contain the two vital elements: information both about the reader and about the titles chosen. Although I had no idea what the "Door-Kewaunee Regional Library Demonstration, 1950–1952" was, these flimsy yellow slips could, I conjectured, form the basis of a new research project—one that would focus on the reading choices of people living in the counties of Door and Kewaunee that together formed the Door Peninsula.

It was not hard to find information about this Demonstration in the professional literature of the early 1950s. *The Wisconsin Library Bulletin*, the journal of the Wisconsin Library Association, included several reports of this new state-funded project. The Wisconsin Free Library Commission produced flyers and pamphlets designed to publicize its efforts, and some of these were to be found in the unprocessed boxes. Most helpfully, the University of Wisconsin library held several copies of a publication titled *The Idea in Action*, which provided an official summary of the project and its outcomes. Articles and editorials in local newspapers, microfilmed and available in the Wisconsin Historical

Society Library, indicated that the Demonstration was considered a red-hot topic in the counties concerned. Other unpublished but archived institutional documents, including memos and correspondence, were preserved in the WHS archives. Before long, I had acquainted myself with the salient details. When the Door-Kewaunee Regional Library experiment came to its abrupt end, official accounts hinted at political controversy, but spelled out few of the details.

Extremely curious to find out more, I could envisage that combined with the other sources of information (newspapers, publications, institutional records, and so on) the Door-Kewaunee circulation records were full of promise—but also held important limitations. Practical difficulties immediately presented themselves. A quick glance at the circulation slips revealed that many were only partly filled out, and that evidently many of the borrowers were children, since the handwriting was often hard to read, and the titles and authors misspelled. The data from the slips would need to be entered into a computer, but how to achieve this was not obvious. The slips, the archives staff made clear, could not leave the reading room. Neither was it practicable to photocopy them. Data entry would have to take place in the reading room itself. Fortunately I was able to hire two student assistants with the aid of fellowship money from the Wisconsin Historical Society, and in this era before the ubiquity of laptops, the archives staff kindly allowed me to keep a small computer for the students' use in a cupboard in the reading room. This system worked well, and over the next few months the students gradually built up a database, transcribing as best they could the information from the circulation slips. In a second stage, a graduate student in library and information science checked the bibliographic data, making particularly extensive use of the catalogs of the Library of Congress and bibliographic cooperative OCLC's WorldCat. This seemingly simple task sometimes took some deft detective work, given the extremely rough state of the records transcribed from the circulation slips. The transcribing students had done their best, and most of the records were unambiguous. However, elementary school students appeared to have filled out many of the slips, and a significant percentage required some adjustment of spelling with respect to author name or title, or both. For instance, "Takamere and Jon Ron" by "Arnett" turned out to be *Takamere and Tonhon, Two Little Red Children in Their*

Prairie Home by Anna Williams Arnett. More bizarrely, we conjectured that "Zwithles" by "Bronson" was actually *Turtles* by Wilfred Bronson. Often books circulated more than once, and by discerning variations on a theme, we could generally arrive at a reasonable estimate of correct bibliographic details. Only a few titles proved impossible to cipher. What, for instance, was "Mee Millorous" by "Anery"? In the end we could find no bibliographic confirmation for 227 titles (just under 4 percent of the total of 5822 records) — some perfectly legible, but simply untraceable.

Beyond these operational difficulties, interpretive limitations were evident. Although the forms made the all-important link between real readers and their texts, they left no evidence about how and why these individuals chose these books or what they made of them. What kinds of questions could a print culture historian answer with their help, and how could one compensate for the very obvious gaps in the records? A related and fundamental issue of principle arose from the relatively recent date of the information in the slips. Confidentiality rules confined me to treating the data as an aggregate and to preventing any follow-up of the information about individuals. By signing the archive's confidentiality policy, I agreed not to make any use of the individuals' names, other than to use them to assess totals, for example, of male and female borrowers. Even though I might eventually encounter elsewhere a name I recognized from the database, I would have to ignore this connection. "Asking the reader" was not, at least in a literal sense, an option.

On the other hand, studying a recent period provided an opportunity denied those studying the more distant past. Since some people involved in the library demonstration project might still be living in the area, even though I was obliged to ignore the evidence of the library records, it might be possible to track down and interview some of these individuals by other means. Talking to residents would help me develop a many-layered description of their social and institutional environment, which combined with the public library records would help me uncover the meaning of reading on the Door Peninsula. In a more general sense, then, it seemed to me that by recognizing that since print is intimately embedded in modern life, by describing the local community and the lives of its inhabitants in detail, it would be possible to describe and analyze how print operates in that setting. This approach would shift the methodological problem from one of trying to enter the individual reader's head to that of locating and describing the embeddedness of print in specific terms, requiring a reorientation away from texts, and even from individual readers per se, and toward communities. Print culture is not an abstract overlay of some more fundamental kind of culture—say, the culture of everyday life. Rather, it *is* the culture of everyday life. Only by chasing after the details of everyday life in specific local communities— by, in Geertz's words, picking one's way through "piled-up structures of inference and implication"—can the print culture historian begin to grasp the specific, local meanings that constitute the many-layered sandwich that constitutes the history of reading.[33]

My Research Journey

In the fall of 2000 I was teaching at the University of Iowa, not so conveniently situated for research on Wisconsin. By this time, however, public libraries were commonly posting at least basic contact information on the web, and in this way I learned that the public library in Sturgeon Bay was the largest in the area and was designated the headquarters of the Door County Library. An e-mail to the director, Rebecca N. Berger, brought a speedy and enthusiastic reply and my second piece of great good fortune. Not only was it likely that people who remembered the Door-Kewaunee Regional Library Demonstration were still living in the area, but the former director of this project, Jane Livingston, was living in a retirement community in Sturgeon Bay and was willing and happy to talk to me.

At Rebecca Berger's suggestion, I also contacted the Friends of the Door County Public Library, who invited me to write a short piece for their November newsletter, asking for anyone with memories of the Demonstration to contact me. This publication produced an immediate result when a former Door County schoolteacher, Emily H., now living in Bailey's Harbor, contacted the library and offered not only to share her memories with me, but also put me in touch with several of

---

33 Geertz, "Thick Description," 7.

her former colleagues and students. Eventually I also contacted the two Kewaunee County libraries, in the cities of Algoma and Kewaunee, where directors Ann Schmitz and Susan Grosshuesch and their staff introduced me to a number of Kewaunee County residents. Librarians of smaller Door County libraries were similarly helpful, as were active and knowledgeable members of various historical societies. The Jacksonport (Door County) Historical Society, for instance, had published illustrated books in which residents recorded their memories of living in the area and attending local schools. Another key informant became Virginia Johnson of the Kewaunee County Historical Society. Over the course of several trips, I discovered that just hanging out in the libraries brought me into contact with some very helpful residents who filled me in on local conditions and culture.

My first visit took place in October 2000, when I took advantage of a light teaching load to undertake the seven-hour drive north from Iowa City to the Door Peninsula. Other components of the research project were already well underway. The data entry students had finished entering the bibliographic and patron information from the yellow circulation slips into a computer database. At the University of Iowa, my graduate assistant was learning to decode the sometimes-mangled versions of the titles and authors in the database and to verify their publication dates. I had exhausted the Wisconsin Historical Society's archival references to the Door-Kewaunee Regional Library, as well as the articles in the *Wisconsin Library Bulletin*, and the official report, *The Idea in Action*. I was also in the process of reading secondary literature, not only research into twentieth-century reading, but more broadly into the history of rural Wisconsin and especially the social history of the Cold War. Before starting this project I knew very little about Wisconsin in the early 1950s, but one aspect that was obvious, even to one so uninformed as I, was that Joseph McCarthy, junior senator from Wisconsin in the early 1950s, came from Appleton, only a few miles from the Door Peninsula. The so-called McCarthy Era had had an impact on libraries, as on other cultural institutions.[34] Did the

---

34 Louise S. Robbins has written extensively on libraries in the Cold War. For a history of the American Library Association's response to McCarthyism, see *Censorship and the American Library: The American Library Association's Response to Threats to Intellectual Freedom, 1939–1969* (Westport, Conn.: Greenwood, 1997). See also *The Dismissal of Miss Jane Brown: Civil Rights, Censorship, and the American Library* (Norman: University of Oklahoma Press, 2000).

failure of the Kewaunee contribution to survive the election of 1952 have anything to do with Cold War politics, I wondered?

I drove north through Madison, bypassing Appleton and Green Bay, and as I approached the Door Peninsula, the traffic thinned out. It was over twenty years since I had been to the area before as a weekend visitor. It was evident that although once famous mainly for its cherry orchards, Door County had become transformed into an important tourist resort. A major highway conveyed me through a small section of Kewaunee County without my even being aware of it. However, I was excited to travel through the Door County village of Brussels and to see signposts to other communities that I had come to recognize from the addresses listed in the circulation database. I arrived in Door County's largest city of Sturgeon Bay in the early evening as dusk was falling and the mist closing in, and checked into my modest motel. Sturgeon Bay boasts a wide range of accommodation, and prices are not uniformly low. Sophisticated restaurants now dot the streets downtown, along with gift shops and boutiques selling fashionable clothes. The character of the town had changed dramatically since my previous visit. It was now far more upscale than I remembered. Nevertheless, despite the appearance of prosperity, the 2000 U.S. Census revealed that average household incomes in Sturgeon Bay stood at just under $38,000, less than the Door County average of just over $45,000, the U.S average of nearly $49,000, and much less than the Wisconsin average of nearly $52,000. In my visits to the area, I would hear many times the complaint that local housing prices were forcing local young people away. It seemed that the prosperity that tourism generated was not necessarily resulting higher incomes for local inhabitants.

Sturgeon Bay straddles a ship canal that connects Lake Michigan to Green Bay, bisecting the Door Peninsula, and the next morning I drove across the bridge to the main part of the city. I planned to visit the Sturgeon Bay Public Library, check out the library's archives for any mention of the Demonstration headquartered there fifty years earlier, and, most important, visit former library director Jane Livingston. On the phone, Jane (as she urged me to call her) had sounded eager to talk about the project. "I've been wondering when someone would pick up on that story," she told me. At the library I met director Rebecca Berger and other staff members, who were welcoming and interested in my project. The library itself was housed in a building dated from 1975 that it shared with a public art gallery. A timeline found in the archives informed me that the Sturgeon Bay library had begun life as a subscription library in 1866. In 1901 the local women's club opened a combination reading and lunchroom for men and boys, and in 1906 the City Council started funding it as a free library open to all. An application for a grant from the Carnegie Corporation resulted in a new building in 1913, and it was this structure that the library occupied until replaced with the present building in the 1970s.

I spent several hours going through the archival resources relating to the Door-Kewaunee project, which mostly consisted of cuttings from the several local newspapers that existed in the early 1950s, many of which have now vanished. Everyone I spoke to showed great interest in the Door-Kewaunee Regional Library, and some had vague memories of hearing about it before, but no one had personal knowledge to share. More than ever, I hoped to get an insider's view from Jane Livingston (although she had married and changed her name in the mid-1950s, I thought of her as still in the role of Demonstration director). With some nervousness, I drove up to the modern apartment building in Sturgeon Bay where she now lived, and parked the car. Jane had given me careful instructions on how to negotiate the building's entry procedure, instructions that I now proved unable to follow—not a good start, I thought. At last, Jane came down to let me in and took me up to her second-floor apartment. In her late eighties and widowed, she had recently decided to move out of the house she and her late husband had occupied for many years, and she was beginning to get used to living in a smaller space. One of her main hobbies was quilting, she told me, and she showed me some of the exquisite examples of her work that decorated her home. To my relief I found her very easy to talk to, and as I sat down on the sofa in her living room and set up my tape recorder, I sensed that she was going to be just the key informant that I had hoped.

Over the next two years I would have four lengthy interviews with Jane Livingston. As director, she was the most involved member of the local staff of the Door-Kewaunee Demonstration, and she had detailed memories of what she obviously considered an important but under-recognized project that she was anxious to share. In subsequent decades as director of the Sturgeon Bay/Door County Public Library, she had also built up a detailed knowledge of people of the Door Peninsula, and she had several contacts who would turn out to be key informants. I quickly realized that if finding the circulation records had been my first piece of luck, talking to Jane was the second.

I was able to talk to about twenty-five other people at some length, a process that opened my eyes to important aspects of life on the Door Peninsula that I might otherwise have missed. All the men and women that I met were generous with their time and enthusiastic in sharing their memories. These interviews also highlighted the need for me to reflect on my own identity as researcher, as a woman, and as an "outsider." As an immigrant from Britain, I was instantly and unavoidably branded as different by my speech, and it was possible that this characteristic, along with my academic status as a university professor, might not only affect whom I could encounter, but also shape the stories that people told me. Born and bred in London, I was also poorly acquainted with the routines of rural or even small-town life. A couple of other characteristics perhaps took the edge off some of this strangeness. I was approximately the age of some of those I talked to, and that along with my affiliation with library education—a connection that several informants let me know that they approved—gave us common ground, as did my midwestern residency. Nevertheless, there were severe limitations to my use of the methods of oral history. I never made contact with anyone who had voiced strong objections to the Demonstration, partly because I never tried very hard to locate such individuals, but also because I learned that the key figures had since died. My representation of opponents' arguments was therefore largely filtered through my conversations with library supporters (along with newspaper editorials and letters to the editor written by library critics). The opposing side certainly did not receive equal time in the resulting account. I also had to remind myself not to fall into the trap of representing the opponents as the "baddies" of the story. Their opposition to the library, initially so inexplicable to long-time library advocates like myself, came to make more sense to me when placed in its geographical and temporal context.

By the time I made my first of several visits to the Door Peninsula, I was beginning to see that my multi-pronged approach had a number of advantages. Tracking down and interviewing participants in the project would indeed give me a way of accessing their reading practices that would not only supplement the evidence of the circulation data, but also give me a much broader sense of what to include under the category of "reading practice." While an important first step in the history of reading is to answer the question "who read what," more interesting but more difficult are questions of "how and why" people read.[35] Pondering the theoretical implications of these questions and thinking of practical ways of answering them prompted me to reflect both upon the particular story I had to tell—that of the readers on the Door Peninsula during the early years of the Cold War—and on research methodologies in book history in general. My close-up view of the Door-Kewaunee Regional Library Demonstration emphasized for me the variability in reading practices in even one small rural area, illustrating how, against the backdrop of an apparently unified national print culture, practices of literacy can still be an intensely local affair.

The Plan of Reading Places

The next eight chapters explore the Door-Kewaunee Demonstration of 1950–1952 in more detail, each relating part of the library story and linking it to some broader trends. As discussed above, a major continuing theme stresses the importance of locality and sociability in understanding the reading practices of ordinary Americans, particularly in the context of public policies designed to shape that reading. As is well recognized by ethnographers of reading, local community values for reading, local history, and politics intertwine with ethnicity, class, and gender to influence not only who read what, but how and why (to paraphrase Robert Darnton). As an expression of organized sociability the institution of the public library can provide a window onto these various reading practices, especially when situated in their geographic

---

35 Robert Darnton, "History of Reading," in *New Perspectives on Historical Writing*, ed. Peter Burke (University Park: Pennsylvania State University Press, 1992), 142.

contexts. According to their early twentieth-century advocates, public libraries sustained local communities by providing residents with the means to involve themselves in democratic processes. Reflective, literary reading, the argument went, produced moral, committed citizens. Access to information also sustained local democratic cultures by giving voters facts and arguments to help them to make well-informed decisions. But despite proponents' fervent belief in the library "faith" and in the power of information, public libraries, mostly poorly funded, found it hard to deliver on these promises. Faced with difficult decisions about what services to offer, what materials to buy, and for whom, library advocates debated and sometimes clashed over their priorities. And the targets of their efforts could be less than receptive. In the case of the Door-Kewaunee Demonstration of 1950–1952, local responses to the initiative ranged from enthusiastic endorsement to implacable hostility.

Chapter 2 focuses on the geography of reading on the Door Peninsula, and discusses how ethnicity, class, and gender patterned the inhabitants' reading experiences. It also sets the Peninsula's ethnic composition within a broader history of migration to Wisconsin, and of national reformers' efforts to link immigration and citizenship to literacy. The Demonstration emerged out of earlier public policy programs to establish universal literacy. Wisconsin's traveling libraries, organized by WFLC librarian Lutie Stearns before World War I, were precursors of the bookmobile, for example. The story of these efforts continues as the subject of chapter 3, and includes the nineteenth-century development of free schools and libraries, the Progressive Era establishment of library commissions, Americanization programs, and the emergence of the Wisconsin Idea. Recognizing that rural communities would always be disadvantaged by the local finance structures for public libraries, librarians sought alternatives, including state and federal funding. The chapter ends with the politics and philosophies that set in motion the Door-Kewaunee Regional library.

The WFLC had taken the key policy decision to focus the Regional Library's efforts on adult rather than young readers. In chapter 4 I review the official reasoning behind this approach, and contrast it with the deeply felt desires of local staff to devote their services mainly to rural children. This chapter also describes the controversy that boiled up around the kinds of books that children and adults encountered, especially on the bookmobile. In the early 1950s, intellectual freedom was a professional value only recently espoused by librarians, but it was put to the test in the tense atmosphere of the early Cold War. The library's opponents adopted an organized strategy of challenging controversial books as a way of drumming up support for their position, but the library also inspired much local support, especially among rural schoolteachers. Chapter 5 shows how, for some young people, school was a gateway to a world that revolved around reading and writing, while for others reading began and ended in the classroom. Rural schoolteachers were usually young women from the area, who had attended the county normal school. In the one-room schools that they had themselves attended, books were few, and the curriculum changed little from year to year. Now, through the bookmobile, the library and the school systems intersected as members of the two organizations came into regular contact with each other, radically enlarging the flow of print through local classrooms.

Women and children were the heaviest users of the new library services. Despite some local residents' misgivings about the effects of the bookmobile on the young, officials claimed that the Demonstration's greatest success lay in children's improved reading skills. In chapter 6, circulation record analysis shows that children of all ages checked out fiction and picture books in large numbers, but also chose books about science and books designed to improve reading skills. However, the diversity of their reading choices was perhaps compromised by the large number of standard texts created by influential reading experts whose stories depicted as normal a suburban world that Door Peninsula children must have found unfamiliar. And the most popular stories selected, like those of Lois Lenski, did little to challenge the children's view of America as normally white, Protestant, and middle-class.

Women's experiences of the library combined with their experiences of other institutions that promoted reading. These included the clubs that constituted women's primary secular social organizations in the postwar period. Chapter 7 turns to their reading activities and reveals that consumer culture was beginning to penetrate even the then-remote Door Peninsula, as women transformed their homes, drawing for inspiration on fictional descriptions as well as books of household hints. Still, although these patterns conformed to the prevailing conservative ethos of the Cold War, for rural women in traditional households they represented a rupture with the past. Moreover, women of various classes and ethnicities engaged in social and cultural activities outside the home, often centering these on print and reading. By acting together in institutional settings, these women increased reading opportunities not only for themselves, but also for their families and other members of their local communities.

Chapter 8 sums up the politics of the referendum and continues the story into its aftermath. Librarians relaxed their reading standards and began to accept popular materials into their collections. At the same time, although still controversial, collaborative county and regional library systems spread across the United States, and small rural schools vanished. As school districts consolidated into larger units, comparatively well-stocked school libraries became common, prompting county officials to drop popular bookmobile services—sometimes in the face of outcry. Still, officially imposed library networks did not necessarily replace small local libraries. The chapter ends with a successful late twentieth-century campaign by a homemakers' club to build a permanent library in the southern Door Peninsula.

In 1956, despite opposition from conservatives keen to unravel the New Deal, for the first time the federal government committed funds to aiding rural public libraries. The final chapter (chapter 9) discusses the effects of successive pieces of library legislation in the light of the Great Society programs of the 1960s, a boom in library building during the 1970s, and the rise of digital technology in the 1980s and 1990s. Despite late twentieth-century arguments that local library spaces would become obsolete in the age of the Internet, communities large and small continued to build them, convinced that they hold value for both rural and urban neighborhoods. As institutions of print, public libraries presented staff and patrons with opportunities to read and write. But some groups found it easier to take advantage of these opportunities than others. Some were deliberately excluded on racial grounds, while others found little congruity between their own cultural and ethnic backgrounds and that of librarians and most library supporters. In a section titled "The 'Right' Reading" I review efforts to establish a hierarchy of texts, and argue that such boundaries sometimes make more sense to cultural authorities than they do to ordinary readers. Lastly, I return to the story of the circulation records. Eight years after I began this research, I found that they had not fared well. *Reading Places* ends with a reflection on the place of public library records in print culture research.

2
The Geography of Rural Reading

When, as often happens, my mental vision sweeps over all the
country to see where the best work in some particular line is
being done, the state most likely to loom up as leader is Wisconsin, to which we of New York always claim a kinship and think of
it as a new New York a thousand miles nearer the sunset.

Melvil Dewey, letter to Lutie Stearns, 1912

Jane Livingston, Director of the Sturgeon Bay Public Library, moved
to Door County in 1945. Born in 1915 and raised on a farm in central
Wisconsin, like many other young women of her day Livingston at first
planned to become a teacher. This in itself was no easy proposition.
During the Depression, "getting an education was a real achievement,"
she later recalled. The state teachers college at Stevens Point was just
twenty miles from her parents' farm, and she traveled home every
weekend, she said, for her mother to hand her the money that would
see her through the next week, and "to stock up on food . . . There
wasn't any extra money." After finishing her degree, instead of teaching school, she worked for a year in the children's department of the
Green Bay Public Library and then attended the University of
Wisconsin–Madison, where she obtained a qualification in library science. Librarianship was one of the few professions that encouraged
women members, and the path by way of school teaching was not
unusual. Librarians who had classroom teaching experience were
likely to forge strong bonds with local schoolteachers, forming alli-
ances that could have political as well as practical consequences. After
graduation, Livingston worked for several years in a Michigan county
library system. However, on a visit home, she found herself recruited
for the directorship of the Sturgeon Bay Public Library, largely on the

basis of her Michigan experience. Four years later, she became Director of the Door-Kewaunee Regional Library.

Although WFLC officials congratulated themselves on having recruited an ideal area for its literacy experiment, in fact the Door Peninsula was less homogeneous than it may have appeared from far-off Madison. In the postwar period, tight ethnic enclaves still patterned the two counties, creating distinct communities that were clearly marked off from each other by "nationality" and even by language. Not only did the counties differ from each other, but within each county one area could diverge from the next. In this the region resembled much of the rest of Wisconsin, a state etched by the flows of immigration it experienced during the nineteenth and early twentieth centuries. These ethnic communities held contrasting views about the importance of books and reading, a matter of concern to reformers, politicians, and officials anxious about the effect of immigration on the quality of democracy in America. In rural areas, it was hard for people to get their hands on books and newspapers even if they wanted to. Improved library services, officials hoped, would open up the distribution of reading materials and encourage reading as a ingrained habit of everyday life. Habitual readers, they felt, were better equipped to exercise the responsibilities of democracy than those with little regard for print.

North and South

Sturgeon Bay was—as it still is—the biggest community on Wisconsin's Door Peninsula, marking the boundary between the north and the south. In the postwar period, the contiguous counties of Door and Kewaunee relied mostly on agriculture. Their total population was just over 38,000, two-thirds of whom lived in country areas, while most of the urban population lived in three cities: Sturgeon Bay (population 7,054), Algoma (3,384), and Kewaunee (2,583).[1] The median annual income for the two counties was similar: $2,438 for families in Door County, $2,323 for families in Kewaunee County.[2] Local industry

---

1 "Door-Kewaunee Regional Library," promotional leaflet produced by the WFLC. Originally found in WHS Series 1111.

2 "Characteristics of the Population, Part 49: Wisconsin," in *Census of Population: 1950*, vol. 2

included shipbuilding in Sturgeon Bay and Kewaunee (where World War II had brought boomtown conditions as shipyards expanded their industrial output), but much of the region was still heavily rural.[3] The southern peninsula relied mainly on farming, and north of Sturgeon Bay extensive cherry orchards attracted Mexican families as seasonal migrants. Fishing villages dotted the northern coast and Washington Island, separated from the rest of Door County by a treacherous strait called Porte des Morts (Door of the Dead). Northern Door County was distinctive for another reason, as picturesque hamlets like Ephraim, Sister Bay, and Fish Creek attracted wealthy summer visitors from Chicago and Milwaukee. Some families had the habit of sailing up Lake Michigan to their Door County cottages for many years, spending the entire summer there. These regular seasonal visitors brought with them middle- and upper-class cultural activities that included concerts, classes on the local environment, and an art association.[4] Few public libraries served the two counties. The cities of Sturgeon Bay in Door County and Algoma and Kewaunee in Kewaunee County each had its own locally funded library. Five northern Door County communities — Bailey's Harbor, Egg Harbor, Ephraim, Sister Bay, and Washington Island — also had small libraries that were, for the most part, run by volunteers, open for restricted hours only and poorly stocked. By contrast, southern Door and Kewaunee counties had no rural libraries at all, though county residents could use the city libraries for a fee.[5]

Once on the Door Peninsula, Livingston soon recognized that ethnicity drew the fault lines along which rural communities divided. Even fifty years later at the turn of the twenty-first century, ethnic difference still created a patchwork effect throughout the two counties in which localities were stamped with the "national" characteristics of their inhabitants. These old patterns were breaking down, though. "Starting at southern end," Livingston told me in 2000, "we have a large

---

(Washington: Government Printing Office, 1952), 49–13; 49–112.

3 William F. Thompson, *The History of Wisconsin*, vol. 2, *Continuity and Change, 1940–1965* (Madison: State Historical Society of Wisconsin, 1988), 96.

4 Writers' Program, *Wisconsin: A Guide to the Badger State* (New York: Duell, Sloan, and Pearce, 1941), 317. In the 1960s, Douglas Waples, library science professor of Chicago's Graduate Library School, retired to Washington Island, where he regularly taught classes in sociology to the inhabitants.

5 Sturgeon Bay charged a fee; Algoma and Kewaunee only instituted fees after 1952.

Belgian group who came in the early 1800s . . . Those people were very poor, very hard-working and even as late as when I came here in 1945 many of those children did not speak English until they went to school. They were a close-knit people and their language was a spoken language—Walloon." The Belgians were practical people, she emphasized. "They were rural people, mostly farmers. They cleared the land. The women went out and worked in the fields along with the men. Had large families." But despite the fact that most were Catholics, they did not support parochial schools. "'We have to pay for public education, we aren't paying twice,'" she said. "The last county superintendent of schools was pure Belgian. That was one of his jokes." In the southernmost part of the Peninsula, she went on, "Kewaunee County had Czech and Bohemian people also in separate little enclaves. Now you can't tell where one group ends and one begins." Working on up the Peninsula, she told me, "Sturgeon Bay itself was settled by a lot of New Englanders, and from New York," while further north still "there's Scandinavian, both Swedes and Norwegians." At the very tip, Icelanders inhabited Washington Island. "They fished," Livingston said. "A lot of the people [in the] north were fishing." Small groups of Poles and Italians could also be found in the south, and German communities were sprinkled throughout.

In addition to experiencing a different ethnic composition from the south, the north also felt the influence of the affluent summer visitors who started to arrive regularly toward the end of the nineteenth century. "The northern part of the county was turned into a summer resort area first," Livingston said. "There were a few big hotels—Ephraim was one of the first places . . . People would come by boat and stay all summer. There was a steamer service. They used to come up from Chicago." The summer people "used to come up loaded down with all their summer reading and then had to tote them back," Livingston went on. But sometimes it was easier for the visitors simply to leave the books behind when they left. "That's how we got a lot of books. We didn't charge them because a lot owned property and don't get much for their property taxes, so they could get library services." These summer migrants from the city had a profound and lasting cultural influence—for the better, she felt. "That was the difference between the north and south. Although there were adults who didn't read (who hadn't been brought up to read), there *were* readers and they also had contact with the summer people who came in from the big cities, and they used to be able to borrow a big box of books."

In its ethnic diversity, the Door Peninsula was not unlike the rest of Wisconsin, a state that during the nineteenth century attracted immigrants, first from the eastern United States and later from Europe. At the beginning of the seventeenth century, an estimated twenty thousand Indians (mostly Menominee, Winnebago, Chippewa, and Sauk and Fox) inhabited the lands that would later form the state. In the early nineteenth century, Stockbridge, Oneida, and Brotherton tribes arrived, displaced from New England and New York. In the decades that followed, some Indians found themselves confined to reservations (mostly in the north of Wisconsin), while in the south others were forced to move west of the Mississippi. When Indian resistance to coerced removal collapsed with the Black Hawk War of 1832, the southern part of the state opened to white settlement, prompting the migration of Yankees in the thousands.[6] In 1850, Wisconsin's population stood at just over three hundred thousand. Over one-third of these came from New York, and another nineteen thousand originated in Vermont. Migrants brought with them institutional blueprints for settlement that included legal systems, churches, commercial enterprises, and schools. In 1836 twelve men from the village of Colebrook, New Hampshire, for instance, formed the New England Emigrating Company. Together with six other New Hampshire families they moved to Wisconsin, where they settled in the Rock River Valley area that is now Beloit. Once there they established a college modeled on Yale. This pattern of institutional mimicry repeated itself as Wisconsin's common schools, too, drew on New England models.[7]

Yankees also brought with them a propensity for reading, as well as formal and informal practices for sharing books. Although subscription libraries were not unusual in New York and New England, much more common were "dense social webs of exchange" that facilitated the non-institutional borrowing and lending of reading materials within

---

6 John D. Buenker, "Wisconsin," in *Heartland: Comparative Histories of the Midwestern States*, ed. James H. Madison (Bloomington: Indiana University Press, 1988), 66.

7 Lois Kimball Mathews Rosenberry, *The Expansion of New England: The Spread of New England Settlement and Institutions to the Mississippi River, 1620–1865* (Boston: Houghton Mifflin, 1909), 241–42.

communities. Such reciprocity depended on participants following unwritten rules of behavior that demonstrated responsibility and care on the part of lenders as well as generosity and trust by borrowers.[8] This shared culture set a standard for the literacy practices that became embedded in the newly settled lands of the Midwest.

Within two or three decades, native-born settlers were joined by large numbers of immigrants from Europe. Between 1846 and 1855, over three million, mostly from Ireland and Germany, landed in the United States. Although many settled in New York and other east coast cities, others headed straight for the developing lands to the west. The 1850 census numbered Wisconsin's German population at about 38,000. Within two decades, this had more than quadrupled to over 162,000. In 1900, 10 percent of Wisconsin's population had been born in Germany, and Germans accounted for just under half of the total foreign-born population. Wisconsin was a prime destination for other ethnic groups, too. Between 1820 and 1910, over a hundred thousand Belgians settled in the United States. These immigrants spoke either Flemish or the French patois known as Walloon, and tended to settle in separate communities. Over time, Belgians came to dominate the area between Green Bay and Sturgeon Bay, which developed into the largest Walloon settlement in the United States.[9]

State-sponsored projects encouraged Europeans to move to Wisconsin. In 1852, the state commissioner of emigration distributed pamphlets in English, German, Norwegian, and Dutch to immigrants as they disembarked in New York, mailed other leaflets directly to foreign countries, and also inserted advertisements and editorials in newspapers abroad. In the late 1860s, complaining that the Civil War had created an acute labor shortage, the Wisconsin legislature encouraged Congress to pass laws encouraging immigration. In 1879 a newly constituted State Board of Immigration published official circulars that lauded Wisconsin not only for its climate and land, but also for its free schools and university, religious freedom, and male suffrage. Individual counties and commercial companies made similar attempts

---

8 Ronald J. Zboray and Mary Saracino Zboray, *Everyday Ideas: Socioliterary Experience among Antebellum New Englanders* (Knoxville: University of Tennessee Press, 2006), 125.

9 Monique Berlier, "Picturing Ourselves: Photographs of Belgian Americans in Northeastern Wisconsin, 1888–1950" (Ph.D. Diss., University of Iowa, 1999), 74.

to entice immigrants to Wisconsin. Their efforts paid off. By 1880, Wisconsin had attracted 24,000 immigrants from Austria, "Bohemia," Poland and Hungary.[10] Nearly one-third of the state's population was foreign born, with Germans, Scandinavians, and Irish leading the British, Czechs, Dutch, and French.[11]

Between 1860 and 1870, most immigrants to Wisconsin took up life in rural areas. In 1870, less than one in five residents lived in towns or cities, compared to a national average of over one-quarter. The state's cities were growing, however, and between 1880 and 1890 most new immigrants were moving to Milwaukee or one of the other expanding cities like La Crosse, Racine, and Oshkosh. As the cities and towns grew, so did the gap that rural and urban residents perceived existed between their respective life styles. In the eyes of rural residents like those on the Door Peninsula, even small towns like Sturgeon Bay and Algoma represented a stark contrast to their own ways of life. Poor rural immigrants resented Yankee townspeople's prosperity and saw city dwellers as exploitative and dishonest. Milwaukee came in for particular hostility from the rest of the state on account of its pattern of industrial life, labor agitation, and financial power.[12]

Although the state encouraged the settlement of Europeans, not all viewed this development favorably. In 1887, the *New York Post* complained that Wisconsin's population contained the highest proportion of immigrants of any state in the Union, with foreign-born voters outnumbering the native born, and suggested that Wisconsin should take steps to restrict immigration.[13] The influx of non-English-speaking— and even worse, illiterate—immigrants threatened the stability of the republic, some believed. Fears about the destabilizing political influence of white immigrant men were reinforced by biological theories about race that cast southern and eastern Europeans as inferior to those from northern Europe. At the University of Wisconsin, renowned

10 Emily Greene Balch, *Our Slavic Fellow Citizens* (New York: Charities Publication Committee, 1910; reissued in 1969 by the Arno Press and the *New York Times*), 217–19, 234; *Wisconsin Dictionary of History*, www.wisconsinhistory.org/dictionary/

11 Reuben Gold Thwaites, *The Story of Wisconsin* (Boston: Lothrop, Lee, & Shephard, 1899).

12 Robert C. Nesbit, *Wisconsin: A History* (Madison: University of Wisconsin Press, 1973), 341–42, 343–44.

13 David P. Thelen, *The New Citizenship: Origins of Progressivism in Wisconsin, 1885–1900* (Columbia: University of Missouri Press, 1972), 6.

sociologist Edward E. Ross ruminated on the implications of immigration in a book he titled *The Old World in the New: The Significance of Past
and Present Immigration to the American People*.[14] "To the practiced eye," he
wrote, "the physiognomy of certain [immigrant] groups unmistakably
proclaims inferiority of type. I have seen gatherings of the foreign-
born in which narrow and sloping foreheads were the rule . . . In every
face there was something wrong—lips thick, mouth coarse, upper lip
too long, cheek-bones too high, chin poorly formed, the bridge of the
nose hollowed, the base of the nose tilted, or else the whole face prog-
nathous." Industrialists, Ross complained, had imported cheap labor
to tend their factories, just as planters had imported slaves to tend their
crops. "Without likening immigrants to negroes," Ross hedged, "one
may point out how the latter-day employer resembles the old-time
planter in his blindness to the effects of his labor policy upon the blood
of the nation." The result of this unrestricted flow of immigrants, Ross,
held, was "race suicide."[15]

Ross's work appeared in a bibliography of fifteen books on "Americanization," recommended by University of Wisconsin Professor Don D.
Lescohier, distributed at a meeting of the Wisconsin Library Association,
and published in the *Wisconsin Library Bulletin* in 1919.[16] It took its place
among a widespread eugenics literature that thoroughly infused mainstream intellectual thought, feeding upon a nineteenth-century debate
over whiteness and citizenship. Out of this debate had emerged a new
racial classification that rested upon the ostensibly scientific term
"Caucasian," a single category that encompassed former racial groupings of Europeans such as "Celts," "Iberics," "Mediterraneans," "Slavs,"
and "Hebrews." What Caucasians had in common was that they were
white, and therefore eligible for citizenship, at a time when law and
practice excluded people of color. At the same time, formerly accepted
racial categories became transformed into "national" or "ethnic" categories such as Irish, Russian Jews, Poles, and Greeks.[17]

---

14 Edward Alsworth Ross, *The Old World in the New: The Significance of Past and Present Immigration to the American People* (New York: Century: 1914).

15 Ibid., 286–87, 299.

16 "Americanization," *Wisconsin Library Bulletin* 15, no. 9 (1919): 237.

17 Matthew Frye Jacobson, *Whiteness of a Different Color: European Immigrants and the Alchemy of
Race* (Cambridge: Harvard University Press, 1998), 7–9.

By the mid-twentieth century, though they had lost the worst of their pejorative connotations on the Door Peninsula, ethnic distinctions had become commonsense categories that continued to structure residents' interpretations of local cultural differences, especially in rural areas. My interviewees saw geography as the key to understanding the region's print culture and drew an especially stark contrast between the northern peninsula and the south. According to Livingston, "The northern part— there were a lot of areas . . . that didn't have much access to books. But they came from a different breed I suppose you'd say. And books were . . . more important to the people in the north." She was anxious not to cast the southerners in a poor light, though. "People in the south were hard workers," she assured me. "They had to be, because the women were out working in the fields with the men and doing all of the housework and raising the kids besides. And so reading was something that they weren't even familiar with. The daily newspaper was something—they didn't have that. And a lot of it was poverty." Despite her efforts to be even-handed, however, for Livingston, women's involvement in fieldwork was a marker of class and ethnic distinction, and, she implied, an indication of inferior domestic arrangements. Such women were to be pitied.

In closely knit southern farm families, everyone, including women and children, shared in the labor. Like other traditional, ethnicity-based midwestern farm families, those that composed these communities were male-centered and male-dominated. Even in the postwar period, little had changed from the early years of the twentieth century. Men ran not only the family farm, but also made the major decisions in that key local institution, the church. Women in German Lutheran farm families, for instance, were expected to focus their energies almost exclusively on the home and children. Even at church, they were responsible for cleaning and kitchen chores, just as they were at home.[18] Describing a rural Iowa region that she called Open Country in the early twentieth century, historian Deborah Fink noted, "A woman's social world of family and close friends blended into the ethnic communities. With people marrying within their ethnic groups (which were in turn geographically consolidated), neighbors, schoolmates, and members of the same church

---

18 Sonya Salamon, *Prairie Patrimony: Family, Farming, and Community in the Midwest* (Chapel Hill: University of North Carolina Press, 1992), 41, 194.

often came to be members of the same extended family." Social events like picnics, sports, dances, and dinners followed the same ethnic patterns. Sometimes these patterns represented cultural rifts. "The Germans, who unlike most others, drank beer at their gatherings," Fink observed, "had a dance hall where they gathered for Saturday night celebrations of weddings, anniversaries, and reunions." By contrast, Norwegians (who tended to be Quaker or Lutheran) neither drank nor danced. The two groups overcame their spiritual differences in favor of ethnic unity in a social setting when the Quakers built a school that provided social space for all Norwegians. Because singing and dancing was "un-Quakerly," other pastimes were devised, some of them print-related, like a literary society, and including a program of traveling speakers who gave talks open to the whole community on religious or political topics such as pacifism.[19] The connection between print and religion fitted traditional Protestant values for reading as a form of piety and source of spiritual development. Gradually, over the course of the twentieth century, the tight nexus between print culture and religion weakened, however. Those interviewed about their memories of the Door Peninsula in the 1950s found it hard to think of significant instances where church and reading went hand in hand. The secularization of reading was mirrored by a gradual decline in the importance of the church in women's lives that accelerated after mid-century.

Just as gender and ethnicity affected the distribution of adult work and leisure, so too did they influence the lives of rural children. In the late nineteenth century farm children of all ethnicities were expected to spend a significant amount of time working on the family farm as a matter of course, and these practices persisted well into the twentieth century. Boys living on Door and Kewaunee County farms were less likely than their sisters to attend school beyond the compulsory eight grades. But daughters were more likely to work in the fields and the barn if they came from homes where their mothers shared these tasks. Many families still spoke languages other than English at home in the middle decades of the twentieth century. Former schoolteacher Clarice F. recalled attending a country school in the late 1920s in southern Door

---

19 Deborah Fink, *Open Country Iowa: Rural Women, Tradition, and Change* (Albany: State University of New York Press, 1986), 91.

County that was strongly German. "The [German] children . . . when they got to fifth grade, then they had to drop out for sixth, seventh, and eighth, and go to school at the church—at the German Lutheran church they had a school in the basement," she commented. "They had to learn German and all that sort of thing, and that's where they graduated [from] the eighth grade . . . A lot of them spoke German." Belgians formed another sizable ethnic group at Clarice's school. "At that time," she said, "if you went into the Belgian community, you really felt out of place because everybody spoke Belgian. You weren't Belgian, so you couldn't speak with them."

The Belgian communities of the southern peninsula featured prominently in present-day residents' accounts as people who lacked an interest in reading. During the nineteenth century, the immigrant Belgians had used French as their written language, employing the patois Walloon in conversation. Well into the twentieth century, Belgian Americans continued to speak "Belgian" at home, at work, and at church. Although the community shared common moral and religious values as well as work practices, it was language that was "the glue which cemented the community together while keeping outsiders at a distance," comments the historian Monique Berlier. After the turn of the century, school instruction was in English only, and children were even punished for speaking Walloon at school, though this did little to stamp out the practice, for even in the early 1950s some Belgian Americans were not fluent in English. Although Livingston was exaggerating when she claimed that Walloon was not a written language, it was true that the Belgians on the Door Peninsula had no newspaper of their own, and that French was generally used in written documents. Whereas other immigrant groups circulated newspapers as a way of maintaining community cohesion, the Belgians in Wisconsin failed to establish this or any other significant form of print culture.[20]

In the middle of the twentieth century, print still did not figure prominently in the lives of Belgian families. "In Southern Door, it was

20 Berlier, "Picturing Ourselves," 111, 113, 118. Berlier notes, "The only hint that a Walloon newspaper might have existed comes from an account in the *Bay City Press* (17 November 1860) stating 'WANTED an interpreter to translate a paper written in an unknown language (some words of which look like French patois) which is now being circulated among the Belgian settlers of the town of Green Bay . . . Address, Republican Committee of the Town of Green Bay'" (111).

mostly children who used the library, because the adults couldn't read," remembered Livingston. "So we had to grow up a generation of readers. The children were starved for it. There would be a few adults who had gone on to [high] school, but there wasn't money for them to go on to school." It was a matter of priorities, she added, with more than a hint of disapproval. "What money there was went back into the farm . . . They bought farm machinery and cars. The barns were always well cared for. The wives didn't have so much." Two library staff members who claimed Belgian heritage confirmed this lack of opportunity for education and reading when they themselves were young. Both remembered the Kewaunee County bookmobile with affection, and emphasized how much they now appreciated a new library in southern Door County. Said one, "I would have been a better reader, if I had had a library like this"—she spread her hands to encompass the ample book shelves and comfortable reading spaces—"when I was growing up."[21] Other Door Peninsula residents, both Belgian and non-Belgian, supported this picture of a hard-working, "practical" Belgian community of non-readers. Former rural schoolteacher Gerald G., who grew up in a predominantly Belgian area in southern Door County, claimed of his own German-origin family that during the 1940s and 1950s they had no books or newspapers at all in their home. But when asked to characterize the surrounding rural area, he commented, "There were a lot of Belgians." This was sufficient, he implied, to account for the whole community's lack of interest in books and reading. Gerald found a way to fill the gap in his own household, even in the days before the advent of the bookmobile. His parents, who owned a small cheese factory, would drop him off once a week at the Algoma Public Library when they went to town to sell their products.

Some residents who lacked interest in print themselves saw no shame in this. "I remember when I first came here [to Kewaunee County]," recalled an Algoma Public Library staff member, "I had to go out to the farms and talk to the farm boys about who was using [the library]—at that time the information was not privileged information. You had to go over the list of names of who was using the library. I remember Jules M. . . . from [the predominantly Belgian] Red River township.

---

21 Conversation with library staff, Door County, 25 May 2001.

He said, 'We don't have anybody that reads in this town.'" For these men and boys of Belgian heritage, reading was low on their list of priorities. Avoiding reading was a matter, even, of masculinity and pride.

By contrast, present-day Door Peninsula residents characterized people of Swedish, Danish, and Norwegian extraction as generally interested in print. "The Scandinavian people are more apt to be readers," flatly asserted Jane Livingston. Noting that Scandinavians were more likely to live in the northern part of the county, she added, "I think people in the north—adults—used the library more. They had more of a background for reading." Moreover, men as well as women were perceived as closely engaged with print. Emily H., a retired schoolteacher who grew up in northern Door County, whose mother was "one hundred percent German" and farmer father was "a hundred percent Scandinavian," recalled that her father "read I think every farm magazine there was. He took at least four. I remember my dad in the evening every evening sitting there, reading his farm magazines. He was a reader." Although still conscious of their heritage, by the 1930s Scandinavians were losing some of their distinct ethnic identity. Lucille K., who grew up in Sister Bay during the 1930s and 1940s, and who claimed Scandinavian heritage on both sides of her family, noted that by that time only older people still spoke the languages of the old countries. "As a child we'd listen, we could sort of figure out what they were talking about," she said with a laugh. "If they didn't want us to know what they were talking about they'd use [those languages]." Lucille's family owned a store and ice cream parlor that provided a social center where customers came from surrounding farms to buy newspapers, use the phone, and visit with each other. "They went to town Saturday night and they stopped at my dad's store and the men would be in the store visiting and the ladies would come and talk to my mother [in the kitchen]. Social hour I guess. Not much going on." Lucille remembers that her family subscribed to the local newspaper— the *Sturgeon Bay Advocate*—and that because her father sold newspapers, the family also read the *Milwaukee Tribune*, as well as several magazines, including *Life*, the *Ladies Home Journal*, and *Good Housekeeping*. Yankee descendants also tended to assume a reading identity. Jane Livingston had herself grown up in an Anglophone family of "readers" on a central Wisconsin farm in the 1930s. The family took a daily newspaper, while the children took magazines like *Youth's Companion* and *Boy's Life*. It was only later that Jane recognized her experience as unusual; "I didn't realize how lucky I was. I remember cousins coming to our house because we had magazines to look at," she recalled.

Reading for Citizens: Schools and Libraries

For most of my interviewees, who included former librarians and teachers, an ingrained habit of reading signaled a form of moral achievement and civic participation. While unwilling to outright condemn those who rejected the habit of reading, these men and women, most of whom had devoted long professional lives to promoting literacy among the young, saw reading as more than a means to individual entertainment and useful information. Reading fulfilled a natural need, the lack of which resulted in "starvation," according to Livingston. It also provided the basis of education that turned children into fully functioning adult citizens. These beliefs drew on a long American tradition that held up informed citizenship as a justification for free and universal public schools and libraries. In Colonial New England, colonies and townships had already passed laws requiring parents to teach their children to read, partly to ensure that they were capable of self-support, partly to ensure their religious faith and spiritual salvation, but also so that they would be able to read the laws governing their lives, especially the "capital laws."[22] In the early republic, print took on even greater significance as citizens participated in civic affairs no longer solely through face-to-face meetings in their local communities, but also through this newly widespread medium of communication. Ideally, an informed citizen was one with the knowledge and virtue to put self-interest to one side and to select as political representatives those best men who would act in the interests of the republic. Print helped enable this universal, as opposed to particularistic, vision of society, making possible both the impersonal voice of the author and the impersonal response of the citizen.[23] To read and to write in print were equally to

---

22 E. Jennifer Monaghan, *Learning to Read and Write in Colonial America* (Amherst: University of Massachusetts Press, 2005), 31.

23 Michael Warner, *The Letters of the Republic: Publication and the Public Sphere in Eighteenth-Century*

participate in civic life as Americans developed political ideas and understandings of citizenship through the medium of what François Furstenberg calls "civic texts." In popular printed items that included pamphlets, broadsides, school grammars, almanacs, newspapers, and sermons, men and women living ordinary lives in rural areas of America encountered the writings of European republican and Enlightenment writers like John Milton and David Hume, and later of Americans like George Washington, Thomas Jefferson, and Alexander Hamilton.[24]

Although the republican vision saw property-owning yeomen farmers as the foundation of an ideal citizenry, an increasing number of white men inhabited the expanding cities and were occupied not as farmers but as artisans and tradesmen. By 1824, the property qualification for voting had dropped away as the franchise was extended to all white male adults in every state. At the same time, states tightened racial restrictions. When in 1790 the Congress passed a law declaring that naturalization was to be confined to "free white persons," the legislators were only codifying an unquestioned belief that citizenship and whiteness went together.[25] No racial restrictions were placed on voting at that time, however. South Carolina added a racial restriction in 1778, and Delaware in 1787, but free blacks generally enjoyed the right to vote in the 1780s, and even as late as 1850 in Virginia. African Americans fought back against the introduction of these restrictions, arguing that in an era of universal manhood suffrage voting (previously considered a privilege) was a right to be enjoyed by all citizens.[26]

With the widening of the white franchise came the extension of education, as states adopted free public—or common—schools for white boys and girls. The link between citizenship and literacy provided legitimation for schooling as an object of public policy. Educational reformers made the establishment of free common schools in both urban and rural areas a goal, backed, at least in the North, by newspaper editorials that promoted literacy as a vehicle for moral and eco-

America (Cambridge: Harvard University Press, 1990), xiii.

24 François Furstenberg, *In the Name of the Father: Washington's Legacy, Slavery, and the Making of a Nation* (New York: Penguin, 2006), 20–21.

25 Jacobson, *Whiteness of a Different Color*, 25, 22.

26 Richard D. Brown, *Strength of a People: The Idea of an Informed Citizenry in America, 1650–1870* (Chapel Hill: University of North Carolina Press, 1996), 157, 172.

nomic self-improvement as well as nation building. As in Colonial times, a common school education was seen as an avenue to personal economic independence (even prosperity) and individual moral wor-thiness. For the developing Republic, however, education provided insurance that cultural values for print and civic participation would be perpetuated through coming generations.[27] At the same time, increased literacy for women as well as men became the object of pub-lic policy, even though women were denied the vote. Advocates of schooling for girls argued that women were as capable as men of bene-fiting from education, and pointed to the important role that mothers played in raising their sons to be citizens. Women's long-established responsibility for teaching young children to read became a powerful justification for including girls in the developing movement to establish free common schools in the early nineteenth century.

In the rural Northeast, white children's school enrollment rose steadily, especially among girls. Drawing on a Protestant value for lit-eracy and the development of a market economy, and taking advantage of the expansion of publications and political calls to dispel ignorance, rural communities increasingly invested in free schooling for girls and boys to the extent that, in New York State, for instance, school enroll-ment of children under the age of twenty had risen from 37 percent in 1800 to 60 percent in 1825. Urban schooling lagged behind that in rural areas, however. In the cities, private, religious, and other charita-ble organizations tended to play the role that community-funded school districts filled in the countryside. Apprenticeship provided another path to education for boys and sometimes for girls.[28] In the middle decades of the century, efforts to standardize and regulate this patch-work of institutional provision became the focus of school reformers, as states began to adopt a unified system of common schooling free to white girls as well as boys. School reform gathered momentum in the decades before the Civil War, drawing on ideas from Europe, includ-ing those of the Englishman Joseph Lancaster and the Swiss Johann Heinrich Pestalozzi, as well as the Prussian model of compulsory free

---

27 Lee Soltow and Edward Stevens, *The Rise of Literacy and the Common School in the United States: A Socioeconomic Analysis to 1870* (Chicago: University of Chicago Press, 1981), 20–22.

28 Carl F. Kaestle, *Pillars of the Republic: Common Schools and American Society, 1780–1860* (New York: Hill and Wang, 1983), 24, 30–31.

education, to advocate for free common schools that would foster moral education and good citizenship. The educational practices that these predominantly Protestant, middle-class Anglo-Americans advocated rested on the belief that literacy could act as a conduit for socialization into a set of moral values that stemmed from the intertwining of republicanism, Protestantism, and capitalism. The values emphasized, among others, were the importance of personal character-building, individual industriousness, the equality of economic opportunity, the need for public intervention to unify an increasingly diverse population, and a limited though respected domestic role for women.[29]

While for most white Americans the nineteenth century saw an expansion of reading opportunities, for African Americans the picture was more somber. For slaves, reading instruction went hand-in-hand with religious instruction, whether through missions, or at the behest of slaveholders. Some slaves taught themselves to read. In the middle of the eighteenth century, although South Carolina (in 1740) and Georgia (in 1755) passed laws forbidding the teaching of writing to slaves, the teaching of reading was legal everywhere in the colonies.[30] Still, in the South, fear of slave rebellion was always present, and a literate slave was seen as a dangerous one. Following the Nat Turner revolt in 1831, fear of slave insurrection prompted the passage of repressive anti-literacy legislation in several states. Between 1829 and 1834 Alabama, Georgia, Louisiana, North and South Carolina, and Virginia all passed anti-literacy laws. By 1850 the legal codes of North and South Carolina, Georgia, and Virginia prohibited teaching slaves to read and write, although Virginia's law did not forbid owners from teaching their slaves.[31] However, in some ways the laws reinforced the abolitionist case, since by using the power of the state to deny slaves the opportunity to read they clearly contravened republican principles. An alternative response to the "problem" of slave literacy was to channel slave reading in ways that encouraged "habits of order, industry, and discipline," comments Furstenberg. Didactic and religious texts targeted at slaves sought to "shore up slavery and protect the Southern social order in a

---

29 Ibid., 71–77.

30 Monaghan, *Learning to Read and Write*, 242.

31 Janet Cornelius, "'When I Can Read My Title Clear': Slave Accounts of the Literacy Process, 1830–1865," *Phylon* 44, no. 3 (1983): 173.

manner more consistent with U.S. nationalism."[32] Reading was to be a means to piety, rather than empowerment.[33] Despite these restrictions, the enslaved recognized the value of literacy and found ingenious though risky ways to acquire reading and writing skills. Following the Civil War, newly freed blacks eagerly sought the means to learn to read and write. Schools for freedpeople sprang up, sometimes with the help of missionary societies or the Freedman's Bureau, but often initiated by ex-slaves.[34]

The cornerstone of the common school curriculum was learning to read. At least in the North, parents as well as legislators supported the goals of the common school movement.[35] Parents were willing to trade control over their children's education for the benefits that they perceived: basic training in skills and literacy, as well as character development.[36] Legislators were convinced that common schooling could head off potential threats to the safety and stability of the republic, particularly in helping reduce urban crime by encouraging the habit of self-improvement. Newspaper editors and authors of school texts and other books targeted at children, too, reinforced this general message. Authors of children's books urged children to "mind their books" and love their schools, competing with each other to impress parents and teachers of the moral worthiness of their publications.[37]

By the time of the Civil War, a model for publicly sponsored literacy in the form of free common schools for white children was in place in many areas of the country, but was especially well established in the Northeast and Midwest. During the antebellum years, a parallel movement to establish the free publicly sponsored library—another institution that aimed to spread literacy—was also under way. In 1776 twenty-

---

32 Furstenberg, *In the Name of the Father*, 171.

33 Cornelius, "When I Can Read My Title Clear," 171.

34 Heather Andrea Williams, *Self-Taught: African American Education in Slavery and Freedom* (Chapel Hill: University of North Carolina Press, 2005), 7–29.

35 In the South in the late 1860s and 1870s, Reconstruction legislatures enacted measures to establish public education for black and white students. White resistance to paying taxes even for the education of white children took the form of violence against schoolteachers, students, and buildings. When the federal government withdrew and Reconstruction legislatures gave way to white supremacists, although public schools for black children remained in place, they were severely underfunded. States designed ways to treat black and white children unequally and to minimize spending on black education (Williams, *Self Taught*, 80–95, 194–99).

36 Kaestle, *Pillars of the Republic*, 160–61.

37 Soltow and Stevens, *The Rise of Literacy*, 71, 73.

nine "public" libraries containing a total of 45,623 books had existed in the thirteen colonies.[38] These libraries were "public" as opposed to privately owned by individuals, rather than freely open to the community, however. Subscription libraries became common in New England and mid-Atlantic states during the first half of the nineteenth century, and by 1850 New England states had established over one thousand "social" libraries.[39] As antebellum Yankee settlers moved west, they brought with them this model for institutionalizing the sharing of books. In thousands of small towns, the same leading families who established local banks, schools, churches, and voluntary and fraternal organizations like the Masons also formalized cooperative groups for the circulation of reading materials based on subscription or the purchase of shares. Use of such libraries, dependent upon a fee or subscription, was mostly confined to the more affluent. Free public libraries were still rare at that time, but in 1849 New Hampshire passed a bill allowing municipalities to tax themselves to set up a free public library, and Massachusetts followed in 1851. The 1854 opening of the Boston Public Library gave major impetus to public library development, and by 1875 all other New England states had passed public library laws.[40] In other parts of the country, too, states passed public library enabling laws during the later part of the nineteenth century, although legislation

---

38 Department of the Interior, Bureau of Education, *Public Libraries in the United States of America: Their History, Condition, and Management. A Special Report* (Washington: Government Printing Office, 1876), xi, xvi, 773. Henceforth, 1876 Report.

39 Jesse Shera, *Foundations of the Public Library: The Origins of the Public Library Movement in New England, 1629–1855* (Chicago: University of Chicago Press, 1949), 69. By "social" library, Shera meant any "voluntary association of individuals who had contributed money toward a common fund to be used for the purchase of books." Not included in his estimate were academic, school, private, and circulating libraries (57).

40 Sidney Ditzion, *Arsenals of a Democratic Culture: A Social History of the Public Library Movement in New England and the Middle States from 1850 to 1900* (Chicago: American Library Association, 1947), 30. The motives of Boston Public Library founders, particularly George Ticknor, have been a subject of controversy among historians. Ditzion's view was that Ticknor was driven by "a deep concern for the preservation of our republican institutions on the foundation of an intelligent population," and that he "loved and trusted the great majority of his fellow citizens as much as he feared and hated what he termed illiterate mobs" (16–17). However, revisionist scholars such as Michael H. Harris have argued for an alternative view; see Harris, *The Role of the Public Library in American Life: A Speculative Essay*, University of Illinois Graduate School of Library Science Occasional Papers 117 (Champaign: Illinois Graduate School of Library Science, 1975). Harris presents Ticknor as "an arrogant patrician" and "narrow-minded bigot" whose principal goals for the new public library were, first, to educate the masses so that they would follow the "best men" and, second, to provide the elite minority who would someday become leaders of the political, intellectual, and moral affairs of the nation with access to "the best books" (7).

did not necessarily translate into actual libraries, at least in the short run. Iowa, for example, passed such a law in 1870, but five years later still had only four public libraries.[41] Wisconsin's enabling law passed in 1872.

Early library leaders shared many of the personal characteristics, values, and strategies of antebellum school reformers. Mostly white male Anglo-American Protestants of the middling sort, leading librarians and library supporters made the link between formal education and the public library a justification for raising public money for the latter. Introducing the first issue of the *American Library Journal*, Melvil Dewey claimed a place for libraries in the developing school system. "[The journal's] founders," he wrote, " have an intense faith in the future of our libraries and believe that if the best methods can be applied by the best librarians, the public may soon be brought recognize our claim that the free library ranks with the free school . . . The time is when a library is a school, and the librarian is in the highest sense a teacher, and the visitor is a reader among the books as a workman among his tools. Will any man deny to the high calling of such a librarianship the title of profession?"[42] By invoking the library "faith" and the "high calling" of librarianship, Dewey also sought to imbue librarianship with a moral legitimacy that the journal's readers would both understand and appreciate. Like teachers, librarians often saw their role in missionary terms. This was a view that fitted very well the increasingly feminized nature of the profession. It also meshed with the language used by leading literary figures, clergy, and other cultural authorities accustomed to discussing the place of reading in American lives.

Gradually the public library idea took hold, and in the developing Midwest, establishing a local library along with other middle-class institutions became one of the ways in which influential members of a pioneering community put down roots and boosted their own value.[43] In the decades that followed the passing of enabling legislation, a network of public libraries sprang up across the country, as at the state

---

41 Daniel Goldstein, "The Spirit of an Age: Iowa Public Libraries and Professional Librarians as Solutions to Society's Problems, 1890–1940," *Libraries and Culture* 38, no. 3 (Summer 2003): 215–16.

42 Melvil Dewey, "The Profession," *American Library Journal* 1 (September 30, 1876): 5–6.

43 For an account of the public library's role in one community, see Christine Pawley, *Reading on the Middle Border: The Culture of Print in Late Nineteenth-Century Osage, Iowa* (Amherst: University of Massachusetts Press, 2001), especially 61–116.

and local level groups of people—the majority of them women—worked to persuade communities that public libraries were worth financing. At the state level, librarians formed library associations and supported the creation of state library commissions. In towns and villages thousands of women joined women's clubs that made support of the local library a high priority.[44] Women found opportunities for paid employment in libraries, too. The Boston Public Library hired the first woman assistant in 1852, and over the next twenty-five years feminized two-thirds of its workforce. By 1910, nearly four-fifths (78.4 percent) of all American library staff were female, and by 1920 that figure was nearly nine-tenths; at the beginning of the twenty-first century women librarians still constituted 85 percent.[45]

Finding the money to fund libraries in small communities was a perennial problem. By 1876, the library of the State Historical Society of Wisconsin (formed in 1849) was the largest in the state, with over 33,000 volumes.[46] By contrast, Wisconsin's local tax-supported libraries, freely open to members of the public, were mostly small and poorly endowed at this time. As elsewhere, the public library movement in Wisconsin had its roots in the library associations that Yankee migrants had brought with them from the East. In its state constitution of 1848, Wisconsin provided part of the income of the school fund to support libraries in the common schools. The State Historical Society formed a kind of central consulting agency, corresponding with libraries across the state, answering questions, and even loaning out materials at the request of local librarians.[47] Most of the early library associations were controlled by boards of directors—usually consisting of nine members—who represented the interests of the association's membership.

---

44 According to Daniel Goldstein, it was the interaction between these three institutions— women's clubs, the state library commission, and the state library association—that contributed to the flourishing condition of Iowa's public libraries during the period 1890–1940 (Goldstein, "The Spirit of an Age," 214).

45 Dee Garrison, *Apostles of Culture: The Public Librarian and American Culture, 1876–1920* (Madison: University of Wisconsin Press, 2003), 173. According to the U.S. Census Bureau, in 2003, 84.4 percent of librarians in the United States were women ("No. 597: Employed Civilians by Occupation, Sex, Race and Hispanic Origin: 2003," *U.S. Census Bureau, Statistical Abstract of the United States: 2004–2005*, www.census.gov/prod/www/statistical-abstract-04.html).

46 1876 Report, xi, xvi, 773.

47 Kathryn Saucerman, "A Study of the Wisconsin Library Movement 1850–1900 (M.A. Thesis, University of Wisconsin, 1944), 69.

In 1872 the state passed a law that authorized Wisconsin cities and towns to establish free public libraries and reading rooms. Drawing on library association experience, the act called for a library controlled by a board of nine members or "trustees" to be chosen by the community's elected representatives—usually the city council (a body of men, elected by men). The act authorized library boards to hire "assistants" (rather than librarians) to run the library on a day-to-day basis.[48]

Rural communities, lacking the resources of big cities, typically lagged behind in providing purpose-built libraries. At the turn of the century, however, public library advocates all over America found an ally in Andrew Carnegie's philanthropic library building program. Between 1886 and 1917, the Carnegie program spurred on the library movement by funding 1,689 public and academic libraries. Many of these were situated in small towns and were modest in scope and vision. Carnegie discouraged the building of monumental libraries. Early recipients often found themselves without money for books and furniture, since construction costs had run over budget. In response, the program administrator, James Bertram, devised a pamphlet titled "Notes on the Erection of Library Buildings," in which he gave advice to library committees. The pamphlet included sample plans, and Bertram suggested functional design features, such as open plan, low bookcases, and glass partitions that drew more inspiration from department stores and factories than the ecclesiastical structures beloved of architects.[49]

States that benefited most from Carnegie's philanthropy lay in the Midwest and the West, where many communities were still new. Over half of all the libraries that Carnegie funded were in the top ten recipient states, consisting of nine midwestern states plus California.[50] Sixty Wisconsin municipalities accepted Carnegie library grants; only six states built more Carnegie public libraries than Wisconsin.[51] However,

---

48 John C. Colson, "The Public Library Movement in Wisconsin, 1836–1900" (Ph.D. Diss., University of Chicago, 1973), 364.

49 Abigail A. Van Slyck, *Free to All: Carnegie Libraries and American Culture, 1890–1920* (Chicago: University of Chicago Press, 1995), 34–40.

50 Percentage calculated from figures in Theodore Jones, *Carnegie Libraries across America* (New York: John Wiley, 1997), 128–30.

51 David I. Macleod, *Carnegie Libraries in Wisconsin* (Madison: Department of History, University of Wisconsin, 1968), 25–26.

not all communities saw Carnegie funding as an unalloyed good. The topic was often controversial, and eleven Wisconsin municipalities went so far as to reject Carnegie offers. Six of these, the communities of Columbus, New London, Racine, Ripon, Sturgeon Bay, and Wausau, subsequently changed their minds, but Manawa, Mineral Point, Monroe, New Richmond, and Portage stood by their refusals.[52] Reasons varied. Sometimes the argument prevailed that Carnegie funds consti- tuted "tainted money" obtained by unscrupulous means. Such objec- tions were not confined to Wisconsin. Bitter memories persisted of Pittsburgh's Homestead strike and lockout of 1892 that pitted the Amalgamated Association of Iron and Steel Workers against the Carnegie Steel Company, in which hired Pinkerton guards battled with striking workers. In Oelwein, Iowa, for instance, the local Trades and Labor Assembly rejected a proposal for a new Carnegie library in 1902, resolving "that if Mr. Andrew Carnegie wants to use some of his super- fluous money to good advantage" he should "send it to the widows who were made widows, and the orphans who were made orphans by the death of their husbands and fathers who were killed at the time of the strike at Homestead, Pa., a few years ago."[53]

Often, though, local objections reflected an unwillingness to spend money on a library. Carnegie grants required local communities to make their own contributions in terms of funding and commitments to staff and equip the library. In Wausau, Wisconsin, voters rejected a proposed Carnegie gift of $25,000 in a referendum in 1903. A petition carrying four hundred signatures argued both that Carnegie was not fit to donate money to the city and that the library would cost the city too much. Class and ethnicity also appeared to play a part. Whereas nearly 60 percent of the men in the ward that voted most heavily to support the new library were businessmen, professional, or clerical workers, 80 percent of those in the ward most heavily opposed were skilled or unskilled workers. Much of the strongest opposition came from residents of German origin, perhaps because the existing library had made little effort to collect books in German. Nearly 75 percent of

---

52 Ibid., 31–32.

53 Quoted in Robert Sidney Martin et al., "Mistaken Pride, Unseasonable Rush: Rejected Grants in Missouri, Iowa and Nebraska," in Martin, *Carnegie Denied: Communities Rejecting Carn- egie Library Construction Grants, 1898–1925* (Westport, Conn.: Greenwood, 1993), 121.

the residents of the ward where library opposition was strongest had parents born in Germany. A German-language newspaper, *Der Deutsche Pionier*, attacked Carnegie in an article titled "Der Tanz um's goldene Kalb" (Dance around the Golden Calf). However, the following year, the Wausau Men's Club, a group of relatively affluent professional and businessmen collected over fourteen hundred signatures in favor of the library, and since more than half the registered voters had supported the petition, the city council agreed to accept Carnegie funds.[54]

Reformist programs for universal literacy were thoroughly enmeshed with concerns about who was—and should be—eligible to participate in democratic processes. In urban areas calls for public education relied on fear of immigrant ignorance, crime, and vice, pointing to frightening implications for the maintenance of a republic based on a virtuous, informed citizenry.[55] Whereas the first naturalization law of 1790 had limited citizenship to the safely unambiguous category of white persons, the massive influx of undeniably white, but often Catholic, sometimes illiterate, and usually not English-speaking immigrants from Europe cast doubt upon the capability of whiteness to stand as a reliable marker of civic virtue.[56] Yet universal male suffrage, essentially complete by 1830, conferred upon white male immigrants the same rights and responsibilities as enjoyed by white native-born American men. In some states aliens could vote: the laws and constitutions of at least twenty-two states permitted this, although in the second half of the nineteenth century states gradually began to withdraw the right, starting with Illinois in 1848. Wisconsin's constitution of 1848 permitted aliens to vote who had lived in the state for one year and who declared their intention to become citizens, a right that immigrants enjoyed until a constitutional amendment withdrew it in 1908.[57]

After the Civil War, emancipation's extension of the franchise to black men implied that white women could come under their protection—a possibility that many white women found difficult to accept. At the same time, immigrant votes were changing the political landscape,

54 Macleod, *Carnegie Libraries in Wisconsin*, 33, 37–38, 146.

55 Kaestle, *Pillars of the Republic*, 36.

56 Jacobson, *Whiteness of a Difference Color*, 7.

57 Leon E. Aylsworth, "The Passing of Alien Suffrage," *American Political Science Review* 25, no. 1 (1931): 114.

particularly in the cities. The older understanding of politics as the disinterested work of morally upright (white) male citizens gave way to a view of politics as the dirty work of corrupt and self-interested "machines," in which "bosses" manipulated voters.[58] Some leaders of the women's suffrage movement reacted with anger to the extension of the franchise to men whom they considered their racial and class inferiors, pointing to ignorance born of illiteracy as a fundamental problem. "Think of Patrick and Sambo and Hans and Yung Tung," fumed Elizabeth Cady Stanton in 1869, "who do not know the difference between a monarchy and a republic, who can not read the Declaration of Independence or Webster's spelling-book, making laws for Lucretia Mott, Ernestine L. Rose and Anna E. Dickinson."[59] Their inability to read significant civic texts condemned such men, since poor literacy skills were a clear indication of racial inferiority and unfitness for citizenship, this rhetoric implied. By contrast, white women's shared ancestry with white men gave them a superior claim to citizenship, argued Frances Willard, leader of the national Woman's Christian Temperance Union (founded in 1874). Willard believed that it was the task of white women to raise men to a standard of morality and behavior that she identified as "a white life," one in which men should avoid alcohol and seek sexual purity, defined as chastity outside of monogamy. Stanton and Willard both favored an educational qualification for the franchise, fearing that the "inferior races" would use their political power to increase the oppression of women.[60]

"The presence of so many culturally alien people in antebellum America greatly reinforced the use of emerging public school systems to teach children a common English language and a common Protestant morality," comments the historian Carl Kaestle. The movement for state regulation of education proceeded, as gradually midwestern states followed the Northeast in establishing offices of state superintendents of education in the 1840s. In the 1850s, further centralization and standardization took place as states introduced teachers' institutes for pro-

---

58 Ratification of the Fourteenth and Fifteenth Amendments to the Constitution took place between 1868 and 1870. See Louise Michele Newman, *White Women's Rights: The Racial Origins of Feminism in the United States* (New York: Oxford University Press, 1999), 56, 59.

59 Quoted in ibid., 6.

60 Ibid., 67–68.

fessional training and development, encouraged support for school libraries, and experimented with supervision at the county level.[61] Still, although in the countryside individual, and in the cities organizational, sponsorship of literacy through schooling was well established in the antebellum years, the extent to which governments should be involved was far from agreed upon. While the mainly Whig reformers pressed for state regulation and centralization of schooling, others—often Democrats—resisted, some on the grounds of local autonomy, others on religious grounds.

Catholics, in particular, objected to the use of public funds (including tax dollars contributed by Catholics) to promote what they saw as Protestant values and beliefs. They especially objected to the practice of reading the Bible in school.[62] A common response among Catholics was to set up independent schools that eventually formed a separate, though parallel system, to that sponsored by the state. Language of instruction, too, was an issue, as even some Protestant immigrant groups resisted the efforts of the common school movement to create linguistic uniformity. Wisconsin's 1848 constitution, for instance, permitted school districts to provide instruction in languages other than English, and local practices varied with the acquiescence of school officials. German was most commonly substituted for English, sometimes for part of the day, sometimes for part of the school year, while in some areas school instruction was predominantly in German. However, local compliance depended on the support of the locally influential, and some rural communities simply ignored official rules that didn't suit them.[63] In the 1880s Yankee calls for state regulation of the common schools founded expression in Wisconsin's Bennett Act of 1889 that enforced attendance at public and parochial schools and required that classes in reading, writing, arithmetic, and American history be taught in English. German Catholics and German and Scandinavian Lutherans in particular were outraged, expressing their anger in true democratic

---

61 Kaestle, *Pillars of the Republic*, 182.

62 Richard Jensen, *The Winning of the Midwest: Social and Political Conflict, 1888–1896* (Chicago: University of Chicago Press, 1971), 125.

63 Kaestle, *Pillars of the Republic*, 165, 180.

fashion at the ballot box.[64] Despite their politically organized opposition, however, the act stood, its provisions not rescinded until 1990.[65]

By the end of the nineteenth century, anxieties about citizenship, race, and immigration had resulted in legislation that mandated literacy qualifications for voting. In the South, poor white and black voters were systematically prevented from voting by literacy tests and poll taxes introduced after the end of Reconstruction. Seven southern states introduced literacy tests for voting between 1890 and 1908, but Connecticut and Massachusetts had already done so in 1856 and 1858. Other states to follow suit included Wyoming (1890), Maine (1894), California (1896), Washington and Delaware (1898), New Hampshire (1906), Arizona (1912), New York (1922), and Oregon (1926). Most states specified literacy in English.[66] Congress also sought new ways to shape the characteristics of those seeking entry to the United States. In particular, legislators tried to encourage the entry of literate Europeans who they felt could be easily assimilated, and to discourage the immigration of Asians altogether. The Immigration Act of 1891 set up the federal Bureau of Immigration, and in 1896 both houses of Congress passed a bill to require literacy of immigrants, but in the face of opposition from employers President Grover Cleveland vetoed it. In 1906, the Naturalization Act included an English language test for naturalization, and in 1911 a body that Congress established to investigate the effects of immigration, known as the Dillingham Commission, published its report, recommending a literacy test. Over the next several years, Congress and successive presidents argued over the desirability of demanding a literacy test. In February 1917 Congress succeeded in passing a bill over President Wilson's veto, excluding illiterate aliens unable to read forty words in some language (not necessarily English).[67]

---

64 Nesbit, *History of Wisconsin*, 377. For details of the political conflict over the Bennett Act, see Jensen, *The Winning of the Midwest*, especially pages 124–47.

65 Harold F. Schiffman, *Linguistic Culture and Language Policy* (London: Routledge, 1996), 233.

66 Michael Schudson, *The Good Citizen: A History of American Civic Life* (New York: Free Press, 1998), 183.

67 Plummer Alston Jones Jr., *Still Struggling for Equality: American Public Library Services with Minorities* (Westport, Conn.: Libraries Unlimited, 2004), 3–7. Other bills deprived women who married aliens of their citizenship (1907), later limiting that to women who married Asians (1922), and set quotas for immigrants from different areas of the globe. Especial discrimination against Asian immigrants continued in a series of bills and court cases during the 1920s. In 1924, the Johnson-Reed Act limited the number of immigrants to be admitted from any coun-

This was a time of deep concern about social unrest, the politics of influence, excessive corporate power, economic depression, and environmental destruction. The 1890s were characterized by profound social upheavals that included labor disputes like the Homestead strike of 1892 and the Illinois Pullman strike of 1894, both of which resulted in violence and military intervention. These strikes coincided with a period of severe economic dislocation. The four-year depression that began in 1893 caused widespread unemployment and social upheaval. In Wisconsin, for example, nearly half of urban workers found themselves unemployed, while in the countryside falling agricultural prices reduced farm incomes. At the same time, stories of bankers' fraud and embezzlement appalled the state. The chasm between rich and poor increased, and public indignation rose at what people saw as betrayal and exploitation by the rich.[68] Trends in publishing reflected the disturbances of the times and fed calls for reform. Muckraking journalists exposed scandal and corruption and drew attention to slum conditions in the cities. In 1891, journalist and photographer Jacob Riis (an immigrant from Denmark) published *How the Other Half Lives*, a shocking exposure of squalid life in the tenements of New York. Novelists such as Stephen Crane, Frank Norris, and Theodore Dreiser told pessimistic tales that depicted people as helpless and suffering in the face of overwhelming social and natural forces.

Reform movements coalesced under the term "Progressivism." A key question for Progressive Era politicians and reformers was, "What is the relationship of the state to society in determining the mode of production and the distribution of resources?" The Progressive Era also explicitly linked consumption with citizenship, constructing consumers as a new group of political actors who exercised their agency through direct means, including, as Lizabeth Cohen puts it, "primaries, initiatives, referenda, recalls, and female suffrage—as well as specific remedies to protect consumers and taxpayers from exploitation, such as municipal and consumer ownership of utilities and fairer tax

---

try to 2 percent of the number recorded from that country in the 1890 census. Not until the McCarran-Walter Act of 1952 were all races made eligible for immigration, although a quota system remained (see Jones, *Still Struggling*, 7, 34; "Immigration to the United States, 1789–1930," Harvard University Library, ocp.hul.harvard.edu/immigration/dates.html).

68 Thelen, *The New Citizenship*, 57–62.

policies."[69] The political system, commerce, labor, health, education, and the lives of working people in the cities and the countryside all came under scrutiny from official bodies as well as from voluntary organizations. Professional social scientists offered their expertise, armed with a panoply of investigative techniques like surveys and systematic observation, along with statistical methods for analyzing the results. Women's clubs set aside projects of personal self-improvement through the study of literature in favor of debates on topics in economics and sociology. In Milwaukee, Wisconsin, bankers and lawyers, clergy and journalists also formed study groups. At Milwaukee's Liberal Club, Socialist leader Victor Berger instructed bankers, merchants, and lawyers on socialism. In Professor Richard T. Ely's economics classes at the University of Wisconsin, students of the new profession of social work learned to construe the poor as "prisoners of their environments, not of their characters."[70]

In the fast-growing cities, reformers organized charities to save immigrant and native working-class boys and girls from the evils of the streets. "Delinquency," these middle-class reformers believed, resulted at least in part from large numbers of poor children roaming the streets or laboring in factories and sweatshops, unlike their middle-class counterparts who were more likely to be safely tucked up at home in the bosom of their (smaller and more affluent) families.[71] Reformers thought that reading was an especially safe and suitable occupation for children. To provide alternatives to life on the streets, the Boston Children's Aid Society started a home library program in 1887. Depositing boxes of twenty books in the home of a child designated as "librarian," the Society arranged for the circulation of the books among groups of children, who then met for weekly book discussions. In 1893 seventy groups with a total of over 630 children took part in the program, which the Society believed would help counteract the harmful influences of dime novels.[72] In the long run, the develop-

---

69 Lizabeth Cohen, *A Consumers' Republic: The Politics of Mass Consumption in Postwar America* (New York: Vintage, 2003), 21.

70 Thelen, *The New Citizenship*, 71.

71 Eric C. Schneider, *In the Web of Class: Delinquents and Reformers in Boston, 1810s–1930s* (New York: New York University Press, 1992), 146.

72 Ibid., 133.

ment of free and compulsory schools and of free public libraries reduced the scope of such charitable efforts, but in the meantime, not only home libraries, but also boys' and girls' clubs, industrial schools, settlement houses, and gymnasiums worked to convert the residents of working-class neighborhoods to middle-class cultural practices.[73]

Urban social reformers also found outlets in new initiatives like the Young Men's and Young Women's Christian Associations (YMCA and YWCA), as well as in the settlement movement. The Hull House settlement in Chicago (founded by Jane Addams in 1889) became one of the best-known projects in the country. In a neighborhood comprised of European immigrants of many nationalities, including Italians, Russian and Polish Jews, Irish, Germans, Greeks, and Bohemians, Addams and her colleagues established services for the neighborhood that included a daycare and kindergarten, employment bureau, art gallery, libraries, and music and art classes. In the process Addams became a model of activism and even a hero for other women, including those flocking to the newly feminized profession of librarianship. Lutie Stearns, a leader of Wisconsin's public library movement, later commented, "I've been called 'a radical' and 'a communist,' but I recall that Susan B. Anthony was termed 'an old hen' and Jane Addams was designated . . . as 'the most dangerous person in America,' so I'm in good company."[74]

The problem of immigration was principally seen as an urban phenomenon, but rural residents, too, came under expert scrutiny. In contrast to the images presented of problem-ridden cities, rural America was often cast in idyllic terms. Even in 1910 the rural population continued to exceed that of urban areas, and farm employment reached an all-time high of 13.6 million in 1916.[75] Country life was still considered the norm for Americans, and until 1920 farming appeared to be a good prospect for young people growing up on farms, as well as for immigrants. Yet even during this period of relative affluence, signs of impending

---

73 Susan Thorne, "Missionary-Imperial Feminism," 39–65, in *Gendered Missions: Women and Men in Missionary Discourse and Practice*, ed. Mary Taylor Huber and Nancy C. Lutkehaus (Ann Arbor: University of Michigan Press, 1999).

74 Quoted in Ruth Kohler, Story of Wisconsin Women (Kohler, Wis.: Committee on Wisconsin Women for the 1948 Wisconsin Centennial, 1948), 89.

75 John J. Fry. "Reading, Reform, and Rural Change: The Midwestern Farm Press, 1895–1920" (Ph.D. Diss., University of Iowa, 2002), 26; The Statistical History of the United State: From Colonial Times to the Present, (New York: Basic Books, 1976), 11.

decline were already evident. Progressive Era reforms were helping improve the quality of urban life. Perceptions grew that it had even over-taken that of the countryside, threatening the very "civilization" that rural life depended on, as young people left for the cities. From being the ideal of American civic participation, rural residents become a source of unease. In 1908 President Theodore Roosevelt appointed an investiga-tive body, the Country Life Commission. The resulting report noted that to stem the exodus from the country to the town, government and other agencies needed to address the social and physical needs of rural people. "If country life is to become what it should be, and what I believe it ulti-mately will be—one of the most dignified and sought-after ways of earn-ing a living, the farmer must take advantage not only of the agricultural knowledge which is at his disposal, but of the methods which have raised and continue to raise the standard of living and of intelligence in other callings," Roosevelt wrote in the introduction.[76]

The Commission pointed to four "fundamental" remedies: Know-ledge, Education, Organization, and Spiritual Forces. Underlying all these remedies were institutions—the United States Department of Agriculture and state-supported agricultural colleges, the public schools, voluntary clubs, and the churches.[77] The report supported the notion of a nation-wide extension service (along with the development of university-based rural sociology and agricultural economics). Rural residents needed help with communications (advanced by such improvements as paved roads) and social organizations, the Commission pronounced, but above all they needed public educational institutions like schools and libraries. The Country Life Commission Report added weight to Progressive Era efforts to extend the reach of educational institutions to rural areas. The responsibility for this seemed to be fall-ing more and more upon the shoulders of the government.

Expanding the reach of government demanded a shift from the old system of partisan politics that mainly functioned to parcel out civil service jobs to loyal supporters, to a new distribution of regulatory power based on principles of meritocracy. The growth of state author-ity and local government responsibility (already boosted by railroad

---

76 U.S. Country Life Commission, Report of the Country Life Commission (Washington: Government Printing Office, 1909), 4.

77 Ibid., 17–18.

regulation) continued, as commissions and other agencies were created to oversee new government operations. At the federal level, efforts during the 1870s and 1880s to regulate interstate commerce demonstrated the struggle for government administrative control of the industrializing economy.[78] In Wisconsin as in other areas of the country, the state legislature responded to pressure from organized groups by assuming new powers to regulate many areas of social life. In 1883 it created a bureau to oversee the enforcement of safety and child labor laws, in response to organized labor. In 1887, sportsmen and resort owners lobbied for, and won, a state system of wardens to enforce fish and game regulations. In Milwaukee after 1885, the Board of Fire and Police Commissioners introduced competitive examinations for employment. In 1895, the state legislature passed a bill to establish the Wisconsin Free Library Commission, and charged it with providing "advice and counsel to all free libraries in the state, and to all communities which may propose to establish them, as to the best means of establishing and administering such libraries, the selection of books, cataloging and other details of library management."[79] With measures such as these, which sought solutions to local issues that would transcend political, ethnic, class, and religious differences, Wisconsin firmly embraced Progressivism, garnering national notice in the process.[80]

The WFLC legislation resulted from the efforts of three people whose interest in libraries grew out of very different experiences. James H. Stout was a reformist Republican state senator and lumber baron from Menomonie, Wisconsin, and a long-time supporter of educational innovation.[81] Frank Avery Hutchins had helped establish the Beaver Dam Free Library Association in 1884 while working as both city clerk of Beaver Dam, Wisconsin, and editor of the Beaver Dam *Argus*. Later, while a library clerk in the office of the state school superintendent, he helped organize school libraries. Along with state education officials, University of Wisconsin faculty, and several members of the American

---

78 For an analysis of the development of Progressive Era administrative structures and relationships, see Stephen Skowronek, *Building a New American State: The Expansion of National Administrative Capacities, 1877–1920* (Cambridge: Cambridge University Press, 1982).

79 Colson, "The Public Library Movement in Wisconsin," 289–94.

80 Thelen, *The New Citizenship*, 35, 31 310.

81 Ann M. Keppel and James I. Clark, "James H. Stout and the Menomonie Schools," Wisconsin Magazine of History 42, no. 3 (1959): 210.

Library Association (ALA), he helped found the Wisconsin Library Association (WLA), in 1891.[82] Lutie Eugenia Stearns had taught in an elementary school in Milwaukee before the Milwaukee Public Library hired her as circulation assistant. She met Hutchins at the first meeting of the newly formed WLA, and both quickly became active at regional and national levels of the expanding world of professional librarianship.

In addition to participating in WLA, Hutchins and Stearns traveled to meetings in other states. At the 1893 Columbian World's Fair in Chicago, they met Melvil Dewey of the State Library of New York, whom Stearns later described as "the country's greatest librarian."[83] There they learned about the traveling library system that Dewey had helped establish in his home state. The following year, Stearns gave a paper entitled "Reading for the Young," at the Lake Placid, New York, meeting of ALA and, in turn, listened to presentations on the state library commissions of Massachusetts and New Hampshire. She acquired copies of the enabling legislation, and on her return home, she and Hutchins set about drafting a similar law for Wisconsin. However, Hutchins credited Stearns with the primary responsibility for founding the WFLC. "Because Miss Stearns wants it and believes in it," he said in 1894, "let us work for a library commission."[84]

The following year, Stout helped steer the necessary legislation through the Wisconsin legislature. With Hutchins as Secretary and Stearns as Librarian, the WFLC set about fostering public library development in Wisconsin along lines already laid out in New England and New York. Their initial budget for 1895 was five hundred dollars, but ten years later this had risen to $23,500.[85] As their work progressed, the WFLC began to break new ground. Based in Madison, over the next few years the WFLC established several programs, or "departments": the Department of Library Extension, the Book Selection and Study Club Department, the Legislative Reference Department, the Library School, and the Traveling Library Department. In different ways, these efforts represented the Progressive Era's efforts to develop an informed

---

82 Colson, "The Public Library Movement in Wisconsin," 289–94.

83 Lutie E. Stearns, "My Seventy-five Years: Part I, 1866–1914," *Wisconsin Magazine of History* 42, no. 4 (1959): 216.

84 "Hutchins and Stearns: Ideas and Energy," *Wisconsin Library Bulletin* (March–April, 1975): 72.

85 Walter S. Botsford, "60 Years of Preparation . . ." *Wisconsin Library Bulletin* 51, no. 5 (1955): 12.

citizenry through reading and helped establish Wisconsin as a leader in the burgeoning library movement. In the eyes of east coast library leaders, Wisconsin, the first state west of New York State to set up a library commission, represented a missionary success story.[86] "When, as often happens, my mental vision sweeps over all the country to see where the best work in some particular line is being done, the state most likely to loom up as leader is Wisconsin, to which we of New York always claim a kinship and think of it as a new New York a thousand miles nearer the sunset," wrote Melvil Dewey in response to an appeal for contributions to a volume celebrating the career of Frank Avery Hutchins.[87]

With the establishment of state library commissions and the spread of libraries, this period saw the rise of the Midwest as a newly powerful center for librarianship. In 1904 a coalition of library commissions from eleven states banded together to form the League of Library Commissions. The League was dominated by midwestern states, and its agenda reflected midwestern librarians' efforts to draw the profession's attention away from a former preoccupation with large city libraries and instead focus on the needs of small communities in rural areas.[88] In 1909 the American Library Association moved its headquarters from Boston, where it had resided since its inception in 1876, to Chicago. Influential behind the move was Henry Legler, director of the Chicago Public Library, and former secretary of the Wisconsin Free Library Commission (Legler had succeeded Hutchins in 1904 when ill health forced the latter to retire).[89] The move recognized the growing influence of the Midwest in the library movement and signaled a shift in professional priorities toward small public libraries.

---

86 Only Connecticut, Massachusetts, New Hampshire, New York, and Vermont predated Wisconsin's establishment of a state library commission.

87 Melvil Dewey, n.d., Frank Avery Hutchins Papers, 1910–1921, WHS. Solicited for a volume of original letters compiled by Lutie Stearns, *Frank A. Hutchins' Worth and Work: Volume of Letters from His Many Friends, 1912*. Dewey's letter is not addressed to Stearns or dated, but some other letters in the volume are addressed to her and are dated May 1912.

88 Alice S. Tyler, "The League of Library Commissions," *Library Journal* (May 1905): 274–77.

89 Wayne A. Wiegand, *The Politics of an Emerging Profession: The American Library Association, 1876–1917* (New York: Greenwood, 1986), 122–23; Joyce M. Latham, "White Collar Read: The American Public Library and the Left-Led CIO: A Case Study of the Chicago Public Library, 1929–1952" (Ph.D. Diss., University of Illinois at Urbana-Champaign, 2007), 51–52. For the next twenty years, ALA was housed in the Chicago Public Library until the library's need for space and a grant from the Carnegie Corporation prompted it to move to new quarters in 1929.

3
Reaching Readers with the Wisconsin Idea

> If the weak ask for justice, the state should see that they get it
> certainly, quickly and surely. If certain social classes are forming
> among us, can we not destroy them by means of education and
> through hope and encouragement make every man more efficient
> so that the door of opportunity may always be open before him?
>
> *Charles McCarthy*, The Wisconsin Idea

Progressive Era institutions systematically channeled reading materials to particular groups of people. Organizations like schools, libraries, women's clubs, and extension agencies cooperated to foster literacy and encourage community participation, especially among immigrant and native-born members of the working class. Through programs of library outreach, Americanization, and, later, adult education, these collaborators institutionalized the distribution of print to those they considered in particular need, sometimes drawing on expert advice from the researchers and professionals populating the developing universities. In Wisconsin, the practice of tapping into university expertise on behalf of all the state's inhabitants became known as the Wisconsin Idea.

In the early years of the twentieth century, WFLC founder Lutie Stearns played a major role in Wisconsin's public library development, gaining a state and even national reputation in the library profession that persisted long after her death in 1943. "I never met Lutie Stearns," Jane Livingston told me in 2000, "though I heard about her for years. She was a legend." During her nineteen years at the WFLC, the passionate and "peppery" Stearns traveled the state's remotest corners, advising, reasoning, and cajoling local communities into establishing free library service.[1] One of her first projects, once the WFLC was approved by the legislature, was to push for the introduction of traveling libraries. Melvil Dewey had established such a system in New York State at least by 1893, followed by Michigan and Iowa in 1895. In 1896 Stearns and her colleague, WFLC Secretary Frank Hutchins, set out to provide books and pamphlets by similar means to Wisconsin's rural inhabitants whether they were English-speaking or not, putting together collections in foreign languages that included Norwegian and Danish, German, Yiddish, Polish, and "Bohemian" (Czech).[2]

Traveling Libraries and Small-Town Libraries

Providing foreign-language materials through traveling libraries formed part of a broader effort at Americanization of immigrants, in which librarians were enthusiastic participants. While early initiatives called for providing English-language materials for immigrants, by the end of the nineteenth century the techniques for assimilation had become more nuanced and sophisticated. Large urban libraries routinely collected books in foreign languages in an effort to attract immigrants—particularly men—to their services. By 1913, 10 percent of the New York Public Library's holdings were printed in twenty-five foreign languages.[3] In the sparsely populated West, librarians also tried "to provide foreign-language materials and to reach diverse audiences," historian Joanne E. Passet notes. "Working in tandem with local residents, they recreated library services that many western residents had previously enjoyed in the East," and "although they sometimes questioned their public's reading tastes, the librarians usually tried to accommodate them, recognizing that recreational reading provided

1 The epithet "peppery" appears in Alan E. Kent, "Frank Avery Hutchins: Pioneer of the Book," *Wisconsin Library Bulletin* 51, no. 5 (1955): 3.

2 Barb VanBrimmer, "History of Mobile Services," in *The Book Stops Here: New Directions in Bookmobile Service*, ed. Catherine Suyak Alloway (Metuchen, N.J.: Scarecrow Press, 1990), 16; Christine Pawley, "Advocate for Access: Lutie Stearns and the Traveling Libraries of the Wisconsin Free Library Commission, 1895–1914," *Libraries and Culture* 35, no. 3 (2000): 441.

3 Dee Garrison, *Apostles of Culture: The Public Librarian and American Society, 1876–1920* (Madison: University of Wisconsin Press, 2003), 217.

western residents with respite from difficult lives in isolated areas."[4] Through such relatively relaxed approaches, librarians hoped to build support for libraries among immigrant and laboring groups who had hitherto been slow to make use of their services. For much of the twentieth century, they would continue to struggle to make contact with those whom Lutie Stearns in 1928 was calling "The Great Unreached."[5]

In Wisconsin, Stout paid for the first traveling libraries out of his own purse, funding a total of sixteen. Other philanthropists and groups followed suit, and by 1902 over three hundred were traveling the state. The WFLC was sending out a greater and greater proportion, and in 1903 the legislature created the Department of Traveling Libraries.[6] The libraries themselves typically consisted of up to one hundred volumes housed in a "strong book case which had a shelf, double doors with a lock and key, a record book for loans, printed copies of the few simple rules, borrowers' blanks, and so complete a line of equipments that it could be set up anywhere on a table, a box or a counter and managed as an independent library," Frank Hutchins wrote in an 1897 account.[7] In addition to general collections for use by individual readers, the WFLC provided traveling libraries for organizations, including lumber camps, tuberculosis sanatoria, and orphanages. On request from study clubs, they also put together collections on specific topics. Hutchins reported in the WFLC's first *Biennial Report*, "About one-third of the libraries are kept in post offices, one-half in farm houses, one at a small railway station, the remainder in small stores."[8] A local volunteer managed each library, overseeing the borrowing process, keeping simple records, and corresponding with the Commission.

Between 1896 and 1914, Stearns helped establish 1,400 traveling

---

4 Joanne E. Passet, *Cultural Crusaders: Women Librarians in the American West, 1900–1917* (Albuquerque: University of New Mexico Press, 1994), 154.

5 Lutie E. Stearns, "The Great Unreached and Why," *Wilson Bulletin* 3, no. 19 (1929): 523–27.

6 Pawley, "Advocate for Access," 442.

7 Frank A. Hutchins, "Free Traveling Libraries in Wisconsin," in *Free Traveling Libraries in Wisconsin: The Story of Their Growth, Purposes, and Development; With Accounts of a Few Kindred Movements* (Madison: Wisconsin Free Library Commission, 1897), 6. Stearns and Hutchins modeled their service on the system of traveling libraries established by Melvil Dewey in New York State during the 1890s; see Wayne A. Wiegand, *Irrepressible Reformer: A Biography of Melvil Dewey* (Chicago: American Library Association, 1996), 148, 203.

8 Reprinted in Frank A. Hutchins, *Traveling Libraries in Wisconsin (Madison: Wisconsin Free Library Commission, 1896)* 82.

libraries and fourteen county traveling library systems. She later recalled that she often delivered the traveling library boxes herself "by stage, sleigh, buggy, wagon, passenger coach and caboose, wearing out five fur coats in succession . . . During the winter I would secure a black bear-skin to wear over my fur-lined muskrat coat . . . I would get a three-seated sleigh, remove the last two seats, and fill the space with books."[9] Other women librarians in the early twentieth century could be equally adventurous. Anne Hadden traveled by horseback and mule to deliver books in remote areas of California's Monterey County, as did Mabel Wilkinson in Wyoming. During the 1930s, "pack horse librarians" distributed books in rural Kentucky, funded by the Works Progress Administration.[10]

In providing materials in languages other than English, the WFLC was venturing into new territory, at least in Wisconsin, where public libraries were dominated by their Yankee heritage. In the 1850s and 1860s the German, Norwegian, Swiss, Italian, Polish, and other immigrants who were pouring into the state did not join the library associations that the Yankees had set up, and very few established their own. Despite many Wisconsin communities' large population of non-English-speaking immigrants, libraries generally failed to collect works in their languages. In Milwaukee, the president of the Young Men's Association (the proprietor of one of the biggest libraries in the state) raised the possibility of adding German language newspapers to the library's collection in 1863, in order to attract "German members." Although the 1870 census showed that one-third of Milwaukee's population was of German birth or ancestry, the Association did not immediately follow up on this suggestion, however. It was not until five years later, following another appeal from another president, that a few German titles did appear in the 1868 catalog.[11]

---

9 Lutie E. Stearns, "My Seventy-Five Years: Part I, 1866–1914," *Wisconsin Magazine of History* 42, no. 4 (1959): 216.

10 Denise Sallee, "Reconceptualizing Women's History: Anne Hadden and the California County Library System," *Libraries and Culture* 27, no. 4 (1992): 351–77; Passet, *Cultural Crusaders*, 92; Jeanne Cannella Schmitzer, "Reaching Out to the Mountains: The Pack Horse Library of Eastern Kentucky," *The Register of the Kentucky Historical Society* 95, no. 1 (1997): 57–77; Donald C. Boyd "The Book Women of Kentucky: The WPA Pack Horse Library Project, 1935–1943," *Libraries and the Cultural Record* 42, no. 2 (2007): 111–28.

11 John C. Colson, "The Public Library Movement in Wisconsin, 1836–1900" (Ph.D. Diss., University of Chicago, 1973), 366, 252–53.

In the early 1900s, Lutie Stearns strongly urged small-town librarians to make foreign language materials a regular feature of their collections, arguing that it was nothing less than an immigrant's right. "Many communities have a considerable proportion of people who read a foreign language more readily than English," she wrote in an advice book for librarians. "These people are usually adults, and many of them are taxpayers. It is both just and politic to please them by providing books in their native languages."[12] Sometimes she resorted to pleading. In 1908 she urged Ashland's librarian to accept a Polish traveling library; "Are there not some Polish people in Ashland—even a few? And may we not send a little group of Polish books (ten volumes) for their use? We shall be glad to do so for the mere payment of the freight on the little box."[13] By such exhortations, Stearns helped raise awareness among Wisconsin's librarians (most of whom had had no formal training) about the reading desires of patrons whose cultural, ethnic, and class backgrounds differed from their own.

In 1904, the WFLC experimented with a new method of distributing books in remote areas when Stearns attempted to deliver books door-to-door in Marinette County (near the border with Michigan's Upper Peninsula) by means of a book wagon. "The books were to be left for the winter," she explained, "neighbor to exchange with neighbor, the entire collection to be gathered again in the spring." In the horse-drawn book wagon, boxes "were arranged with shelves for the ready display of the volumes." The experiment foundered, however, because of the great distances between homes, so the Commission arranged instead for a schoolhouse meeting.[14] In the same year Mary Titcomb, librarian of the Washington County Free Library, Hagerstown, Maryland, initiated a longer-lived experiment when she arranged for traveling library collections to be exchanged by the library's janitor by means of a hired wagon and horse.[15] Before long,

---

12 L. E. Stearns, *Essentials in Library Administration*, 2nd ed. (Chicago: American Library Association Publishing Board, 1912), 27.

13 Lutie Stearns to Miss C. M. Fennelly, 3 April 1908, WFLC Series 1112, WHS.

14 Lutie E. Stearns, "Travels of the Book Wagon," *Wisconsin Library Bulletin* 1, no. 1 (1905): 14.

15 Eleanor Frances Brown, *Bookmobiles and Bookmobile Service* (Metuchen, N.J.: Scarecrow Press, 1967), 14–15. For details about Mary Titcomb and the Washington County Free Library, see also Deanna Marcum, "The Rural Public Library at the Turn of the Century," *Libraries and Culture* 26, no. 1 (1991): 87–99.

such services were being motorized. In 1912, Mary L. Hopkins was delivering books by car in Seaford, Delaware, and in 1918 the township of Hibbing, Minnesota, bought a "bookbus" that was perhaps the first "walk-on" book vehicle in the country.[16] By mid-century bookmobiles conveyed by motorized buses were not uncommon, although at that point, few Wisconsin communities had invested in them. A 1947 report recorded that 377 bookmobiles were operating in the continental United States. The area with the most was the South Atlantic region (Delaware, Maryland, Virginia, and West Virginia) with 127, 117 operated by county libraries. The East North Central area (Illinois, Indiana, Michigan, Ohio, and Wisconsin) operated 76 bookmobiles, 53 by county libraries.[17]

Despite the male-dominated nature of libraries' official governing bodies, in many communities it was a local women's group that took the initiative in establishing a free public library. Although such clubs were not new, after the Civil War they greatly increased in number. Aiming to promote individual self-improvement in an era when women's access to higher education was limited, most started as isolated groups of individuals. Before long, though, women began to organize on a state and national level. In 1890, east coast activists founded the General Federation of Women's Clubs (GFWC) as a national organization with which local clubs could affiliate. By 1896, the GFWC had grown from 60 clubs that took part in an organizing meeting in 1889, to 495 clubs, representing a hundred thousand women.[18] Study clubs in which women met regularly to read plays and poetry or to give papers on literary or current affairs topics were common in cities and towns across the nation. Women in Wisconsin self-improvement clubs, for example, tended to pick such subjects as literature, art history, religion, and broad studies of particular nations. Shakespeare, as well as modern American and English writers, was especially popular.[19]

With their interest in cultural uplift, promoting public libraries

---

16 VanBrimmer, "History of Mobile Services," 20.

17 "Large Number of Bookmobiles Operate in the U.S.," *Library Journal* 73 (3 April 1948): 574.

18 Theodora Penny Martin, *The Sound of Our Own Voices: Women's Study Clubs, 1860–1910* (Boston: Beacon Press, 1987), 57.

19 Janice Steinschneider, *An Improved Woman: The Wisconsin Federation of Women's Clubs, 1895–1920* (Brooklyn, N.Y.: Carlson, 1994), 4.

seemed a "natural" fit for women's clubs.[20] In West Allis, Wisconsin, the Women's Club organized the first public library in 1883. The women's club of Kenosha wrote into their constitution, "It shall be one of the objects of this club to aid in all movements toward the establishment of a free public library."[21] In Marshfield, Antigo, and Fort Atkinson, the Woman's Christian Temperance Union took the lead. When the National Federation of Women's Clubs met in Milwaukee in 1899, one of the most popular places to visit was the "Library Bureau," a room set aside in the Milwaukee Public Library where clubwomen who wanted to establish or promote a library in their own communities could find information and advice. In charge was Lutie Stearns, herself a long-standing member of Wisconsin's women's club and suffrage movements.[22]

Not everyone approved of the spread of public libraries. Clergy were sometimes dubious about the value of the library's reading materials, and a library's link to a local women's club could be a hindrance. An important part of Stearns's job as WFLC Librarian was to advise communities on the establishment of local libraries, and over the course of her career she helped set up 150 of these. In Oconto Falls, Stearns encountered the opposition of the Catholic priest, who, she was told, had forbidden the Catholic children to visit the library. When a deputation of clubwomen visited the priest to inquire the reason for his opposition, he told them that he objected to the presence of the *Northwestern Christian Advocate*—a Methodist weekly—on the library's reading table. The clubwomen protested that the library also stocked the *Catholic Citizen*, but "Father Loos" asked that both periodicals be removed. The reading materials themselves were not the only problem; the women's club was made up entirely of Protestants, "*without design*," commented Stearns. "Owing to the smallness of the homes in which the club meets, the membership has been restricted to 16 persons." The advantages of having the village take responsibility for the library off clubwomen's shoulders seemed clear. "Since objection to the club has been raised, the members have withdrawn the restriction, thus doing everything

---

20 Paula D. Watson, "Founding Mothers: The Contribution of Women's Organizations to Public Library Development in the United States," *Library Quarterly* 64, no. 3 (1994): 235.

21 Quoted in Kathryn Saucerman, "A Study of the Wisconsin Library Movement 1850–1900" (M.A. Thesis, University of Wisconsin, 1944), 34.

22 Ibid., 41, 32.

within their power to promote good feeling," she reported. "The club-women are, however, anxious for the village to take the library . . . I suggested that a petition signed by as many as possible be sent to the village board asking for the appointment of a library board."[23] In South Byron it was the Methodist minister who objected to the library, on the grounds that "novels and kindred 'light literature'" were harmful.[24] On the other hand at Potosi, the Rev. R. C. Bennett, "a popular congregational clergyman," agreed not only to have the library sent to him next time, and to look after it in the village, but also to pay the freight.[25]

In 1914, after changes in the Post Office's rules for the delivery of parcel post, the WFLC introduced an additional system of sending books by mail upon written request from state residents.[26] "Carnegie Must Look to His Laurels Since Matthew S. Dudgeon of the Wisconsin Free Library Commission Is Employing Parcels Post and Free Rural Delivery to Reach Those Down on the Farm," proclaimed the *Free Press Sunday Magazine*. Under the new plan, which was aimed at country dwellers with no other access to libraries, books could be borrowed not only from the WFLC itself (45,000 volumes), but also from the State Historical Society Library (183,000 volumes), the University of Wisconsin library (210,000 volumes), and the library of the Wisconsin Academy of Arts and Sciences (5,000 volumes), making a total of 442,000. "While country-life commissions have been discussing means for making the farm more attractive to the youth of America, Mr. Carnegie's rival has shortened the long winter evenings and has filled them with opportunity," the article told its readers. "While Mr. Carnegie has been building libraries, his rival has been teaching the people to read—to read good books, whether they be books of facts or

23 Lutie Stearns, 12 June 1905, Library Visitor's Reports, WFLC series 1108, WHS. Emphasis original.

24 Lutie Stearns, 2 April 1904, Library Visitor's Reports, WFLC Series 1108, WHS.

25 Lutie Stearns, 2 May 1904, Library Visitors Reports, WFLC Series 1108, WHS. Use of the Osage, Iowa, Public Library during the 1890s correlated with religious denomination. Congregationalists were the heaviest users, with Methodists not far behind. Catholics and Lutherans were least likely to make use of the library (Christine Pawley, *Reading on the Middle Border: The Culture of Print in Late Nineteenth-Century Osage, Iowa* [Amherst: University of Massachusetts Press, 2001], 74).

26 Pawley, "Advocate for Access," 454.

books of fiction."[27] A few months later WFLC Secretary Dudgeon (Legler's successor) himself explained the system to farm readers of the *Wisconsin Agriculturist*. No forms were necessary, but requests should be made in a "simple letter" that set out author and title and also named a second or third choice. Alternatively, the WFLC would select suitable books if the writer explained the subject of interest. Books could be retained for three weeks in the first instance, but could be kept for longer on request. "We have books of adventure, books about the countries at war, books about our own country, books for mother and the home, books of fiction, books of good cheer, college and athletic stories, and, possibly most important of all, the very best books on all phases of agriculture," Dudgeon assured his readers.[28]

Ben Logan, who grew up on a southwestern Wisconsin farm in the 1920s and 1930s, related in his autobiography how his mother wrote to the WFLC to request books by mail, and saved the resulting parcel for a special treat at Christmastime:

> After [Christmas] dinner Mother would bring out the package of books. Each year, just before Christmas, she sent off a letter to the State Lending Library, asking them to send us about thirty books for three adults and four boys. She gave our ages and a few words about each of us. She'd never let us read what she said, though sometimes she'd include our suggested additions, things like "Please don't send Black Beauty again this year." Then someone in the library in far-off Madison would read the letter and would, we liked to think, sit down, close their eyes, see us, and decide what books to send.[29]

For the Logans, like other farm families, books marked the season— they were particularly associated with the coldest of snowy winter days. The Logans saw bad weather as providing a reading opportunity, and Ben's mother saved up books especially in the event of bliz-

---

27 "Uncle Sam Now Aid to Libraries," *Free Press Sunday Magazine*, 11 October 1914.

28 M. S. Dudgeon, "Wisconsin's Free Library System: How We Are Able to Use It," *Wisconsin Agriculturist*, 15 April 1915.

29 Ben Logan, *The Land Remembers: The Story of a Farm and Its People* (Minnetonka, Minn.: NorthWord Press, 1999), 254, 263.

zards. "She gave me Bambi on a day like that," he recalled. "When I reread it years later, I was surprised to find it wasn't always snowing in the book."[30]

Local control of public libraries usually fell to more affluent members of the community. Although subject to three-year terms, board members sometimes held office for successive terms, even for as much as twenty-five years or more. In 1907, the Madison city council appointed a workingman to the library board in an effort to attract more factory workers as patrons, but this experiment in crossing the usual social boundaries was an exception. Women board members tended to be members of women's clubs or such organizations as the WCTU, and to support a genteel cultural agenda for their local libraries. Library boards controlled many details of library management, including book selection, building management, and the hiring of the librarian. For the most part, the librarians they chose were young women whose character, background, and interests matched that of the board members themselves. Knowledge of literature could be another significant criterion for employment. In 1910 the board of the Madison Public Library set an examination for those seeking the librarian's position at a branch that served an industrial part of the city. Five of the questions related to literature and asked the applicant to "classify novels according to genre or subject and to list works by various literary men and historians." Another question focused on children's books, and yet another on magazines. The only question relating to science or technology asked what five men, including Edison and Westinghouse, had invented. More mundanely, desire for economy played an important part. The board of the Waukesha Public Library preferred to pick a woman from the immediate locality because, they considered, she would be willing to work for less, and in any case, she could supplement her income by cleaning the library.[31]

Everywhere, librarians were underpaid. As a condition of funding, Carnegie demanded only an annual budget of $1,000 or $2,000 to cover all the running costs, including the librarian's salary. Addressing the

30 Ibid., 263.

31 David I. Macleod, *Carnegie Libraries in Wisconsin* (Madison: Department of History, University of Wisconsin, 1968), 64–68, 71, 58–69.

ALA Woman's Meetings in 1892, Mary Salome Cutler of the New York State Library listed as reasons for poor salaries the uncertainty of librarians' employment that often depended on politics, the supposed gentility of librarianship (compared with teaching), library trustees' lack of understanding of modern librarianship, and women's willing-ness to work for low pay.[32] Recognizing that libraries were unlikely to attract energetic and talented librarians as long as sweeping the floors was part of their job description, WFLC gave a boost to more profes-sional working conditions and education for librarianship. Traveling the state, Stearns realized the difficulties that the—mostly—women who ran public libraries encountered in securing basic conditions of employment. "It is always a pleasure to visit this library as it is one of the best in the state," wrote Stearns, from the small town of Plymouth, Wisconsin, in 1906. "The librarian at Plymouth, Miss Grace Prescott, asked me to assist her in securing a vacation this summer, never having been granted one by the board, though her hours are from 10 a.m. to 9 p.m. daily."[33] What to pay the librarian was also a matter of contention. In 1905, the Fond du Lac librarian earned the same as the janitor. The Waukesha librarian earned $35.00 a month.[34] At Mosinee, Stearns found "employment of the librarian at a salary $40 per month was the greatest bone of contention" and the library board in favor of employ-ing another candidate (the daughter of one of the board members) for a salary of twelve dollars a month. Pointing out that "Miss Dean was giving fifty-one hours of service each week for the same salary paid a teacher for thirty hours," Stearns eventually won the board over.[35] In this case, appeal to fairness had a powerful effect, but longer-term suc-cess at establishing librarianship as a profession that deserved a decent salary and humane working conditions required setting up a system through which aspiring librarians could learn the necessary special skills and expertise.

---

32 Joanne Passet. "'You Do Not Have to Pay Librarians': Women, Salaries, and Status in the Early 20th Century," in *Reclaiming the American Library Past: Writing the Women In*, ed. Suzanne Hildenbrand (Norwood, N.J.: Ablex, 1996), 211.

33 Lutie Stearns, 26 March 1906, Library Visitor's Reports, WFLC Series 1108, WHS.

34 Macleod, *Carnegie Libraries in Wisconsin*, 71.

35 Lutie Stearns, 14 March 1906, Library Visitor's Reports, WFLC Series 1108, WHS.

Seeking Expert Advice

From the beginning, Wisconsin Free Library Commission officials made a regular practice of consulting University of Wisconsin–Madison faculty for expert help, particularly in compiling specialized reading lists and lists of books in languages other than English. Such collaboration with the university fitted the spirit of the times. The Progressive Era ushered in new appreciation for expertise that rested on access to timely and accurate information. Reforms accelerated the production and distribution of such information genres as government reports, scientific journals, newspapers, and pamphlets. State and federal legislators were faced with making far-reaching decisions about a whole range of "issues" that often required the rational weighing up of competing ideas, rather than voting according to party loyalty. Searching for sources of trustworthy and easily assimilated information, politicians in Wisconsin and elsewhere across the nation turned to resources close at hand. The state university was one of most readily available.

Originally founded in 1848, the year that Wisconsin gained statehood, the University of Wisconsin gained impetus from the United States Department of Agriculture (USDA) and passage of the Morrill Land-Grant Act in 1862. The establishment of the land grant colleges gave an enormous boost to university-based research and teaching in departments of agriculture, rural sociology, agricultural journalism, and home economics. For example, at the University of Wisconsin the money helped fund a new college of agriculture.[36] The Morrill Acts also stimulated an arguably even more widespread and far-reaching agricultural institution: the extension service. In 1887, Congress passed the Hatch Act, providing federal funds to help set up "experiment stations" in the land grant colleges. In 1892, Pennsylvania State College (followed by Cornell University and the University of Illinois) took a lesson from the Chautauqua movement to create a system of agricultural outreach that they called "extension," by which university experts traveled from community to community, introducing rural residents to

---

36 Robert C. Nesbit, *Wisconsin, a History* (Madison: University of Wisconsin Press, 1973), 227, 289.

new ideas and techniques. Wisconsin also fitted its outreach efforts to the extension model, with legislative funds for farmers', teachers', and mechanics' institutes being appropriated in the 1880s and 1890s.[37]

In Wisconsin, the leader of Progressive Republicans was Wisconsin-born Robert La Follette, state governor from 1901 to 1906, and U.S. senator from 1906 to 1925. La Follette's passionate advocacy for voter control of government institutions gave him wide exposure, and he became identified across the nation with progressive ideals. He was also identified with the "Wisconsin Idea," a phrase often traced to 1904 when University of Wisconsin president Charles R. Van Hise declared, "the beneficent influence of the university [should be] available to every home in the state." In other words, a service relationship should exist between the university and the state by which the expertise of social scientists, economists, legal scholars, and scientists should be brought to bear on solving Wisconsin's problems. But the idea that the university should put its expertise to the service of the state was neither new in 1904 nor confined to Wisconsin. Rather, it was the outgrowth of the state support of universities during the latter half of the nineteenth century.[38] The work of the WFLC's innovative Legislative Reference Department particularly exemplified the reformist approach to government based on rational decision-making rather than party politics. Though a branch of the WFLC, the Legislative Reference Department resulted primarily from the efforts of one individual: Charles McCarthy.

Born in Brockton, Massachusetts, in 1873, McCarthy, son of struggling Irish immigrants, had moved to Wisconsin to attend graduate school, attracted by the presence there of famous scholars Richard T. Ely, Charles Homer Haskins, and above all, Frederick Jackson Turner, who became McCarthy's adviser.[39] In 1902, after receiving his Ph.D. and on Turner's recommendation to Frank Hutchins, McCarthy took a position as chief document clerk at the Wisconsin state capitol. The

---

37 Edmund deS. Brunner and E. Hsin Pao Yang, *Rural America and the Extension Service: A History and Critique of the Cooperative Agricultural and Home Economics Extension Service* (New York: Teachers College, Columbia University, 1949), 4–8.

38 Nesbit, *Wisconsin, a History*, 427.

39 Marion Casey, *Charles McCarthy: Librarianship and Reform* (Chicago: American Library Association, 1981), 15.

State Historical Society had recently moved to a new building on the university campus, and most of the books formerly at the capitol had been transferred to the new library. According to the legislation that authorized the WFLC to hire a "document cataloger" at the salary of $1,500 a year, a library was to be set up under WFLC direction "for the legislature, the several state departments, and such other citizens as may desire to consult the same," making available to them "the several public documents of this and other states."[40]

Writing to a friend, McCarthy described his job; "Whenever the legislature is to meet I will have to write to all the members and find what bills they are to present and then I will hunt up everything upon those matters and make such a comprehensive bibliography that they will know exactly where to find out what they want—incidentally, I am to make myself familiar with the questions." The work would be similar, McCarthy surmised, to that done by a "Young Ph.D." recently hired by Melvil Dewey to help fill the needs of New York State legislature.[41] Indeed, the Wisconsin vision for the new library meshed very well with the Progressive Era drive for efficiency and effectiveness that Dewey was anxious to promote in librarianship. However, although McCarthy felt that he needed to take some training in library work at the WFLC summer school before he started work, he left after only five weeks, "unable to stand" Dewey's "rubbish."[42] Whether he meant by that the detailed organizational instructions or the inculcation of the almost religious library "faith" or "spirit" that were both hallmarks of Dewey's approach to library education is not clear. McCarthy himself went on to invent a modus operandi for what came to be called the Legislative Reference Library that was as detailed as anything Dewey could have devised, and found himself equally imbued with fervor for his calling, albeit adopting scientific and utilitarian rather than religious language.

McCarthy personally directed the Legislative Reference Library's research division, often staying late at night in an effort to anticipate and collect the information that representatives working on a particu-

---

40 Ibid., 28.
41 Ibid., 29.
42 Quoted in Wiegand, *Irrepressible Reformer*, 206.

lar piece of legislation might need. Arguing that books went quickly out of date, McCarthy devoted most effort to accumulating newspapers, periodicals, pamphlets, bills, letters, organizational leaflets, and other ephemeral material that he recognized were hard to organize, keep current, and make accessible. Like other Progressive Era reformers, he saw in information the capability to save society and cure its ills. In 1907 the service was officially recognized, and McCarthy was made chief of the Legislative Reference Library, serving in this capacity until his death in 1921. Wisconsin's Legislative Reference Library became the model for other states and the federal government to set up similar organizations.[43] In 1914, Congress passed legislation to establish the "Legislative Reference Service" (subsequently the Congressional Research Service) as a separate department within the Library of Congress.

In 1912, McCarthy wrote a book titled *The Wisconsin Idea* in which he trumpeted Wisconsin's reform achievements, outlining a movement that had been underway for several decades. In the introduction, Theodore Roosevelt endorsed the philosophy, claiming that thanks to the La Follette brand of Progressivism, Wisconsin had "become literally a laboratory for wise, experimental legislation aiming to secure the social and political betterment of the people as a whole." The whole country could learn from the Wisconsin lesson of "scientific popular self-help," Roosevelt maintained, as well as from its gradual approach and "patient care in radical legislation."[44] Written in haste, and largely a list of Wisconsin's legislative accomplishments rather than an exploration of the principles underpinning the admittedly hazy concept of the Wisconsin Idea, the book ended with an appeal to fairness and education. "Whatever has been accomplished in Wisconsin seems to have been based upon this idea of making practice conform to the ideals of justice and right which have been inherited," McCarthy wrote. "If the weak ask for justice, the state should see that they get it certainly, quickly and surely. If certain social classes are forming among us, can we not destroy them by means of education and through hope and encouragement make every man more efficient so that the door of

---

43 Paul D. Healey, "Go and Tell the World: Charles R. McCarthy and the Evolution of the Legislative Reference Movement, 1901–1917," *Law Library Journal* 99, no. 1 (2007): 36.

44 Charles McCarthy, *The Wisconsin Idea* (New York: Macmillan, 1912), vii, x.

opportunity may always be open before him?"[45] State responsibility for eradicating class and other distinctions through education was clear, according to McCarthy.

In the library field another source of expert advice was a growing cadre of mostly male researchers and managers, who were being trained in newly established graduate programs based in universities from the late 1920s on. In launching the first library training classes at Columbia in 1887 and then in Albany in 1889, Melvil Dewey had taken steps toward a university-based education for librarianship, but not all agreed that formal classes were preferable to learning on the job. Some argued in favor of an apprentice-style training delivered by practicing librarians. Graduates quickly fanned out from New York, however, planting the seeds of the Dewey vision in new library schools across the country. They were especially popular among women. Gilded Age and Progressive Era college-educated women saw in librarianship an alternative career to teaching and mission work, albeit one that shared some of the same reformist and civilizing goals. Encouraged by library leaders like Dewey, they not only found work in public libraries, but sought to further their education by enrolling in the formal library education programs that were proliferating at the turn of the twentieth century. Pratt Institute (New York City) opened in 1890, Drexel (Philadelphia) in 1892, and the Armour Institute (Chicago) in 1893. As was typical in some other states, the WFLC program started with summer courses first held 1895. In 1906 the Wisconsin Library School opened as a full-time program, the ninth in the nation.[46]

Popular periodicals drew attention to librarianship as a suitable occupation for women. In 1900, a *Ladies Home Journal* article titled "What It Means to Be a Librarian" stimulated a flood of requests for more information. In 1906, Mary Emogene Hazeltine, Preceptress of the Wisconsin Library School, was complaining at unwanted publicity. "The Ladies Home Journal for the current month also struck Wisconsin!!" she wrote to a friend. "I assume that every mail from this time on until I land in the lunatic asylum will be followed up with simi-

---

45 Ibid., 302–3.
46 Valmai Fenster, "The University of Wisconsin Library School, a History, 1895–1921" (Ph.D. Diss., University of Wisconsin–Madison, 1977), 19.

lar requests."[47] A graduate of Wellesley College, Hazeltine had come to Madison in that year from Jamestown, New York, to take charge of the newly constituted full-time library school. Like Dewey she had been born in the "burned over district" of western New York State (so-called because the area had been thoroughly evangelized during the second Great Revival) that had produced many reformers at the University of Wisconsin, including John Bascom, university president from 1874 to 1888, and Richard T. Ely, controversial economics professor who had come to Wisconsin from Johns Hopkins University in 1892.[48] In the Progressive Era, Yankees continued to exert great cultural influence in Wisconsin.

Essential to satisfactory performance in library school was evidence of "library spirit," the belief that Melvil Dewey promoted, that book collections housed in publicly sponsored libraries and managed through a librarian's special professional expertise would create a public eager to further their education through reading.[49] "When faculty at the Wisconsin Library School perceived that a student's 'spirit was not right,' they required her to report to the preceptress for a talk," notes Joanne E. Passet. Graduates emerged from their studies infused with a sense of "missionary zeal" and filled with enthusiasm for their potential role as civilizers. Some early library school graduates found fulfillment, Passet demonstrates, in sparsely populated western states where "library work provided them with a significant degree of flexibility and autonomy." As independent "cultural crusaders" these women contributed to the political as well as the cultural development of the West, aiming to stamp settlers with an American identity in the process of converting "farmers, lumbermen, ranchers and miners to the library cause."[50]

---

47 Passet, *Cultural Crusaders*, 2. The title of the female head of Wisconsin's Library School later changed to "Principal."

48 Charles Seavey, "Laying the Foundation: The Hazeltine Years, 1906–1938," in *Tradition and Vision: Library and Information Studies at the University of Wisconsin, a Centennial History*, ed. Louise S. Robbins, Anne H. Lundin, and Michele Besant (Madison, Wis.: School of Library and Information Studies, 2006), 16; J. David Hoeveler, "The University and the Social Gospel: The Intellectual Origins of the Wisconsin Idea," *Wisconsin Magazine of History* 59, no. 4 (Summer, 1976): 294.

49 Wayne A. Wiegand, "The Socialization of Library and Information Science Students: Reflections on a Century of Formal Education for Librarianship," *Library Trends* 34, no. 3 (Winter 1986): 389.

50 Passet, *Cultural Crusaders*, 2, 151, 153.

Librarianship's feminization was largely complete by the early twentieth century, resulting in low status for the profession, lamented the 1923 Carnegie-funded *Training for Library Service* (known as the Williamson Report, after its author, Charles C. Williamson).[51] To boost librarianship's standing and efficiency, the Williamson Report recommended two-tier staffing for libraries. Clerical staff (assumed to be mainly female) would perform routine filing and typing, managed by administrators educated in specialized, graduate-level library schools and assumed to be predominantly male.[52] To this end, in 1926, the Carnegie Corporation helped fund a new educational establishment: the University of Chicago's Graduate Library School (GLS). Over subsequent years, the GLS promoted a research agenda that drew heavily on the empirical, positivist, social sciences to create a discipline known as "library science." Strongly influenced by the GLS, other library schools also began to award doctoral degrees in library science, mostly to men who in turn became library school faculty and administrators of large research libraries, thus institutionalizing a gender gap between a small number of mostly male library managers and university faculty and a comparatively large number of mainly female clerical staff. Small public libraries continued to be managed mostly by women, however, and there the distinctions between those with professional training (if any) and those without were slight.

In the first quarter of the century, a small number of research theses had appeared that took a social scientific approach to studying reading habits. In 1929, educational researchers William S. Gray and Ruth Munroe published a summary of their major findings in a book titled *Reading Interests and Habits of Adults*.[53] Now library science researchers, too, were becoming interested in uncovering "facts" about people's reading preferences and patterns. The GLS became the center of research production in the developing field of library science. During

---

51 Charles C. Williamson, *Training for Library Service: A Report Prepared for the Carnegie Corporation of New York* (New York, 1923), in *The Williamson Reports of 1921 and 1923*, ed. Sarah K. Vann (Metuchen, N.J.: Scarecrow Press, 1971), 142.

52 Ibid., 136.

53 William S. Gray and Ruth Munroe, *Reading Interests and Habits of Adults: A Preliminary Report* (New York: Macmillan, 1929). Gray was professor of education at the University of Chicago. At this time, too, Gray started his collaboration with William H. Elson to create their famous reading series "Dick and Jane," published by Scott Foresman. See also Chapter Five.

the late 1920s and the 1930s, drawing inspiration, theories, and techniques from the influential social sciences at the University of Chicago,
faculty and students at the GLS undertook an extensive research program into Americans' reading, publishing their results in a new journal
devoted to library science research, titled *The Library Quarterly.*

One of the most prominent GLS researchers was Douglas Waples,
whose study with Ralph Tyler, *What People Want to Read About* (funded
by the Carnegie Corporation and ALA, through a joint Committee on
the Reading Interests and Habits of Adults) appeared in 1931.[54] The
study focused on "contemporary nonfiction" and excluded "pure fiction, humorous writing, historical subjects, and subjects addressed primarily to particular vocational groups." Waples and Tyler sampled and
classified the topics appearing in contemporary magazines and surveyed groups of adults about their preferences. "Perhaps the most
important fact to emerge," they reported, "is that groups of adults
express genuine interest in reading about matters of real importance.
The particular subjects of interest and the relative amount of interest,
of course, vary from group to group. But it is somewhat contrary to
popular opinion to know that interest in reading about such significant
social issues as 'personal hygiene,' 'the next war,' 'the courts and the
administration of justice,' and the like, is nearly universal among adult
members of all classes of society." They also pointed out that "*people like
to read about themselves.* The more closely a subject relates to what is
familiar to the given reader, the more interesting it is. The common
denominator of reading interest, in the field of non-fiction at least, is
self." However, they reported clear differences between men and
women. "The reading interests common to all men . . . are 'sociability,'
'laws' and 'war.' The reading interests common to all groups of women
are 'self-improvement and happy living,' 'nature of human nature and
intelligence,' 'personal qualities analyzed,' and 'successful marriage.'"[55]
These findings accorded with contemporary views of separately gendered spheres of interest and activity that seemed natural and
enduring.

---

54 Douglas Waples and Ralph Tyler, *What People Want to Read About: A Study of Group Interests and
a Survey of Problems in Adult Reading* (Chicago: American Library Association and University of
Chicago Press, 1931).

55 Ibid., xxi, xxii–xxiii, 192.

Other research studies focused on community, rather than individual, reading patterns. As we have seen, Louis Round Wilson's *Geography of Reading*, published in 1938, provided a comprehensive overview of library services across the United States. In 1941, Wilson's graduate student Eliza Atkins Gleason (the first African American woman to earn a Ph.D. in Library Science), published *The Southern Negro and the Public Library*, carefully documenting the lack of library service to the nearly nine million African Americans living in thirteen southern states where segregated libraries were the norm. This study, based on Gleason's doctoral dissertation at the University of Chicago, found that although library service of some kind was available to 44 percent of the white population in the thirteen states, it was available to only 21 percent of the black population. Moreover, the services provided to African Americans fell far short of those provided to whites.[56] Whereas previously librarians had tended to view readers from a missionary perspective as individuals to be transformed and even redeemed, studies such as these by Waples and Tyler, Wilson, and Gleason began to signal a shift toward thinking of readers as consumers of reading materials whose wants libraries should work to fill. By drawing comparisons between states, they also emphasized the importance of libraries to national and state educational policy-makers.

Beyond Americanization: Adult Education

Influential voices were calling for new directions in librarianship, particularly a new focus on information and adult education. An advantage, some library leaders believed, was that they might attract more men to use the public library, and might at the same time divert the many women who already used the library away from reading fiction. One of these leaders was Carl Milam, ALA executive secretary from 1920 to 1948. Despite the fact that the Nineteenth Amendment to the Constitution had at last given women the suffrage in 1919, women's

---

56 Eliza Atkins Gleason, *The Southern Negro and the Public Library: A Study of the Government and Administration of Public Library Service to Negroes in the South* (Chicago: University of Chicago Press, 1941), 184–85. Gleason graduated from the Graduate Library School at the University of Chicago in 1940.

worth as citizens rarely received equal attention from library leaders with that of men. According to the historian Patti Clayton Becker, "Milam and other library leaders often acted and spoke as though the mostly female librarians—and the women their collections catered to—were sources of shame for the profession."[57] Children's library services, too, were undervalued. Work with children was considered especially appropriate for women; some even held that children's librarianship constituted a calling analogous to the spiritual calling to a religious vocation.[58] A dramatic growth in children's services in the early twentieth century was librarianship's great success story, but the ALA leadership chose to focus its attention and resources instead on adult education and other ALA initiatives that were in part attempts to raise the status of librarians and the cultural level of library users.[59]

The Carnegie Corporation frequently partnered with ALA in these initiatives. After Carnegie's death in 1919 the foundation continued to support library development, but drew back from the building program so dear to Carnegie's own heart, recognizing that bricks and mortar were not enough to ensure successful library service. In 1924, William S. Learned, of the Carnegie Foundation for the Advancement of Teaching, published *The American Public Library and the Diffusion of Knowledge*, a title which made direct reference to language contained in the Carnegie Corporation's charter: "To promote the advancement and diffusion of knowledge and understanding among the people of the United States."[60] Learned had already written a report on teacher education, published in 1920, recommending four years of college-level study for those planning to become teachers, no matter what kind of school they expected to teach in. Now he turned his attention to public libraries and their role in coping with the "rapid accumulation of vast masses of information which makes imperative some means of selec-

---

57 Patti Clayton Becker, *Books and Libraries in American Society during World War II: Weapons in the War of Ideas* (New York: Routledge, 2005), 15.

58 Christine Jenkins, "The Strength of the Inconspicuous: Youth Services Librarians, the American Library Association, and Intellectual Freedom for the Young, 1939–1955" (Ph.D. Diss., University of Wisconsin–Madison, 1995), 59.

59 Becker, *Books and Libraries in American Society*, 13.

60 William S. Learned, *The American Public Library and the Diffusion of Knowledge* (New York: Harcourt, Brace, 1924), 3.

tion, digest, or abridgment."[61] Learned's publication was notable not only for its picture of what he considered the most forward-looking library practices of his day, but also as a marker of a point in which an older value for character formation through reading serious literature was becoming upstaged by the progressive ideal of useful, quantifiable information. The belief that librarians' work would gain significance (and, not incidentally, status) through providing useful factual information rather than encouraging the sustained reading of literary works (let alone the entertaining fiction that most library patrons actually sought) was reinforced by the library science researchers in the 1930s, and would gain an enormous boost through the documentation movement of the later 1940s.

In complaints that sound eerily familiar in the age of the Internet, Learned commented on the "phenomenal improvement in speed and accuracy of communication" and bemoaned the fact that "even the trained student finds the time required thoroughly to examine a topic in an unfamiliar field almost prohibitive." In consequence, he said, the "daily losses in energy and material that result from sheer ignorance on the part of otherwise intelligent persons . . . must be colossal beyond all calculation."[62] One solution was already underway in "many progressive cities," however, in the form of "an institution where a great range of useful information available in print may be secured authoritatively and quickly." Ideally, such a center would be "as familiar to every inhabitant as the local post-office." It would constitute "the central intelligence service of the town not only for 'polite' literature, but for every commercial and vocational field of information."[63]

To Learned, the obvious institution to provide such a center was, of course, the tax-supported public library. While libraries should continue to make available the literary works that supported moral development in individual readers, they should prioritize the distribution of knowledge that would have practical, useful application in the lives of citizens. Learned's language may seem prescient today, but complaints about being inundated by information were not new, even in the 1920s.

---

61 Ibid., 8.
62 Ibid., 8, 12.
63 Ibid., 12.

Many of the essential components of Learned's proposed "central intelligence service" already existed in some public libraries, and much of his book was devoted to providing examples. He praised the Cleveland, Ohio, public library for its open shelves, adult education program (with services to "immigrant foreigners," and "illiterate or partly educated natives"), its provision for children and youth, and its branches and delivery stations distributed in schools and neighborhoods throughout the city.[64] Learned pointed, too, to other cities' provision of specialized services, such as the Business Library at Newark, New Jersey, the Teachers' Library in Indianapolis, and technology departments in cities like Detroit and Pittsburgh. [65]

Learned included a lengthy quotation from a Seattle public library report that lauded the library's Americanization work, especially among Scandinavians, Germans, Finnish, Russians, and Italians. Not all immigrants were alike, this report claimed. Among these ethnic groups Russians (mostly refugees from the Revolution) were "destitute of all but courage, fine breeding, and a sustaining spirit of adventure." For these well-educated and formerly affluent immigrants, the library's challenge was to find suitably challenging material, since Seattle was "still rather a crude western city, affording little scope for the employment and the intellectual and cultural talents of these ex-patriates." Scandinavians presented "no problem," and constituted "one of the most reliable of the foreign elements of the city, making use of every school and library facility in qualifying for a place in the ranks of the progressive farmers, skilled mechanics, or competent merchants." Italians and Greeks, by contrast, need to be "enticed to the library," though once there, responded "with that graciousness which is characteristic of southern peoples, to the invitation extended them through the night schools or their own societies."[66] Although the report took pains to praise each group for its specific characteristics, it also made it clear that some ethnic groups brought with them to America a greater affinity for books and reading than others, an affinity that smoothed their path toward assimilation.

---

64 Ibid., 29.
65 Ibid., 33–35.
66 Ibid., 42.

The Seattle library's Americanization collection consisted of "civics manuals, histories of the new country in easy English, and biographies of the foreign-born whom America now proudly claims as her own." The library printed its leaflets in thirteen languages and publicized its services in Seattle's "foreign press." Librarians regularly visited night school classes for the foreign born, where they saw "the tired faces of the Beppos and Johanns, the Ivans, Ingas, and Sophies, light up at the prospect of a diversion; their bodies, drooping in their cramped seats with weariness from the day's toil, straighten up," and "the whole atmosphere become electrified with attention, as the library's importance to them [was] set forth in carefully chosen, simple words, and an invitation extended to visit it."[67] Class mingled with ethnicity in the report's analysis of the life circumstances of these disadvantaged immigrants.

Gradually in the 1920s, the adult education movement replaced older Americanization efforts. At the GLS, Waples argued that it was not enough for libraries to make the best materials available and hope that readers would educate themselves. His studies showed, he said, that more active intervention was needed.[68] The Carnegie Corporation and ALA had already taken steps in that direction. In 1926, the ALA was a charter member of the American Association of Adult Education, founded with financial support from the Carnegie Corporation of New York, and in the same year had published *Libraries and Adult Education*, setting out this new direction for the profession.[69] ALA also published a series of pamphlets titled "Reading with a Purpose," written by subject experts and dealing with a variety of topics, from psychology to sculpture.[70] In 1932 the Carnegie Corporation helped sponsor a series of "forums" on current affairs initiated in Des Moines, Iowa, by the school superintendent, John Studebaker (later U.S. Commissioner of Education), and hired Lyman Bryson to head the program. Although the Des Moines forums were run through the public school system,

---

67 Ibid., 43.

68 Evelyn Geller, *Forbidden Books in American Public Libraries, 1876–1939: A Study in Cultural Change* (Westport, Conn.: Greenwood, 1984), 150.

69 Jean L. Preer, "'This Year—Richmond!': The 1936 Meeting of the American Library Association," *Libraries & Culture* 39, no. 2 (Spring 2004): 141.

70 Jean Preer, "Lyman Bryson and ALA: Adult Education, Discussion, and Democracy in the Mid 1930s" (paper delivered at the Library Research Seminar, Kansas City, Mo., October 2004).

Bryson later used this experience to encourage librarians to set up similar groups.[71] He praised Des Moines library director Forrest Spaulding for fostering a "new tradition of free speech," and for inviting Communist groups to meet in the Des Moines library on Sundays, and socialist groups to do likewise on alternate Sundays. These radicals were suspicious of the Carnegie Corporation's forums, but nevertheless became active and vociferous participants.[72]

Still, librarians continued to worry about what Lutie Stearns in her 1928 address to the Wisconsin Library Association termed "the Great Unreached." Stearns had long complained about the difficulties that working people encountered when trying to make use of the public libraries that their tax dollars supported. At a meeting hosted by the Wisconsin Free Library Commission in 1906, members of the public had criticized libraries for their restricted opening hours, especially in view of the long days that many labored. "Interviews with over one hundred working men were epitomized as follows," Stearns reported. "'[T]he men of wealth who conduct business and head the lists of contributors who pay for library buildings have shut against the working man the door of opportunity to enjoy what they have so generously provided, by their demand that he shall labor from seven o'clock in the morning until six o' clock at night.'" Another speaker proposed, "The public library and reading room should be open during all those ordinary waking hours when the common people are off duty. It should be open evenings until 10 o'clock. It should be open Sundays and holidays, all day and all evening."[73]

Now in 1928, Stearns was again drawing attention to inequalities in access to libraries. Fifty million, or 46 percent of the American population, were still without library service, she pointed out. Even in towns and cities like Cleveland "with its magnificent new library and branches," she contended, only one-third of the population was registered at the library. A major problem was the refusal of library administrators "to give library patrons the books for which they ask."[74] She

---

71 Ibid.

72 Geller, *Forbidden Books in American Public Libraries*, 152.

73 Lutie E. Stearns, "An Innovation in Library Meetings," *Library Journal* 31, no. 2 (1906): 56–57.

74 Lutie E. Stearns, "The Great Unreached and Why," *Wilson Bulletin* 3, no. 19 (1929): 523.

pointed to the narrow principles of selection that were keeping books for working people out of the library, demanding, "Why not have both sides of all questions—for and against Christian Science, Spiritualism and all the other isms. Why not have an Open Forum right in your library lecture room and thresh out all sides of every question of interest to humans?" Arguing that librarians should emulate department stores and mass market advertisers in their efforts to attract patronage, Stearns railed against rule-bound circulation clerks and advised librarians to "Put the soft pedal on all this patronizing chatter about Adult Education as if the lives of men were not filled with records of those like Edison and hosts of others who have educated themselves."

Finding the Funds

Librarians recognized that despite the efforts of state library commissions and the generosity of the Carnegie building program, the funding structures for public libraries continued to put small communities at a great disadvantage. Dependence on local taxes placed severe restrictions on what individual communities could achieve. During her years at the WFLC, Lutie Stearns advocated tirelessly for county systems of traveling libraries, but met with limited success, often finding it hard to convince county boards of supervisors of the value of libraries. The state of Wisconsin was willing to play an advisory role through the WFLC and to help finance education for librarianship, but not to provide direct funding for public libraries. Lacking alternatives, and frustrated by what they felt was continued low level of library service, especially in rural areas, in the 1920s some librarians were beginning to feel that the answer lay in seeking assistance from the federal government. In the 1930s, the government's response to the economic and social effects of the Great Depression seemed to provide a model.

In debates about the New Deal, most librarians aligned themselves with the advocates of intervention and construction and against those who argued for government restraint and resistance to higher taxes. Funding libraries made sense, the American Library Association argued, because they offered information about how to overcome unemployment and other effects of the Depression. ALA secretary

Carl Milam told listeners to a radio show, "There is more demand now than at any time in a generation for facts and ideas on economic, social and governmental questions." Frank L. Tolman (Director of the Library Extension Division at the New York State Department of Education) claimed that libraries were storehouses "of solutions of difficulties, of helpful hints, of forgotten clues, of missing links."[75] Using an argument that would have been familiar a century earlier, leading librarians argued that library use also had the effect of mitigating social unrest if the unemployed occupied themselves safely in reading rather than fomenting revolution.[76]

Although the Depression hit many libraries hard, in some other ways libraries benefited directly from the New Deal.[77] Between 1933 and 1935, the Women's Division of the Federal Emergency Relief Administration (FERA) prioritized library work and sent directives to all states to initiate library projects. FERA workers made astonishing gains, especially in areas where the Depression had severely reduced library services, and in some cases ended the reductions entirely. In rural Mississippi, for instance, workers ran book collection drives, opened reading rooms and deposit stations, operated houseboat libraries to serve fishermen, and transported books by car to rural reading stations.[78] In Des Moines, Iowa, library director Forrest Spaulding opened a Men's Reading Room, with the help of nine FERA workers. During a single month (November 1934) 5,633 men and boys used the room to read newspapers, magazines, and books. Librarians dubbed the room, which was open until nine o' clock on weekdays and on Sunday afternoons and was located directly on the Des Moines River, "The Water Front University."[79]

With the creation of the Works Progress Administration (WPA) in

---

75 Quoted in Brendan Luyt, "The ALA, Public Libraries, and the Great Depression," *Library History* 23 (June 2007): 94.

76 Ibid., 91.

77 Carleton Bruns Joeckel and Leon Carnovsky, *A Metropolitan Library in Action: A Survey of the Chicago Public Library* (Chicago: University of Chicago Press, 1940), 121.

78 Martha H. Swain, "A New Deal in Libraries; Federal Relief Work and Library Service, 1933–43," *Libraries & Culture* 30, no. 3 (1995): 266–67.

79 Jeannette Hyde Eyerly, "A Special Reading Room for Unemployed Men," in *Helping Adults to Learn: The Library in Action*, ed. John Chancellor (Chicago: American Library Association, 1939), 86–89.

May 1935, further opportunities opened for library programs. Between 1935 and 1942, for example, the number of libraries in the state of Georgia grew from 44 to 210. In New York City, workers ran open-air reading spaces and operated bookmobile services. With WPA help, the Boston Public Library reclassified its collection, and in Philadelphia workers contributed five million cards to a union catalog project encompassing the city's public and private libraries.[80] "To the librarian one of the compensating features of this depression has been the vastly increased use of library facilities by the general public," commented a *Wisconsin Library Bulletin* report in 1936. "Gratifying as this steady stream of new customers has been, it has also brought dismay to the librarian who was forced to contemplate helplessly a steady stream of worn-out books being removed from the shelves." At precisely the time when libraries needed to repair books and expand their services, shortages of funds and staff meant that they were forced to curtail them. The WPA had stepped in to save the situation, however. Approximately 650,000 books had been repaired and renewed by Wisconsin's WPA workers, "most of them women with families to support," taking them from "relief rolls and giving them employment in scores of libraries throughout the state."[81] When the Manitowoc high school burned, the WPA helped salvage books damaged by smoke and water. WPA workers also indexed and organized materials and even helped extend library services into rural areas where none had previously existed. Other workers compiled scrapbooks for state institutions, and transcribed books and pamphlets into Braille.[82]

For most librarians, New Deal programs provided their first experience with federal assistance, and many found it a positive one. In June 1934, at its annual meeting in Montreal, ALA endorsed the principle of federal aid to public libraries, and later the same year the ALA Council adopted a resolution calling for an appropriation of between fifty and one hundred million dollars in federal assistance. Not all librarians supported this move, however. Fearing higher taxes, an increased national debt, bureaucratic interference, and perhaps worst of all, death

80 Swain, "A New Deal in Libraries," 268–70.

81 "Libraries Receive WPA Aid," *Wisconsin Library Bulletin* 32, no. 9 (1936): 105.

82 "Libraries and the WPA," *Wisconsin Library Bulletin* 33, no. 3 (1937): 61–62.

of the "library spirit" that relied on community civic pride and self-help, opponents sent out a letter to ALA members, demanding, "Do you want Federal Supervision?" Thirty prominent librarians signed the letter.[83] In an impassioned speech delivered in March 1935, C. Seymour Thompson, Librarian at the University of Pennsylvania, denounced ALA's "abdication" of responsibility for leadership. Fearing that federal involvement would lead to "compulsory library service," Thompson accused its supporters of "seeking to impose upon our education system, always recognized as the vital organ of democratic government, an autocratic management." "Do men gather democracy of autocracy?" he thundered. "Can we save our democracy by subjecting our schools and libraries to the domination of a federal agency—remote, impersonal, and at least semi-political?"[84]

Opposition to federal aid persisted through the 1930s, though within ALA it dwindled, perhaps because many opposed members resigned over the issue.[85] At the 1936 conference, held in Richmond, Virginia, federal aid was again on the agenda. Following a contentious debate, ALA Council members accepted a report that committed ALA to continue to campaign for a federal library agency and to seek federal funding on a permanent basis. This commitment, argued Louis Round Wilson, meant that librarians needed to focus more on community involvement, to be prepared to collaborate with other social agencies, and to seek new groups of users. It was no longer enough, he argued, to focus on traditional concerns such as bibliographic organization.[86]

In recognition of "the fundamental importance of citizen interest in libraries," the program committee designated one day of the conference, May 13, "Citizens' Day." In support of their plan to launch a campaign to seek federal aid for libraries, the organization invited farm, education, and women's groups to take part in Citizens' Day, hoping to enlist their support in the campaign for federal funding. At a luncheon held in the Commonwealth Club, the mayor of Richmond welcomed the more than four hundred guests to the city. The president

---

83 Michael S. Blayney, "'Libraries for the Millions': Adult Public Library Services and the New Deal," *Journal of Library History* 12, no. 3 (1977): 237.

84 C. Seymour Thomson, "The Abdication of the ALA," *Library Journal* (1 May 1935): 371.

85 Blayney, "Libraries for the Millions," 238.

86 Preer, "This Year—Richmond!" 144–45.

of the College of William and Mary, John Stewart Bryan, read a letter from President Franklin Roosevelt that praised public libraries as a "distinctly American contribution to civilization." The president of the British Library Association made an address by short-wave radio from Edinburgh, and Secretary of the Interior Harold Ickes broadcast a speech from Washington.[87] From a technological and social point of view the event seemed to have been a resounding success.

However, the concept of citizenship that ALA organizers envisaged was one limited to white Americans. Despite protests in the professional library literature before the conference about the choice of venue, ALA had persisted in its decision to meet in Richmond, which in the 1930s was a segregated city. In accordance with local laws, African American librarians and library supporters who attended the ALA conference were denied accommodation in many hotels and restaurants, were obliged to sit in separate sections at conference sessions held in hotels, and were excluded entirely from many social events of the conference, including the Citizens' Day luncheon in the Commonwealth Club.[88] Before and after the conference, librarians wrote to periodicals like *Library Journal*, the *Wilson Bulletin* and the ALA *Bulletin*, dismayed at ALA's acquiescence in Richmond's racist policies. Some organizations had successfully contested segregationist policies when making conference arrangements, they pointed out, while others simply refused to meet in segregated venues. Jesse Shera excoriated ALA in an article in the *Wilson Bulletin*. "Even the most passive will confess that the conference got off to an unfortunate start," Shera wrote. "The interjection of race antagonism, however it may be 'defended' as being necessary or expedient, could have been avoided by the proper action, and was most certainly not calculated to win the admiration of those who desire to look upon the American library movement as a great force for the service of *all* mankind."[89]

Despite its efforts at Richmond, ALA's push for federal aid met with

---

87 Ibid., 146–47.

88 Ibid., 150–51.

89 Jesse H. Shera. "Richmond—and Beyond!" *Wilson Bulletin for Librarians* 10, no. 10 (1936): 648. Shera, who later became a leading library science researcher and educator, at this time was a bibliographer at the Scripps Foundation for Research in Population Problems, Miami University, Ohio.

no immediate success. When war broke out in Europe in September 1939, Milam saw a new opportunity to make the case for libraries to the federal government. A few months later, Roosevelt announced plans to build up American defense industries and military, telling the country, "We must be the great arsenal of democracy." Milam was eager to map out for ALA a role in this mobilization process, and in August 1940, ALA published a bibliographic essay titled "Our American Democracy," setting out the part that libraries could play in national defense. All over the country, libraries noticed a decline in the number of books circulating but increased demand for scientific, technical, and business materials—prime representatives of the very information genres that library leaders were anxious to promote. Alice Farquar, reader's adviser at the Chicago Public Library and chair of ALA's Adult Education Board, urged librarians to stimulate interest in defense preparations.[90] Still, not all citizens or even librarians responded with great interest. In Wisconsin, the WFLC Secretary, Clarence B. Lester, explained, "I come from a state with many small libraries, and I say to you that I fear the impact of the present situation has not touched many of those small libraries, that they may not open the doors to these avenues or proceed very far along them toward the information that is being so splendidly organized for us."[91] To small-town Wisconsin, despite its heavy concentration of immigrants of European origin, the war seemed a long way away.

The December 1941 attack on Pearl Harbor jolted even the sleepiest community out of its self-absorption, however. ALA saw America's entry into the war as its chance to demonstrate the value of libraries by collaborating with government and other agencies to provide special services and materials. For instance, in a program that it called the Victory Book Campaign, ALA coordinated a public library, Red Cross, and the United Service Organizations (USO) effort to collect books to supplement armed services reading collections, and through cooperation with the Red Cross to send books to American prisoners of war in Europe and Japan. Some libraries also sent books to German and

---

90 Becker, *Books and Libraries in American Society*, 38, 40–41.
91 Quoted in ibid., 45.

Japanese soldiers imprisoned in the United States.[92] Japanese Americans were forcibly relocated to concentration camps far from the West Coast, run by the War Relocation Agency (WRA). Although the WRA organized schools in the camps, less assistance was available for libraries. However, camp inmates succeeded in setting up libraries with some help from ALA's Victory Book Campaign, state librarians, and other agencies.[93]

Despite being energized to provide new services and play an active role in supporting the military effort, wartime brought mostly hardships to public libraries.[94] Finances were cut, staff left to join the armed forces or take up jobs in industry (now booming for the first time since the Depression), and public use as measured by circulation numbers was reduced. To help shore up dwindling budgets ALA again attempted to secure support for federal funds by drawing attention to inequalities. In 1943, the organization argued in a pamphlet entitled *The Equal Chance: Books Help to Make It*, "Books are the universal medium of education whether in school or outside—books to find the facts behind the news reel or broadcast—books to fit us for a job, or help us to find it—books to explain the economic picture and the world changing before our eyes—books for our children—books to enjoy." And yet, the pamphlet pointed out, books were more readily available in some areas than in others: "There are thirty-five million people in the United States who have no public libraries within reach. Of these thirty-five million citizens, thirty-two million live in small villages or in the open country, and having few books of their own, they are deprived of a basic means of education."[95] As in the past, rural readers were the main source of concern.

The end of the war in 1945 raised national spirits, but the optimism was short-lived. On March 5, 1946, less than a year after the Allies declared victory, Winston Churchill delivered his "Iron Curtain" speech in Fulton, Missouri. The press and politicians were quick to rediscover their old bogey, Communism, and the lines of the Cold War

---

92 Ibid., 134.

93 Andrew Wertheimer, "Public Libraries for Detained Japanese Americans during World War II" (Ph.D. Diss., University of Wisconsin–Madison, 2003). See especially pp. 74–119.

94 Becker, *Books and Libraries in American Society*, 207.

95 *The Equal Chance: Books Help to Make It* (Chicago: American Library Association, 1943).

solidified.[96] Like other Americans, librarians emerged from the war somewhat fearful and unsure of the way ahead. Some looked to the past for reassurance about the significance of the old library faith. On the eve of the public library movement's centennial, in 1947, the American Library Association published a history of the public library's first fifty years. Its author, librarian Sidney Ditzion, titled the book *Arsenals of a Democratic Culture*, in an echo of Roosevelt's speech of 1940. Ditzion argued that the "tax-supported public library not only answered the criteria inherent in the democratic premise but also offered an instrument as responsive to varying social requirements as democracy itself." He pointed to a number of mid-nineteenth century ideologies, including republicanism, a religiously inspired value for individual moral worth, self-culture, nationalism, and "the forward march of science and technology" that contributed to a climate of democracy that fostered the free library movement. The strongest "threats to democracy" were believed to have come from "ignorant classes who would vote for the wrong parties either because of their own untutored choice or because of the scheming leadership of city politicians. America would be the victim of its own humane spirit if it did not educate and inform its 'illiterate blacks and foreign born.'" While Ditzion was critical of, for example, temperance reform that "aimed to deprive others of free expression and action," he was supportive of the link that librarians believed existed between a democracy's need for informed citizens and the library faith that good reading had the power to shape good character.[97]

Ditzion's work, with its celebratory tone and militaristic metaphor, sounded like propaganda, and indeed it was perhaps intended to persuade as much as to enlighten. Librarians were desperate for political support. The problem of providing all Americans, no matter who they were and where they lived, with access to books and information still seemed insoluble. Although the Depression years had seen an extraordinary expansion of federal and state government, a process that World War II only accelerated, both during and after the war federal funding

---

96 David Halberstam, *The Fifties* (New York: Villard Books, 1993), 9.

97 Sidney Ditzion, *Arsenals of a Democratic Culture: A Social History of the Public Library Movement in New England and the Middle States from 1850 to1900* (Chicago: American Library Association, 1947), 51–59, 65, 109.

for libraries still lay in the future. And not all supported the idea of government intervention in what they thought of as local issues. While some politicians had become accustomed to central government's management of the economy and involvement in welfare programs, others in the postwar period believed that peace and prosperity provided an opportunity to cut down on the range and extent of government activity. The Truman administration had responded to demands for a reduced government role by cutting expenditure on the military. By early 1947 America's armed forces had fallen from their wartime strength of twelve million to less than two million, and the annual military budget was cut to just over 10 percent of its wartime high.[98] Some deplored the reduction in military preparedness and called for rearmament as a response to the threat of Soviet aggression, but others saw this as an opportunity to divert public funds from military to peaceful uses such as the GI Bill and public libraries. The debate about where federal dollars should be allocated grew tenser as the Cold War deepened, even surfacing on the Door Peninsula as an argument against the Door-Kewaunee Regional Library. In the postwar years, ALA made repeated attempts to persuade Congress to pass a bill allocating federal funds to state public library initiatives, but just as repeatedly, Republican opposition ensured that their efforts failed. Not until 1956 was federal funding finally secured for library service to rural Americans.

The Wisconsin Idea in Action

Painfully aware that exclusive reliance on local community funding had produced extreme disparities in library services, librarians searched for alternative models of support as public libraries moved into the second century of their existence. In the 1930s state commissions had began to draw on a "demonstration" technique that the agricultural extension services used in the early years of the twentieth century to persuade farmers to adopt innovative methods, reasoning that if people only saw for themselves how valuable good library service could be,

---

98 Halberstam, *The Fifties*, 28.

they would readily agree to fund it. Better still, officials believed, if small communities could be persuaded to band together to pool their resources, much waste and duplication of effort could be avoided. The first county library had begun in Ohio in 1898, and between 1900 and 1910 Wisconsin, Oregon, and Minnesota had provided some county support for libraries.[99] By 1935, only in California and New Jersey were county libraries widespread. Even in Ohio, only seven out of fifteen counties had county library service in 1935. In Illinois, one county out of 102 had county library service, and nine counties had no libraries at all.[100] In Wisconsin, the first effort at pooling resources across county boundaries occurred when the WFLC launched its modest but significant project to set up a regional library in Door and Kewaunee counties.

A key figure in Wisconsin's proposed demonstration was ALA's former Adult Education specialist, John Chancellor. Chancellor had joined ALA's headquarters in 1934.[101] There he worked closely with the staff at Chicago Public Library and the Public Library of Des Moines to codify a new professional stance in support of intellectual freedom.[102] Chancellor was passionate in support of a vision of democracy for America that accepted and even celebrated the right of multiple voices to be heard. "Help to keep alive the spirit of tolerance, understanding, and good will toward minority political, racial, and cultural groups," he urged librarians in an *ALA Bulletin* article in 1941. "America, of all the nations in the world, should lead the way in making the world safe for differences. Deeply rooted in our heritage are the principles, legal standards, and practices that recognize the rights and freedoms of minority groups—religious, racial, political, or cultural."[103] Chancellor (a Quaker) was deeply opposed to ALA's active involvement in military preparations. He also opposed centralized planning and funding. "Doubts persist in my mind," he told *ALA Bulletin* readers," about

---

99 Robert Ellis Lee, *Continuing Education for Adults through the American Public Library, 1833–1964* (Chicago: ALA, 1966), 32–33.

100 Mildred W. Sandoe, *County Library Primer* (New York: H. W. Wilson Co., 1942), 15–16.

101 Jessie W. Luther, "Adult Education and the Librarian," *Wisconsin Library Bulletin* 30 (November 1934): 194.

102 See Chapter Four for further discussion of this movement.

103 J. M. Chancellor, "For a Free and Enlightened People," *Bulletin of the American Library Association* 35 (April 1941): 199.

the possibility of really effective mass education from the professional level downward."[104] Local solutions were best, he argued. "The job of jobs for the ALA is to make libraries strong in themselves, self-reliant, to a degree self-sufficient. They are weakened by encouraging them to look to Federal government or any other remote national leadership for their initiative or by implying that appropriations must be increased before they will try to progress."[105]

In 1942 Chancellor resigned his position at ALA, at least in part in protest against the organization's support for America's engagement in World War II.[106] With his wife and sons, he moved to Mount Horeb, a small town a few miles south of Madison, Wisconsin, and took up the life of a farmer on fifty acres. By June 1947, he had joined the six-member Wisconsin Free Library Commission, and the following month he assumed the position of vice-chairman. In his personal life and professional prescriptions, Chancellor seemed to be drawing on beliefs that would have been familiar in the early republic. The opportunity "to work alone in the open, with tangible things, and with a degree of independence and self-sufficiency" attracted him, but he was also turning away from "some of the old methods" of adult education, even those that he himself had worked so closely to promote. In an open letter in 1947 to the Wisconsin library community he wrote a strong condemnation of two adverse social trends that he felt together constituted the main problem facing America. First was the tendency toward centralized organizations and the domination of economic life by large-scale monopolies. Second was the growth of commercially motivated popular media industries, "powerful communication industries . . . dominated, for the most part, not by motives of enlightenment or social service but by a profit motive." Chancellor saw the answer to the resulting audience passivity and powerlessness in a reinvigorated public library— a "virile library system"—which might permeate "the everyday lives of the people in every city ward and every rural village with personnel

---

104 "John Chancellor Resigns," *Bulletin of the American Library Association* 36 (May 1942): 370.

105 John Chancellor, "The Diffusion of Knowledge: A Memorandum," *Bulletin of the American Library Association* 36, no. 7 (July 1942): 558.

106 Joyce M. Latham, "White Collar Read: The American Public Library and the Left-Led CIO: A Case Study of the Chicago Public Library, 1929–1952" (Ph.D. Diss., University of Illinois at Urbana-Champaign, 2007), n. 143, p. 107; Becker, *Books and Libraries in American Society*, 78.

and materials—printed, audio and visual—focused on making daily living more intelligent, creative, healthy and hence enjoyable."[107] To Chancellor it was clear that library strengths lay in the provision of useful information to citizen-consumers.

In 1948, John R. Barton, Professor of Rural Sociology at the University of Wisconsin–Madison and another newly appointed member of the WFLC, followed up Chancellor's masculine polemic with hard facts and some rhetoric of his own. Barton was just beginning a research project into Wisconsin's public libraries, aided by his graduate student Franklin E. Rector (known as Eugene or Gene).[108] Here could be seen the Wisconsin Idea in action, as Barton made his policy-oriented university expertise available for the benefit for ordinary citizens. In a *Wisconsin Library Bulletin* article about his research, Barton wrote, "At a time when most of us grow more ignorant hour by hour unless we keep pace with the best experience and expanding information of a rapidly changing society, the per capita book circulation of Wisconsin libraries is decreasing. In 1922 the per capita annual book circulation for the state was 5.5 volumes. In 1947, it was 3.94 volumes circulation per capita." Prevention of a further deterioration was essential, Barton contended. "The competition for people's minds and thoughts today is terrific and unless we use effectively some of the newer communications techniques and methods, Americans will become less and less a reading, and one might add, a thinking people." To forestall such an eventuality, Barton envisaged newer techniques for "taking library services to the people or for keeping library values before the public," including regular news columns about new books and library activities, a children's story hour, book talks for adults, book exhibits at group meetings, and radio programs.[109]

The following year, the WFLC published a sixty-four-page booklet that set out its vision for the future of public libraries in Wisconsin, and

---

107 John Chancellor, "An Open Letter from a New Commission Member," *Wisconsin Library Bulletin* 43, no. 9 (1947): 143–44.

108 Rector went on to base his Ph.D. dissertation on the library demonstration: Franklin Eugene Rector, "Social Correlates of Eighth Grade Attainment in Two Wisconsin Counties" (Ph.D. Diss., University of Wisconsin–Madison, 1954).

109 John Barton, "Information Preview," *Wisconsin Library Bulletin* 44, no. 9 (1948): 170, 174. The full report appeared in 1951: John R. Barton and Franklin E. Rector, *The Public Library in Wisconsin: An Inquiry into Its Social and Educational Resources* (Madison: Department of Rural Sociology, Wisconsin Free Library Commission), 1951.

echoed many of Chancellor's and Barton's concerns.[110] In *The Wisconsin-Wide Library Idea* the WFLC emphasized the state's and the university's responsibility for involving as partners-in-democracy all of Wisconsin's citizens, including those living in remote rural areas. The vehicle was to be the rural public library—but not the old "small recreational depot" that was "unfortunately the total picture of a library carried in the minds of most people and public officials today." Downplaying the value of reading for pleasure (especially the reading of fiction or "stories") in favor of a more instrumental value for information, the WFLC emphasized the need for an "efficient, flexible institution for informal education, information, inspiration and recreation easily accessible and easily used by all people of all ages everywhere in the State."[111] By the middle of the twentieth century, then, the earlier "civilizationist" justifications for the public library (with their religious overtones) were being challenged by a more secular rhetoric that claimed to hearken back to Jeffersonian republican values of educating an informed citizenry.

The WFLC planned four objectives for the "reinvigorated" public library that would try to balance these competing ideas about the purpose of the library. First was informal adult education, by providing materials for study to groups or individuals on any subject, at any time. Second, the library would be a source of information, able to "supply quickly special facts needed in the serious work or living of any citizen or organization." Citizens could also use the library for recreation, of course. But here the WFLC did not hesitate to be prescriptive; the library should provide "not only wholesome stories to read but insights into other lives and places and interests to help us out of the ruts of monotony and routine." And finally, the library materials should be inspirational, by giving suggestions and incentives "for creative activity of all kinds and improved living for the individual, the family and community groups."[112]

Behind the WFLC's rhetoric, which echoed concerns that the

---

110 Drawing on its historical antecedents, the Commission titled the pamphlet *The Wisconsin-Wide Library Idea for Voluntary Education through Reading: A detailed but tentative statement from the Wisconsin Free Library Commission.*

111 Ibid., 3.

112 Ibid.

Country Life Commission had expressed early in the century, lay the belief that the existence of ordinary people—especially rural residents—was dull, uninspiring, and circumscribed by lack of spatial and social mobility. The Commission's four fundamental remedies of Knowledge, Education, Organization, and Spiritual Forces, to be supplied by such institutions as the U.S.D.A. and agricultural colleges, the public schools, voluntary clubs, and the churches, had failed to stem the flow of people from the countryside to the cities, and during the 1920s and 1930s farm incomes had continued to slide. Now at the end of the 1940s, the WFLC proposed that access to useful information and the right reading could cure the alienation and isolation of country life. The WFLC would supply the expertise that would identify the necessary materials. These would, however, consist mainly of informational reading in preference to the reading of stories.

Seeking to forestall criticism from Wisconsin's librarians and to reassure them that the possibility of a state plan for county or regional libraries did not constitute a threat to their local autonomy, WFLC consultant Gretchen Knief Schenk drew on a metaphor that she doubtless felt would appeal to her mostly female readers. In an article in the *Wisconsin Library Bulletin* titled "Afraid of Our Shadow?" she argued that cooperation at a regional or county level would only free librarians from the drudgery of "library housekeeping." Rather than have the "specter of book ordering, cataloging, mending, binding etc. hovering over you," she wrote, librarians would have time for the "real task of 'homemaking'—working with readers and books."[113] Thus Schenk added her voice to those calling for an expanded role for the librarian in mediating between readers and library materials. She added a paternalistic touch, presumably intended to soothe rather than irritate; "Would you lose your job? No, of course not. The county or regional library is there to *help you do a better job*, not to give your job to someone else . . . There is nothing to fear as long as the State Library Commission,

---

113 Gretchen Knief Schenk, "Afraid of Our Shadow?" *Wisconsin Library Bulletin* 44, no. 5 (1948): 90. Schenk, a native of Milwaukee, had worked in libraries in several states, including California, Illinois, and Washington. She retired from full-time librarianship in 1945 to become a library consultant. In 1948, she was editor of the "County Libraries" section of the *Wilson Library Bulletin*. Her correspondence with Commission officials suggests that she enjoyed a close working relationship them, and that on occasion she played the role of friend and confidante. See also Chapter Four.

always the best friend of the state's library service, leads the way. The Commission, like the adult of our childhood, will never allow any plan to be approved which would not better the public library service for the citizens whom we serve."[114]

According to the *Wisconsin-Wide Library Idea*, ideally, the community library should be a site and focus of educational activity similar to the public schools and university. Librarians, library trustees, and the WFLC field workers would be partners in reforming libraries. In particular, the state would facilitate county or regional cooperation among libraries, to share essential library operations such as purchasing, cataloging, and processing. A new but crucial organizational feature of library service in Wisconsin would modify the influence of the experts, however. Communities could not expect the state to foot the entire bill for local improvements in library service, and local control was essential to garner local support and thus local funding. The vehicle for this local control was to be a new voluntary body: the People's Library Committee. The problem in the past, *The Wisconsin-Wide Library Idea* argued, lay in the image of the public library as a "kind of cloister for the cultured, retiring and bookish people." This unfavorable image had influenced not only the type of trustee and librarian selected, but also the kind of printed material stocked, and even the kind of buildings built and the locations chosen for them. In fact, the whole pattern of public library service had "fostered a rarefied type of culture designed not so much to improve daily living in the home and community as to provide a refuge from the inevitable difficulties of daily living."[115]

Instead, the library needed to attract a wider clientele, that would include children, "out-of-school" teenagers "through with school and trying to establish themselves in new homes and new livelihoods," homemakers (especially rural homemakers), farmers and townspeople, and those working in industry, business, and the professions. In short, everyone would have a stake in the community library. At the same time, every county, and every community with at least three hundred members, should be represented by a people's library committee composed of those with "a genuine interest in the educational potentialities

114 Schenk, ibid., 90. Emphasis in the original.
115 *The Wisconsin-Wide Library Idea*, 3, 6, 9.

and social services values of a library system." This should be the main criterion for inclusion, not "geography, existing institutions (schools, churches) or organizations (women's clubs, legion, business clubs) or of picking overworked leaders and people of prominence and dominance in the community." Having put its finger on the obvious danger that the people's committee would consist of those already occupying leadership positions, however, *The Wisconsin-Wide Library Idea* had few practical suggestions of how to avoid it.[116]

The other key to the reinvented library consisted of a regional pool of circulating materials that would be passed from community to community, either via their local libraries or by means of a traveling bookmobile. With the aid of a bookmobile, the Commission hoped that the regional pool would help iron out the differences between wealthy and poorer districts, so that even the smallest library would have access to specialized or expensive materials. Echoing long-standing concerns about the value of fiction, and drawing a sharp distinction between "information" and "stories," the Wisconsin-Wide Library Idea would revolve around the provision of nonfiction. All in all, the Commission felt that "the whole regional project may stand or fall on the quality of the bookmobile service." "Experience has shown," the writers argued, "that a community will use two or three times as much non-fiction as fiction if served by a bookmobile rather than a station."[117] The proposed vehicles should not only carry a very wide selection of books (at least a thousand volumes) but informational genres—pamphlets, magazines, booklists, and reading suggestions. "Pamphlets, especially agricultural pamphlets," the document asserted, "can answer many needs more adequately than books and also save space and weight."[118]

Librarians should resist the notion that rural readers' needs would be different from those of city readers, bookmobile advocates advised. "Rural readers get their information about books from the same sources as do city readers; from the book review sections of city newspapers and magazines or from radio book review programs," pointed out Ohio librarian Mildred Sandoe in 1942. "Some bookmobile librarians claim

---

116 Ibid., 10.
117 Ibid., 19.
118 Ibid., 20.

that rural patrons read better things than their city cousins." [119] On the bookmobile, expert aid would be readily at hand to help borrowers make the right choice for them, the Wisconsin-Wide Library Idea assured its readers. Past failures at interesting people in reading non-fiction would be overcome by the presence of "an able librarian . . . on hand to fit it to the serious interests of people." Thus even more essential to the success of the project than the availability of the right reading materials were "personnel fitted by personality and experience to introduce the wealth of reading on the wayside." Moreover, only the mobile library had the capacity to provide access to the most hard-to-reach members of the community—farm families.[120]

The Demonstration under Way

However confident state officials were that they had identified an ideal region for the Demonstration, during the selection process area librarians and library supporters feared that local politicians and residents might not be easily persuaded. Both county boards of supervisors were due to vote on November 9, 1949, the Kewaunee County board in the morning and the Door County board in the afternoon. Since Kewaunee County had a history of funding only a restricted formal education, project supporters were far from sanguine about their willingness to match the state funds for the library. However, to many people's astonishment, at their morning meeting the Kewaunee supervisors voted to fund the library. Still shaking her head in wonderment fifty years later, Livingston commented, "It was a miracle . . . They were so tight-fisted—and they still are!" In her opinion, one woman's activism contributed to the positive vote. Mrs. Olga Dana, widow of a beloved doctor, who used to visit and donate art prints to Kewaunee rural schools, appeared before the county board and told them they "should be ashamed not to allow that money for the library, because the children needed it," said Livingston.

George Miller, district attorney for Kewaunee County at the time,

---

119 Sandoe, *County Library Primer*, 73.

120 *The Wisconsin-Wide Library Idea*, 20.

believed that the prospect of state funding was especially attractive. "It was sort of a controversial thing right from the beginning," said Miller. "The thing that sold it to the Kewaunee County taxpayers was that the State . . . probably paid one-third of the amount of the cost of it. Country schools—either one room or two room—most had very limited facilities as far as libraries were concerned." The idea of getting something for nothing had appeal. "The other thing is the rural areas where the schools were supposedly needed it the most, and that's where the most conservative people were . . . So the state part of it was very important." Whether inspired by Mrs. Dana's example as cultural civilizer, or attracted by the prospect of state aid, the Kewaunee Board voted in favor of the project.

Their decision presented the Door County supervisors with little choice in the afternoon. Impelled by a sense of their own cultural identity and inter-county rivalry, they too voted to fund the project. "The Door County board prided themselves on being more progressive than the Kewaunee board," said Livingston, "so they couldn't not." It helped that Livingston had already laid the groundwork in Door County. When she was hired as director in 1945, rural residents could use the Sturgeon Bay Public Library for an annual fee of fifty cents, but even this modest sum was too much for many families, and few took advantage of the arrangement. Even before the Demonstration received state approval, a county system that included bookmobile service had seemed to be the answer, Livingston decided, and Door County school superintendent Curtis Tronson agreed. County supervisors and library board members, however, however, were harder to convince. Originally skeptical, Stanley Greene, mayor of Sturgeon Bay and an influential library board member, became a county system advocate after he attended a Wisconsin Library Association meeting in Madison.

Others were impressed by a bookmobile demonstration at the 1949 Door County fair, using a borrowed vehicle. "We snared every [supervisor]," Livingston commented. "All we did was tell them we wanted to show them what it was. We didn't put any pressure on them . . . But we got most of them." One supervisor from the north of the peninsula missed the show, however. "On Monday morning the bookmobile was still here. . . So we took off and went up there and stopped at his house." Fortunately for Livingston and Tronson, the man's wife was a library supporter. "He's off out in the woods up there, but you can get through," she told them. Following her directions, Livingston and Tronson drove the bookmobile off the highway into the woods. Perhaps it was their persistence that he found convincing, but from then on they could count on his support. "I think it impressed him that we chased him down," Livingston recalled. "The Door County board voted 15–4 for the project with one abstention Wednesday afternoon," reported the *Sturgeon Bay Advocate*, on November 10, 1949. The state-sponsored Demonstration seemed all set to go.

But although local library supporters and the WFLC rejoiced, not everyone welcomed or even accepted the result. Frugality rapidly emerged as one key issue, and attachment to local autonomy was another. Some opponents felt that their forebears had fled oppressive economic and political regimes in their native lands, and some ethnic groups had a tradition of protecting their freedom from government interference in America.[121] Moreover, libraries and reading had never featured prominently in some ethnic cultures. After all, in Wisconsin, early public libraries had mostly been organized by groups of Yankees for themselves and those who shared their values. Now the opposition, centered on southern townships dominated by people of Belgian and eastern European descent, was quick to organize. Reported the *Algoma Record-Herald*, "A resolution was presented to the [Kewaunee] county board in which Montpelier town electors at their April 4 annual meeting unanimously opposed the action of the county board in setting up the demonstration bookmobile library in Door and Kewaunee counties without giving the people of Kewaunee county an opportunity to vote on the question in a referendum."[122] Supervisor Jim Nejedlo, a Montpelier tavern-owner, was particularly opposed, at least in part because the project involved "giving up some of their powers," George Miller remembered.

In June 1950, three Kewaunee County supervisors, including Nejedlo, proposed a countywide referendum on the Regional Library. "It surely is a fine muddle when something like this can be put over without the taxpayer knowing until it has cost twelve to fifteen dollars a year

---

121 Robert C. Nesbit, *Urbanization and Industrialization, 1873–1893*, vol. 3 of *The History of Wisconsin* (Madison: State Historical Society of Wisconsin, 1985), 45, 52.

122 *Algoma Record-Herald*, 15 April 1950. In Wisconsin a "town" is unit of local government (a six-mile square area) similar to a township elsewhere, rather than an urban area. This Kewaunee County "town" was actually a rural district.

in additional taxes," fumed a Kewaunee County newspaper reader. "About the only thing we may be able to learn about this demonstration set up is that it will be very expensive reading. I think the town of Montpelier electors are very wise to try and stop this fine set up, as it is called, before it costs them any more of their hard-earned tax money."[123] At their June meeting, the county supervisors considered the Montpelier request for a referendum. Three residents (two from Montpelier) spoke against the library, reported the *Kewaunee Star*, while Jane Livingston and the library's administrative assistant also attended the meeting, to put the case for the project. Perhaps the library staff spoke more persuasively, or perhaps the supervisors felt the library should be given more of a chance to prove its worth, but in the end, the request was turned down on a vote of seventeen to three. "Only Supervisors Wodsedalek of Casco town, Ledvina of Franklin and Nejedlo of Montpelier favored the referendum," recorded the newspaper under the headline "REFERENDUM REQUEST IS DENIED BY COUNTY BOARD."[124]

Although the way seemed clear for the Demonstration to swing into action, it was obvious that some groups and individuals already strongly resented being obliged to contribute to it. From the start, the Door-Kewaunee Regional Demonstration was the subject of dispute that ran along political fault lines complicated by ethnic, religious, and cultural differences. Indeed, as the librarians were painfully aware, controversy would continue to dog the project throughout its existence.

For the project's three years these opponents would tenaciously exploit any controversy that might cast the library in a poor light. In doing so they made sophisticated use of the democratic processes available to them, suggesting that their ability to participate as citizens in local affairs was already well developed and rested not one whit on the availability of library services. One of their most promising lines of critique rested upon the kinds of materials that the library, and especially the bookmobile, was introducing into the rural areas. But in issuing challenges to particular books, they ran headlong into a relatively new ethical stance for librarians: defense of intellectual freedom.

---

123 Alvin M. Cherney to the editor, *Kewaunee Enterprise*, 13 June 1950.
124 *Kewaunee Star*, 22 June 1950,

4
Reading—for Whom, and What?

If a public library, supported by tax, is to receive and merit
public support, it must have books that give pleasure. If it is
to hold the esteem of the community, and so win continued
support, the books must be wholesome and must give sane
views of life, inspiration and reliable information.

—Lutie E. Stearns, *Essentials in Library Administration*

Books and other reading matter selected for purchase from the
public funds should be chosen because of value and interest to
the people of the community, and in no case should the selection
be influenced by the race or nationality or the political or
religious views of the writers.

—*The Library's Bill of Rights, 1939*

From early in its history, the WFLC had maintained a close relationship
both with the Wisconsin Library Association (WLA) and with the Wisconsin Library School at the University of Wisconsin in Madison.
WFLC founders Lutie Stearns and Frank Avery Hutchins were heavily
involved in the establishment of the WLA, and the WFLC Secretary
also had the title of Director of the Library School.[1] The close ties generally enjoyed between the professional library community and the WFLC
must have helped the Door-Kewaunee Regional Demonstration project
get off to a good start. Yet most Commission board members were not

---

1 Charles A. Bunge, "The History of the Wisconsin Library School–School of Library and Information Studies 1895–1997," (polyglot.lss.wisc.edu/slis/about/historyproject/form.htm). Commission secretaries were invariably male, while the executive heads of the Library School in its early
years—known first as Preceptor (or Preceptress), then as Principal, were always female.

themselves librarians.[2] These high-profile and predominantly male board members defined and justified the Demonstration in broad philosophical terms, appealing to the lofty principles of fostering democracy and adult citizen participation. Such an approach undoubtedly helped recommend the project to legislators and others of influence, but it also represented the deeply held convictions of Commission members like John Chancellor and John Barton. In the two counties, the (mostly female) librarians too felt a passion for their cause. They took a more pragmatic line, but one that still bore a strong resemblance to a cultural civilizationist approach that they had absorbed through their training for librarianship. To the librarians, their most important task was to foster "readers" — people who liked to read, and who read often. This mismatch of goals between state officials and local librarians was chiefly evident in the matter of providing library services to children.

Children or Adults?

Having identified adults as the spearhead for the renewal of democracy, officials felt that the project's ability to win adult users was now a major yardstick of its success. The WFLC recognized that, in general and on average, children accounted for three-quarters of public library circulation, but nevertheless made the decision to split the budget fifty-fifty between young people and adults. From the beginning, though, officials were nervous about the proportion of adult library use. "The thing that has bothered us for some time is what you warned us about

---

2 Although the Wisconsin Free Library Commission had a salaried staff headed by the Commission Secretary, overall authority rested with a volunteer board. In 1949, this included three ex officio members and four citizens appointed by the governor. The ex officio members were: John Callahan (State Superintendent), Edwin B. Fred (President, University of Wisconsin), and Clifford L. Lord (Director, State Historical Society). Citizen members were librarian Ella Veslak, of Shawano, Wisconsin, William J. Deegan Jr., City Manager of Superior, Wisconsin, John P. Barton, University of Wisconsin–Madison Professor of Rural Sociology, and John Chancellor. Walter S. Botsford, formerly head of the department of political science at the University of Wisconsin's Extension Department, was WFLC Secretary. In addition, the Commission employed full-time "field-workers" (usually librarians), and consultants on an ad hoc basis.

and what we tried to prevent—that is, too much of the budget and the expenditure of time goes to the children," Walter Botsford wrote to Gretchen Schenk. "They're an eager and avid public and there can be no doubt that it is easier to serve that group than other groups among the population, and it is just for that reason that we are calling the program to a temporary halt and re-examining our objectives."[3] In their push for enhanced democratic participation, the WFLC was keen to attract new categories of patrons to the library, particularly adult males. Political considerations perhaps also made it unwise to focus heavily on children, who neither voted nor occupied positions of influence in the community. Care of children on the postwar Door Peninsula fell to their mothers, and few women exercised significant political power in that patriarchal environment. Teachers, too, were mostly female. Poorly paid, and dispersed throughout a decentralized school system, they were likely to carry little weight. Moreover, children's librarianship (also female dominated) was not a prestigious arm of the profession.

By contrast to the officials in the WFLC central office, local librarians were only too happy to focus their energies on the children of Door and Kewaunee counties. In their eyes, providing reading materials to young people and thus helping turn them into devoted adult library patrons constituted a major rationale for the Demonstration. In recounting to me their memories of the project, the former librarians tended to divide the adult world into two groups of people: readers and non-readers. Readers were those whom they could count on to support the public library, while non-readers were likely to be at best indifferent, and at worst hostile to the idea of their tax dollars supporting so frivolous—or even subversive—an activity as reading. It was librarians' job to mold children into readers, as least partly because failure to do so meant that they would grow into non-reading adults and perhaps library opponents. When pressed, however, former librarians justified their own fervor for reading by appealing to the library faith.

Professional librarians included not only those employed on the Door Peninsula, but also Commission field workers based in Madison.

---

3 Walter S. Botsford to Gretchen Knief Schenk, 22 December 1950, Series 1967, WHS Archives.

In 1949, the Wisconsin Free Library Commission hired Anne Farrington, a native of southwest Wisconsin, to liaise with local staff in Door and Kewaunee counties. Farrington and Livingston had been colleagues in Michigan, and now their professional collaboration flowered into a close friendship.[4] It was Anne Farrington who was responsible for recruiting another key employee: bookmobile librarian Shirley J. Shirley was working at the public library in Ashland, Wisconsin, but had taken time off to attend summer classes at the Library School. "The middle of the summer school I [heard] from Anne saying that she knew there was going to be a job opening up in the library experiment which of course I had been reading about," Shirley J. later remembered. "I was delighted with the job because the first thing that Jane said was, 'Well, you're going to be working with rural children who had never had library service.' I grew up going to a one-room school, so I thought, oh, what a great opportunity!" For Shirley J., as for Jane Livingston, there was no doubt that children would be the bookmobile's main focus.

Local library staff hired for the project fulfilled administrative, professional, clerical, and technical roles. Headquartered in the basement of Sturgeon Bay's Carnegie library were project director, reference librarians and catalogers, technical services staff who processed materials, clerical staff who dealt with day-to-day administration, and bookmobile personnel, consisting of a librarian and driver. "The quarters in the basement of the city library have been made extremely attractive with new lighting and bright colors in paint," announced a Green Bay newspaper. "The walls are a medium green, contrasted with book shelf backings and trim of Castilian red. Yellow and grey complete the color scheme." Office space was provided in the "west room" recently vacated by the high school art department. Bookmobiles were able to pull directly up to a former storeroom near the west entrance.[5]

Each of the local library units—in the cities of Algoma and Kewaunee in Kewaunee County, and in several villages of northern Door County—employed their own library staff. In contrast to the project

---

4 Walter S. Botsford to the Anne Farrington Memorial Committee, (n.d.) February 1954. Series 1967, WHS Archives.

5 *Green Bay Press Gazette*, 16 June 1950.

director and some of the headquarters employees who had professional qualifications, most of the women who worked in the local libraries had no formal training in librarianship. But local workers, despite their lack of formal library education, were qualified by virtue of their insider status—something the trained library staff born elsewhere lacked. Although she was a Wisconsin native, Jane Livingston realized that to the inhabitants of the Door Peninsula, she was not one of them. "They used to say that you had to be born here to belong here," she admitted. "That's what they used to say, 'She's an outsider' . . . I was an outsider too." Local staff strengthened links to other organizations in the district that were often invaluable. Olivia Traven, librarian at the village of Bailey's Harbor, was an active member of the local woman's club. As such, she was not only a visible and respected member of the community, but she also had the organizational experience and ability that made her a valuable participant in the Demonstration.[6] Bookmobile driver Andrew Kroeger was another local worker whom other Demonstration staff appreciated. "Andy was a nice man, and he probably made as many friends for us in Kewaunee County as anyone else," recalled Shirley J. "He had been a county officer at one time, an elected official. He had worked all his life in Kewaunee—his wife was from Kewaunee. He had long roots in the county and people liked him. He was a friendly, friendly man." Kroeger had what it took to be an ideal driver of the Kewaunee County bookmobile. "He did a very good job on the bookmobile, loved kids, and that was a real plus. He was meticulous about records and about the bookmobile. The bookmobile got serviced." He attracted people onto the van who might otherwise have stayed away. "There would be people who would stop in, the woman was shopping for groceries," Shirley J. said, "and [the husband] would stop in and talk to Andy. Andy made friends for us."

Together the library staff did their best to attract adult users, Shirley J. stressed. "We tried. We always had adult materials on the bookmobile, and we tried very hard if there was a request from anyone to supply it—it was not always easy because interlibrary loan was not as easy as it is now and it was not near as fast." Local newspapers joined in the

6 Interview with Olivia Traven's son, Lee Traven, 25 May 2001.

task of educating the adult population about the library's potential to meet their needs. "LIBRARY OFFERS AID AS SOURCE OF INFORMATION," announced the *Sturgeon Bay Advocate*. "'If it's in Print, We'll Get it for You,' Speaker asserts." Emphasizing the library as a supplier of useful information, librarians James Mitchell and George Babcock told the reporter, "The library is thoroughly familiar with information sources of all types, as well as having on hand many books for direct reference. Among the latter are Thomas's Register in four volumes, listing all products and manufacturers in the United States. When you have a problem in your business, knowing where to find the answer is our job."[7]

Shirley J. found the mix of WLFC experts, project librarians, and local employees congenial and productive. "It was the best job I ever had. Jane was a good boss, and it was a group of people who worked very hard and were very enthusiastic . . . We had great supervision and advice from the Madison people." The Commission workers were tactful about making suggestions. "They never interfered, but they offered to help. They would come up and do things at staff meetings that were very *very* good for the people at the unit libraries because none of them had any library background—I mean they were readers but that was it." Anne Farrington loved her work for the project, too. Although based in Madison, she bought a cottage on the shore near Sturgeon Bay and spent as much time there as she could. "Anne had such great hopes for things," recalled Livingston. "I can remember sitting looking out over Green Bay and watching the sunset and talking with her about things we were going to do. She was just that kind . . . [she] inspired people to want to do things." The librarians used Anne's cottage as a social and strategic center. "We would all go over to Anne's for dinner," remembered Shirley J. "She would say, 'I'll provide the place—you bring the food. I'm not much of a cook!'"

Together, they formed themselves into a closely knit group—"almost like a family," Shirley J. related. "A lot of us who worked there were young and unattached. That creates an enthusiasm. We could do things that people who were very settled sometimes won't take the time for

---

7 *Sturgeon Bay Advocate*, 14 December 1950.

... Because we were so far from the city as we were, there was an isolation that made us hang together. We had each other . . ." Evaluations that staff wrote at the end of the project confirmed that other employees, too, found their work rewarding. "The most valuable part of the program to me personally," wrote one staff member, "has been the sharing of professional training and experience in the monthly staff meeting." "I am proud to be a member of this staff," wrote another, and "I have utmost pride and confidence in our director," wrote a third.[8] For these library workers, the rich social and professional interactions that the Demonstration afforded outweighed other benefits.

As the project's three years went by, it attracted national and international interest, with visitors from as far away as Burma, the Philippines, and New Zealand. In 1952 Thein Swe, president of Rangoon's Bogyoke Library, wrote appreciatively to Botsford, expressing gratitude for his hospitality; "I will never forget the journey to Sturgeon Bay with your car, and the dinner at that cottage with Miss Anne and Jane."[9] More prosaically, performance measures, too, indicated success. Between 1942 and 1948, circulation ranged from a low of 71,140 in 1946 to a high of 77,682 in 1944. But once the project got under way, these figures rocketed.

Using the "Kaiser Charging System," bookmobile and unit library patrons recorded their own circulation information on preprinted yellow slips. "The Kaiser Charging System, first inaugurated by Walter Kaiser, Librarian of the Wayne County Library, Detroit Michigan, is being established in modified form in the Door-County Regional Library," wrote Livingston in a memo to her staff in 1950. "It has proven to be economical—in terms of materials and personnel—is non-mechanical, involves a signature charge, and is easily adaptable to a regional library system, permitting free exchange of books and materials between all agencies in the system."[10] A disadvantage of the system, as the accompanying manual admitted, was "that part of the charging

8 Anne Farrington, "The Last Lap," in *The Idea in Action: A Report on the Door-Kewaunee Regional Library Demonstration, 1950–1952* (Madison: Wisconsin Free Library Commission, 1953), 12.

9 Thein Swe to Walter S. Botsford, 12 May 1952, Series 1967, WHS Archives.

10 Memo from Jane Livingston to the Staff of the Door-Kewaunee Regional Library, May 1950, DCLA.

process has been transferred from the librarian to the patron. However," the manual continued, "the U.S. Post Office, bank, and many stores request and receive willing assistance from the public for numerous operations. After a period of adjustment, the public will be pleased to cooperate in a small task to improve its own services at less cost."[11] In practice, some patrons were better equipped to cooperate than others, though. Young children, in particular, were likely to need help filling out the forms.

Circulation information recorded on such ephemeral and flimsy slips was never intended to endure. Most were probably discarded once borrowers returned books to the library. But between five and six thousand survived. No document remains to suggest why these records in particular should have been saved, but Jane Livingston remembered that the WFLC had suggested that librarians should retain a sample of records from across the whole region, "just in case." This seems plausible. The surviving records appeared to come from every area, from Washington Island at the northern tip of the Door Peninsula to the village of Denmark in the far south. Although a large number (about one-third) was undated, the dates of the remaining two-thirds clustered into two groups. The smaller group (44 percent) represented materials borrowed from the bookmobile and the libraries around the end of October and the beginning of November 1950. The larger cluster (56 percent) represented books borrowed in July 1951.[12] Of the library charges that survived, 5,059 (87 percent) appeared to have been made by children. About 25 percent of these (1,281) were identifiable only as "children." The other 75 percent (3,778) of these younger patrons were identifiable as girls or boys from their names. Sixty-two percent of these were girls (2,353), while boys (1,425) accounted for 38

---

11 *A Manual for the Installation and Operation of the Kaiser Charging System for the Door-Kewaunee Regional Library, 1950*, DCLA.

12 Despite the lack of statistical "representativeness" (since the sample was not randomly drawn) there are reasons to encourage generalization from these records to the project as a whole. First, the sheer number of records is in itself quite substantial—enough to assume a normal distribution. Second, the WFLC's own samples provide a validity check with respect to the age categories. Since the findings with respect to age were quite similar between the bookmobile database and the two samples taken by the WFLC, it may be safe to assume that the gender distributions were also approximately the same. See Appendix 2 for a description of the database of the records.

percent. The ages of these students ranged from six or seven to four-teen or fifteen.[13]

In 1950, circulation showed an 83 percent increase over 1949. Two years later, it had risen again, to 222,151—an increase of 160 percent over 1949.[14] But, encouraging as they were, these gross circulation fig-ures failed to provide the sort of detail that the WFLC needed to gauge the likelihood of their political success, as a lack of detailed manage-ment information hampered their efforts. It was clear in retrospect that planning time for the Demonstration had been far too short. At the time, library supporters had congratulated themselves on their fast start out of the gate. "REGIONAL LIBRARY IS COUNTY'S NEWEST, PROUDEST ACHIEVEMENT" proclaimed the *Green Bay Press Gazette* in a 1950 "vacation issue." "It's First in State; Two Bookmobiles Now in Daily Operation." Jane Livingston, "diminutive city librarian" and "a dynamo of organization," received most of the credit. "Appointed head of the new project, by May 1 she had 80 per cent of her personnel and had them working overtime on the $6000 worth of books which had been purchased, delivered, and are now distributed via the bookmo-bile. In New York State," crowed the paper, "there was a similar proj-ect that took nine months to purchase its first book."[15] Perhaps, how-ever, the project had taken off before the WFLC had had sufficient time to think through the administrative details. Since state legislators had cut funding for the evaluation phase, staff could not implement a registration scheme that would have allowed them to collect detailed user statistics. Instead, they had to rely on data collected from two sample studies carried out in late spring of 1951 and 1952.[16]

Data from the two sample surveys indicated that WFLC suspicions that children's use would dominate were justified. According to these studies, adult use of units and bookmobiles combined accounted for only about 30 percent of circulation. Once the figures were split

---

13 While bookmobile patrons sometimes failed to include their names on the charge slips, they always recorded the site. Presumably most patrons at school stops were students. It is also likely that the children who failed to write in their names were among the younger pupils.

14 See Appendix 1, Table 1.

15 *Green Bay Press Gazette*, 16 June 1950.

16 See Appendix 1, Tables 2 and 3.

nization plans at the county committee," editorialized the *Algoma Record-Herald*, "the calm was broken by the charge of a Krok [Kewaunee County] farmer who said that three books were found in his area that were unfit for children to read—they had been distributed on the Door-Kewaunee bookmobile."[21] No details of what books came under fire have survived, but if opponents hoped to have *The Grapes of Wrath* removed from the shelves, they failed, since circulation records show that a schoolgirl from Tisch Mills (on Kewaunee County's southern border with Manitowoc County) borrowed the book in July 1951.

Since librarians as well as members of the public saw the act of reading as freighted with moral significance, book selection was a matter of vital professional concern. Nineteenth-century educational reformers believed that reading had the capability to shape a student's character for good, or ill. To some, reading had become a virtuous activity in its own right, while the ability to read marked the good child, as opposed to the bad.[22] Yet the question of what materials children—and adults—should read was highly contentious. In Colonial times, cultural authorities had already segmented the print universe into areas of greater and lesser value. Especially troubling to early religious and political leaders were popular, if ephemeral, genres of street literature, "chapbooks" including crime confessions and captivity narratives. Other forms of publication that became increasingly popular in the eighteenth century included newspapers, history, biography, and self-improvement books that ranged from reading-and-writing aids (such as dictionaries, primers, readers, and penmanship books) to etiquette and fashion books. Newspapers were the first genre of popular publication to circulate extensively in the late eighteenth and early nineteenth centuries. In 1810, 376 newspapers of all political stripes enjoyed a readership of twenty-two million male and female readers, some of whom also contributed opinions and columns to their relatively open and uncontrolled pages.[23]

None of these publication formats came in for more attention—or

---

21 *Algoma Record-Herald*, 15 February 1951.

22 Lee Soltow and Edward Stevens, *The Rise of Literacy and the Common School in the United States: A Socioeconomic Analysis to 1870* (Chicago: University of Chicago Press, 1981), 65.

23 Cathy N. Davidson, *Revolution and the Word: The Rise of the Novel in America* (New York: Oxford University Press, 1986), 41, 18, 160.

censure—however, than the new genre of the novel. American critics, mostly drawn from a well-educated elite, borrowed from the critical tone of articles in British periodicals that complained of novels' lack of didactic purpose and social responsibility, as well as their appeal to the imagination and to emotions (dubbed sensations). Such critics voiced concern, as Cathy Davidson comments, "for a different class of readers whom they *perceived* as being barely capable of reading fiction but eager to do so and, no doubt, highly susceptible to its dubious charms . . . Would not the farm boy and servant girl become discontent with the station in life to which providence had consigned them and fulfill the duties of that station grudgingly or not at all?"[24]

By the middle of the nineteenth century, the expanding market place for publications had called forth not only a greater diversity but also a wider distribution of print than could have been imagined at the end of the eighteenth century. Some of these printed publications, it was feared, could have a corrupting influence on impressionable (literally printable) minds.[25] Anxieties centered particularly on the effects of new kinds of publication—such as the novel—on the reader's moral development. Since the exercise of responsible, virtuous citizenship depended on informed moral character, what individuals and groups selected to read (in a world of increasing choice) was a matter of vital social concern. It was this understanding of the power of print that prompted Americans to invest so heavily in public education for future citizens—white boys (and white girls as future mothers of citizens)—in the middle and later years of the nineteenth century. It also prompted the establishment of public libraries, primarily to serve white adults and youth.

Leading members of the developing profession of librarianship joined the debate about reading. Seeking to reassure those who saw in free public libraries a mixed blessing since they offered such a wide variety of materials to the undiscriminating, Justin Winsor of the Boston Public Library and later Librarian of Harvard University drew an analogy between reading and eating. "There is doubtless a universal

---

24 Ibid., 49.

25 Isabelle Lehuu, *Carnival on the Page: Popular Print Media in Antebellum America* (Chapel Hill: University of North Carolina Press, 2000), 16–17.

goodness in literature as bread is in diet," he wrote, "but no one wants to live on bread solely, and it is the variety, and to a considerable extent condiments and relishes in food and in books, that give health to the appetite and vigor to the digestion." With help, readers could learn to be more discriminating. Librarians should "strive to elevate the taste of their readers" by giving them "such books as they ask for and then conducting them, say from the ordinary society novel to the historical novel, and then to the proofs and illustrations of the events or periods commemorated in the more readable of the historians."[26]

Librarians helped keep alive debates about the place of fiction in the lives of American citizens. Long after British criticism of novels had died down at the end of the eighteenth century, and as fiction moved into the literary mainstream, American critics continued to fulminate against the genre in the pages of elite periodicals and in the expanding world of professional publications. Cultural authorities assumed a distinction between worthwhile reading that served to inform or instruct and reading that aimed to amuse or divert, and reading as an exercise in reason as opposed to reading as evoking passion. They struggled, too, over who would establish and maintain a hierarchy of reading that left no doubt as to who and what were on the top and at the bottom. Throughout the nineteenth century, reading fiction continued to be a controversial topic in the developing public institutions of the school and library.[27]

Censorship: A Contested Professional Practice

For their early founders, public libraries served to disseminate knowledge that elites recognized as valuable in increasing opportunities for self-education and social mobility among the less privileged, and thus likely to contribute to the success of the republican experiment. The enemies of the freedom to read, early library leaders understood, were religious intolerance and political privilege. At a time when newspa-

---

26 Justin Winsor, "Reading in Popular Libraries," 1876 Report, 431–33.

27 For details of this debate during the latter part of the nineteenth century, see Esther Jane Carrier, *Fiction in Public Libraries, 1876–1900* (New York: Scarecrow Press, 1965).

pers and other periodicals showed intense religious and political partisanship, "neutrality" in the library meant adherence to the principle of the separation of church and state and an avoidance of political faction. "In that tense period between the Missouri Compromise and the publication of *Uncle Tom's Cabin* to the outbreak of Civil War," argues Evelyn Geller, the library was "a place where differences could be forgotten as people met in terms of what they shared. The intent of exclusion was not opinion control but the affirmation of religious and political freedom and, more, of tolerance." However, at a time when character and virtue were held to be vital to the exercise of citizenship, the link between morality and democracy was clear. That libraries should provide access only to morally acceptable books was indisputable. Popular novels stood on the margins of what counted as morally acceptable, however, and some argued that public libraries should refuse to include them, just as public schools did.[28]

The period after the Civil War saw a rapid expansion in the publication of popular novels that prompted leading men of letters to debate in print about the quality of reading materials now widely and cheaply available. They agreed that reading could be both a source of self-improvement and a sign of a moral character, and that on the other hand, the wrong reading could lead to moral downfall. But what counted as the wrong reading and what to do about it were not self-evident. Some took a strong stance against "immoral" literature. Fears of social upheaval had intensified during the Civil War. In July 1863, riots against the draft swept New York City. This breakdown in law and order prompted anguished self-examination in print. A report issued by the YMCA in 1866 pointed to the "vile weekly newspapers" and "licentious books" that corrupted young workingmen living alone in the cities, and campaigned for a state obscenity law that would combat such evils. In 1873, Anthony Comstock founded the New York Society for the Suppression of Vice, an organization that he was to lead for the following forty years. Later the same year, a similar organization appeared in Boston, and other cities soon followed, including St. Louis, Chicago, Louisville, Cincinnati, and San Francisco. All were

---

28 Evelyn Geller, *Forbidden Books in American Public Libraries, 1876–1939: A Study in Cultural Change* (Westport, Conn.: Greenwood, 1984), 11, 13, 12.

supported by leading men who believed, as Paul Boyer puts it, "that by money and influence they could impose upon their present 'neighbors' the moral precepts and taboos that had pervaded their own earlier years," and that these would successfully counter the social upheaval that they especially associated with the expanding cities.[29] The so-called Comstock Laws that resulted from these organizations' activities forbade the mailing of any "obscene, lewd or lascivious book, pamphlet, picture, paper, writing, print or other publication of an indecent character." In the vice societies' rhetoric, "obscene" printed material constituted a particular threat to youth, especially the children of affluent families.

Librarians joined the debate over "the fiction problem" in the columns of their new professional journal, the *American Library Journal* (founded in 1876).[30] In its second issue, William Frederick Poole of the Chicago Public Library answered complaints about the moral and intellectual standards of some books, by describing a ladder of moral and intellectual development. Those on the lower rungs, he argued, might well benefit from books of a lower quality. Neither did Poole agree with those who railed against "prose fiction." "The writers of such prose fiction as is found in our libraries were as eminent and worthy men and women as the writers of poetical fiction," he asserted, adding tartly, "or . . . the fiction that passes in the world as history and biography." Moreover, in public libraries "fully four-fifths of the money appropriated for books is spent in works adapted to the wants of scholars." It was then "hardly becoming," he argued, "for scholars who enjoy the lion's share, to object to the small proportional expenditure for books adapted to the wants of the masses who bear the burden of taxation."[31] Over the next decade, articles continued to appear that argued on one side of the question or the other. Some writers, like Mellen Chamberlain of the Boston Public Library, argued that to burden people with taxes and then not give them what they asked for was

---

29 Paul S. Boyer, *Purity in Print: Book Censorship in American from the Gilded Age to the Computer Age* (Madison: University of Wisconsin Press, 2002), 2, 4, 9–10.

30 In 1877 *American Library Journal* became the *Library Journal*.

31 William F. Poole, "Some Popular Objections to Public Libraries," *American Library Journal* 1, no. 2 (1876): 45–51.

unfair.[32] Others, like Samuel Swett Green (Worcester, Mass. Public Library) supported the "ladder of achievement" view of reading, claiming that immature—"simple"—readers would progress from sensational fiction to a better class of book if given the right guidance and encouragement.[33]

In their efforts to find an acceptable alternative to the reading of fiction, librarians created a contrasting category: nonfiction. The *Oxford English Dictionary* credits Justin Winsor with its first use in his Boston Public Library *Annual Report* of 1867. According to this librarian's usage, all the library's circulating works fell into the category of either fiction or nonfiction. By the latter, he meant works of history, biography, science, as well as (usually non-circulating) reference works. Since fiction was so problematic, the residual category of "nonfiction" took on an aura of respectability and even desirability. To steer readers toward higher rungs on the ladder, many libraries implemented a "two book" policy. Readers could borrow more than one book, as long as the second book was nonfiction.

Some categories of reading that had previously been considered questionable had become culturally acceptable and even valued. For example, librarians increasingly prized newspaper reading. The traditional nexus of journalism and politics, by which newspapers were understood primarily as organs of political parties, was giving way to a concept of newspapers as a product to be sold in the commercial marketplace. "The paper became less like an editor's scrap-book," says Michael Schudson, "and more an organization's product" that adopted new stylistic conventions like the interview and the summary lead. These innovations helped construe the newspaper-reading public less as political partisans whose loyalty needed to be fostered than as consumers whose opinion and taste newspapers needed to cultivate.[34] In the 1876 Report, William Cogswell Todd lauded the reading of newspapers and called for free public reading rooms to take their place as

---

32 Mellen Chamberlain, "Report of Fiction in Public Libraries," *Library Journal* 8, no. 8–9 (1883): 209.

33 Samuel Swett Green, "Class Adaptation in the Selection of Books—The Fiction Question," *Library Journal* 5, no. 5 (1880): 141.

34 Michael Schudson, *The Good Citizen: A History of American Civic Life* (New York: Free Press, 1998), 179–80.

"important means of public education" alongside schools and libraries. "A nation with many papers and magazines must be well informed," he declared. "Their circulation can almost be taken as an exponent of its intelligence." Moreover, he claimed, "Everybody reads the newspaper; book readers are comparatively few."[35] In 1893 Todd made a gift to the Boston Public Library of $2,000 a year until his death to be spent on newspapers, and in 1897 he made a second gift of $50,000 for the same purpose.[36] Even without the generosity of such a benefactor, many public libraries, especially in large cities, did indeed provide reading rooms, stocking them with hundreds of periodical titles, often in multiple copies, and sometimes including papers in a variety of languages. Librarians carefully kept note of readership statistics. In Chicago, for instance, Director Poole reported in 1885 that the main branch of the library had given out periodicals 282,613 times for use in the library; by 1896 that number had grown to 589,931.[37]

Librarians took well to the new philosophy of information that was gaining currency as the nation moved into the Progressive Era. Constructing information as a neutral, quantifiable entity opened it to manipulation by technical and administrative processes—it could be accumulated, sorted, classified and filed.[38] Management techniques to control the explosion in printed publication included Melvil Dewey's "Decimal System" published in 1876; other library classification systems quickly followed. By the end of the nineteenth century, cataloging had become a core practice of the new profession, along with the selection and acquisition of books and periodicals. Another core practice was reference service. In 1876 Samuel Swett Green drew attention in the first volume of the *American Library Journal* to the need for an intermediary to link readers with books.[39] In the decades that followed,

---

35 William C. Todd, "Free Reading Rooms," in 1876 Report, 460, 462.

36 "The Todd Tablet," www.bpl.org/research/newspapers/index.htm.

37 Reported in Charles Johanningsmeier, "Welcome Guests or Representatives of the 'Mal-Odorous Class'? Periodicals and Their Readers in American Public Libraries, 1876–1914," *Libraries and Culture* 39, no. 3 (2004): 270.

38 Geoffrey Nunberg, "Farewell to the Information Age," in *The Future of the Book*, ed. Nunberg (Berkeley: University of California Press, 1996), 116–17.

39 Samuel Swett Green, "Personal Relations Between Librarians and Readers," *American Library Journal* 1 (October 1876): 74–81.

the new discipline of library science came increasingly to rest on professional techniques of collection building, cataloging, and reference, making an ever-increasing body of books and periodicals more openly available at least to adult readers.

In small libraries during the nineteenth century, library trustees rather than librarians had often undertaken to choose materials for the collection. In the later part of the century librarians began to publish guides to help in the selection of "the best reading," a move that both encouraged the professionalization of collection development and raised questions about selection principles. In 1872 appeared *The Best Reading: Hints on the Selection of Books; on the Formation of Libraries, Public and Private, on Courses of Reading*, a work that came out with several subsequent editions that were edited by Boston Public Librarian Frederic Beecher Perkins.[40] Librarians were making distinctions within the category of fiction, so that "literature" no longer had an all-encompassing connotation, but referred principally to belletristic genres—poems, plays, and the "better" class of novels. In this way they recognized and reinforced distinctions between more popular types of fiction (such as dime novels), cheaply priced and designed for mass appeal, and "serious" fiction with aspirations to count as "literature" (according to Perkins, works by Walter Scott, William Wilkie Collins, and George Eliot ranked among the highest, though Herman Melville and Anthony Trollope failed to reach this standard). Librarians took pains to assign classification numbers to literary works (the Dewey Decimal Classification placed them in the 800s), but devoted little cataloging effort to novels they valued less highly.

In 1893 the American Library Association produced its own first selection tool, *Catalog of A.L.A. Library*. In 1890, ALA had constructed a model small public library for the 1893 Chicago Columbian Exposition. A selection committee drew up a list of about five thousand volumes and put these on display in Chicago. The printed catalog aimed to help practicing librarians in the selection and purchase of books, and also in classification and cataloging. Although the *Catalog*'s compilers denied

---

40 *The Best Reading: Hints on the Selection of Books; on the Formation of Libraries, Public and Private, on Courses of Reading, etc.* (New York: G. P. Putnam, 1872).

that they wanted to create a definitive collection, librarians undoubtedly construed it as such.[41] The *Catalog* recommended an allocation of only 15 percent of the collection to fiction, at a time when fiction actually accounted for around three-quarters of circulation.[42] A new edition appeared in 1904, with the purpose of guiding "in selecting books, whether to read or buy," and contained a list of 7,520 volumes "specially adapted to small libraries and those just starting, but suitable also for any public library."[43] Two supplements appeared, in 1912 and in 1923, before ALA published another enlarged edition (10,000 volumes) in 1926. From the mid-1920s to the early 1940s, three more supplements were issued, each with about three thousand titles (1926–1931, 1932–1936, and 1937–1941). For the very smallest public library, ALA also published its *Buying List for Small Public Libraries*, with editions in 1910, 1912, 1920, 1925, 1935 and 1940.[44] These lists contained between one and two thousand titles and included not only fiction and classified nonfiction but also children's books.

At the same time, commercial companies were also producing aids to professional selection. In 1898 Minneapolis publisher H. W. Wilson started the comprehensive trade catalog *Cumulative Book Index*. In 1905 he introduced *Book Review Digest*, followed in 1909 by *Children's Catalog* and the *Standard Catalog for Public Libraries* in 1918. State library commissions, too, issued guides. In 1902 the Wisconsin Free Library Commission's *Suggestive List of Books for a Small Library* instructed selection committees to remember that the tax-supported public library should provide "books that give pleasure." But at the same time, the Commission warned, the public library had a duty to "train" readers to

---

41 *Catalog of "A.L.A." Library: 5000 Volumes for a Popular Library* (Washington: Government Printing Office, 1893). On the process by which the Catalog was constructed, see Wayne A. Wiegand, "Catalog of 'A.L.A.' Library (1893): Origins of a Genre," in *For the Good of the Order* ed. Delmus E. Williams et al., (Greenwich, Conn.: JAI Press, 1994), 237–54.

42 Wayne A. Wiegand, "Tunnel Vision and Blind Spots: What the Past Tells Us About the Present; Reflections on the Twentieth-Century History of American Librarianship," *Library Quarterly* 69, no. 1 (1999): 4.

43 Melvil Dewey, ed., *A.L.A Catalog: 8,000 Volumes for a Popular Library, with Notes* (Washington: Government Printing Office, 1904), 7, 6.

44 The first and subsequent three editions were published by the New York State Library, intended for the small libraries of New York State. However, ALA reprinted the lists for use in other states, and in 1935 took over responsibility for publishing new editions.

choose better and better books.[45] In 1909, under its new Secretary, Henry Legler, the WFLC took over an ALA serial publication titled *Booklist* that aimed to provide guidance to book selectors on a regular basis. *Booklist* first appeared in 1905, published in Boston. Issued several times a year, it included not only a "current buying list of recent books" but also "brief notes designed to assist librarians in selection." It particularly aimed to assist "persons who buy for small libraries."[46]

Librarians still entertained few doubts as to which books counted as "better." The early years of the twentieth century saw heightened activity by those who, like the vice societies, sought to restrict what books the public might read. The purification theme that Progressive reformers applied so effectively to politics and good government also worked in the case of social life and literature. Wealthy and well-connected contributors to vice organizations who also contributed to libraries and other cultural organizations included Andrew Carnegie himself.[47] Adopting the metaphor of social hygiene, reformers endorsed the work of such groups as the New England Watch and Ward, assuming that "obscenity" in books and magazines was to be combated as vigorously as sweatshops and adulterated food.[48] The language of pollution could be applied to literature as well as the environment, and "wholesome" became an attribute of books as well as food.

Librarians, taking their cue from the prevailing contemporary discourse, took it for granted that it was part of their professional responsibility to exclude "polluting" literature from their collections. As libraries increasingly opened their doors to children, concerns intensified about how to regulate what young people might find on their shelves (now more likely to be directly accessible to the public). The inclusion of "profane" language in Stephen Crane's controversial novels *Maggie* (published at Crane's own expense in 1893), a story of prostitution and drunkenness set in the streets of New York, and *Red Badge*

---

45 *Suggestive List of Books for a Small Library Recommended by the State Library Commissions of Iowa, Minnesota, Wisconsin, Nebraska, Idaho and Delaware* (Madison: Wisconsin Free Library Commission, 1902), 3–4.

46 *A.L.A. Booklist* 1, nos. 1–2 (1905): 2–3.

47 Boyer, *Purity in Print*, 25.

48 Ibid., 24.

of Courage (1895), a decidedly non-romantic treatment of the Civil War, raised new issues for librarians. In 1896, librarians met in open session to discuss a supplement to the 1893 ALA *Catalog*. More than half of those present agreed that *Red Badge of Courage* should be excluded from the supplement.[49]

Early public libraries had excluded young children entirely, but by the late nineteenth century, book publishing for children was a rapidly growing sector, and children's librarianship was developing as a specialty in which practitioners claimed the expertise to pass judgment on children's literature, an authority that librarians following Dewey's focus on technique and management had never claimed in the case of books for adults. Children's librarians also took it upon themselves to work with parents, especially mothers, to provide guidance about controlling their children's reading. Some libraries started Mother's Clubs to foster knowledge about child development, targeting immigrant and working-class families in particular.[50] The work of such women as Caroline Hewins starting from the 1880s, and Anne Carroll Moore from the 1890s, carved out a new field, in which librarians not only managed specially designed children's rooms and services (such as storytelling), but also established themselves as knowledgeable and authoritative with respect to the fast-growing area of children's publishing.[51]

The new building of the New York Public Library allocated over three thousand square feet to children's services; this room circulated over two and a half million books in the first year of its operation.[52] Moore, the New York Public Library's first Superintendent of Work with Children (a post she held from 1906 to 1941), supported a vision of children's literature as a cultural field valuable in its own right,

49 Wayne A. Wiegand, *An Active Instrument for Propaganda: The American Public Library during World War I* (New York: Greenwood, 1989), 4.

50 Alison Parker, *Purifying America: Women, Cultural Reform, and Pro-Censorship Activism, 1873–1933* (Urbana: University of Illinois Press, 1997), 100, 102.

51 Ibid., 197; Anne Lundin, "Anne Carroll Moore: 'I Have Spun out a Long Thread,'" in *Reclaiming the American Library Past: Writing the Women In*, ed. Suzanne Hildenbrand (Norwood, N.J.: Ablex, 1996), 187–204.

52 Jacalyn Eddy, *Bookwomen: Creating an Empire in Children's Book Publishing 1919–1939* (Madison: University of Wisconsin Press, 2006), 31.

rather than merely as a means to fostering technical facility in reading and writing. For Moore, a librarian's job was to put "the right book into the hand of the right child at the right time."[53] Dime novels and other mass-market fiction definitely counted as the wrong sort of book. Moore was adamantly opposed, for instance, to the Wizard of Oz series that grew out of L. Frank Baum's *Wonderful Wizard of Oz*, published in 1900, and excluded it from the collections of the New York Public Library.[54] She also rejected the "ladder of reading" argument that reading popular fiction could lead to the reading of better literature, objecting primarily on social and aesthetic, rather than moral grounds.[55] Moore reviewed and wrote about children's books, and partnered with publishers to establish Children's Book Week in 1919 and the Newbery and Caldecott awards (1922 and 1938). Under her leadership, children's librarians became literary critics whose expert assessment of quality was sought after by publishers as well as schoolteachers and parents.[56] Those who attended one of the new library schools could also learn about the specialty of children's librarianship. In 1900, Lutie Stearns gave lectures in "Children's Work" to students attending the WFLC's summer classes in librarianship.[57]

When in 1906, Wisconsin opened the first full-time library school in the country that was run under the auspices of a state library commission, the school's faculty members undertook not only to teach in the school, but also to provide advice and make visits to local public libraries. Under Mary Emogene Hazeltine's direction, library school students learned the skills they would need to work to serve the information needs of legislators in a reference bureau as well those of small-town public library patrons. Each fall, Hazeltine herself taught a book selec-

---

53 Christine Jenkins, "The Strength of the Inconspicuous: Youth Services Librarians, the American Library Association, and Intellectual Freedom for the Young, 1939–1955" (Ph.D. Diss., University of Wisconsin–Madison, 1995), 61.

54 Beverly Lyon Clark, *Kiddie Lit: The Cultural Construction of Children's Literature in America* (Baltimore: Johns Hopkins University Press, 2003), 133.

55 Eddy, *Bookwomen*, 41.

56 Anne Lundin, *Constructing the Canon of Children's Literature: Beyond Library Walls and Ivory Towers* (New York: Routledge, 2004), 26.

57 Valmai Fenster, "The University of Wisconsin Library School, a History, 1895–1921" (Ph. D. Diss., University of Wisconsin–Madison, 1977), 98.

tion course. To prepare for this, students entering the program were required to become "intimately acquainted" with books on a list they were sent before they arrived in Madison.[58] Students were also asked to send in a list of "from ten to twenty books that they have read for their own pleasure within the last two years." The earliest required list (dating from 1906) consisted of a number of novels, including Jane Austen's *Pride and Prejudice*, Mark Twain's *Million Pound Bank-note*, Charles Dickens's *David Copperfield* or *Oliver Twist*, *Cranford* by Mrs. Gaskell, Nathaniel Hawthorne's *House of Seven Gables*, William D. Howells's *The Rise of Silas Lapham* or *The Kentons*, Walter Scott's *Kenilworth* or *Ivanhoe*, and *Henry Esmond* or *Vanity Fair* by William M. Thackeray. Students were also expected to read essays by Emerson, Hazlitt, Lowell, Ruskin, and others, biographies of Shakespeare, Emerson, Hawthorne, and Henry Clay, Jane Addams's *Democracy and Social Ethics*, Washington Gladden's *Applied Christianity* or *Social Salvation*, and anthologies of poetry by Palgrave or Stedman.[59]

These standard and unexceptionable works formed the basis of Hazeltine's required Book Selection class. A later list, printed in 1912, warned students to bring the list with them to the first meeting of the class, where they would take part in "an oral discussion of the required reading."[60] From the very beginning of their training, then, students were taught to judge what counted as suitable reading, and understood that they should pass these principles on to their patrons, once out in the field. During Hazeltine's tenure between 1906 and 1938, hundreds of students passed through her Book Selection Course, and then dispersed into the world, sowing the seeds of her reading philosophy across Wisconsin and beyond. Many carried on correspondence with Hazeltine for years after they left the school, asking her opinion about book selection, or discussing their personal reading. Somehow Hazeltine found time to reply. In 1918, she wrote to Harriet Louise Kidder, "Do you see the Publishers' Weekly? The number for January 12, 1918 has an interesting article on the house of George H. Doren, pages 130–132 . . . The Publishers' Weekly, as you know, is one of my

58 Ibid., 176–77, 174.
59 Library School Student Records, UWA.
60 Library School Student Records, UWA.

favorite periodicals. I hope you read it every week." In 1921 Kidder wrote, "I'm just reading Queen Victoria—dropped it a few moments to write to you (stopped reading about a Queen to write to a Queen). I *do* think it fascinating, and I all thru it think of things you said about it. One cannot but feel richer for having read it." Three days later Hazeltine replied. "I am delighted that you are enjoying Queen Victoria. I think it is a charming book. Read Queen Alexandra when you have time. You will like that too. It is different, and yet it is just the right kind of difference to supplement the older queen. Be sure to read My Brother, Theodore Roosevelt."[61]

Former students informed Hazeltine about their employment (including their salary), communities, and libraries. Often they provided references for prospective students and reports on current students carrying out fieldwork, and asked for advice in filling positions in their libraries. Some dropped in on Hazeltine in her Madison home. Harriet Kidder even wrote asking to stay unexpectedly on Christmas Eve. Hazeltine's reply gives some indication of why students remained so devoted to her;

> It will be quite convenient for me to have you with me next Wednesday night. I wish I might tell you that we could plan for a jolly Christmas Day together, but I am in the midst of a very important piece of work that must be completed immediately, so that my Christmas Day must be spent in intensive work. But we shall have our Christmas Eve together and a cosy [*sic*] breakfast on Christmas Morning, which will give us time for a good visit, I am sure. Please let me know when I may expect you, thought I regret to say that I am so very busy that I shall not be able to go to the train to meet you.[62]

Students must have found her dedication and hard work inspiring.

---

61 Mary Emogene Hazeltine to Harriet Louise Kidder, 11 February 1918; Harriet Louise Kidder to Mary Emogene Hazeltine, 7 November 1921; Mary Emogene Hazeltine to Harriet Louise Kidder, 10 November 1921, Library School Student Records, UWA.

62 Mary Emogene Hazeltine to Harriet Louise Kidder, 17 December 1924, Library School Student Records, UWA.

Although their letters sound full of admiration, it is clear that they found her far from intimidating or aloof. Rather, she appeared to them a mentor whose concern they appreciated for many years after they left the school. Urged to keep in touch through letters, alumnae (nearly all were women) helped to build up a network of mutual support and influence that stretched far beyond Wisconsin. Their letters show, too, how successfully Hazeltine instilled in them the library "spirit" that drove their concern for their work, even when they were no longer employed. Still anxious for Hazeltine's good opinion, one student, the former Gladys Hook (now married and pregnant), wrote of her volunteer work for the local library in her community of Berwyn, Illinois. "We have a nice little library, all gifts, with the exception of some new books purchased with money given us by the Woman's Club. They voted us $100, and we bought some new fiction for which we charge, thus bringing in more money. We have now about one thousand volumes." She had recently resigned from being chairman of the library committee, she admitted, but added, "And so you see, even a retired WLS graduate can be useful as a 'missionary of the book' if only in a small way. I wish you might come out to see us and our library some time."[63]

Imbued with a civilizationist ethic, librarians did not hesitate to censor on the basis of moral judgment. But they had taken a hands-off approach in the case of political matters, in an effort to maintain neutrality. However, the First World War changed this. When war broke out in Europe in 1914, libraries' responses reflected the mix of reactions in America at large. Many established collections of books, pamphlets, and maps that fed their patrons' desire for information about the war. Materials in German flew off the shelves, although some readers responded to ideas they considered controversial by annotating magazine articles and defacing pictures. When the British embargo disrupted the normal trade in books and magazines between America and Europe, librarians found their foreign-language book collections impossible to update. In Wisconsin, with the largest German-speaking population in the United States, librarians complained that the WFLC ceased to supply books in German in 1916. The Commission also stopped printing a

---

63 Mrs. Lester Benson Orr to Mary Emogene Hazeltine, 9 June 1924, Library School Student Records, UWA.

bibliography of books from Bohemia.[64] During the period before the United States entered the war, German and British propagandists struggled to influence American public opinion, as both set up networks for channeling gifts of reading materials to public libraries, the British with probably greater success. As time wore on, the weight of American public opinion moved toward the British side, and many librarians shared this sentiment. Still, they attempted to avoid partisanship. In January 1917, the *Wisconsin Library Bulletin* noted that a book recommended for library selection constituted "probably the strongest presentation of the German side since the outbreak of the war."[65]

The following month America broke diplomatic relations with Germany, and in April 1917 declared war. Neutrality set aside, librarians eagerly joined the war effort. Just how to do this was not obvious, however. The WFLC urged public libraries to provide materials on patriotism, the flag, and military training, and to make their buildings available to such organizations as the Red Cross and state councils for defense. Librarians might help the recruiting effort by posting information about where to enlist, names and addresses of war-related organizations, and local service opportunities. Libraries should also post and distribute federal and state information about the war, including speeches by the president, proclamations, and legislation, the WFLC instructed.

As the war progressed, librarians found themselves moving into an ever more active role as anti-German sentiment resulted in the outright suppression of German language reading materials. All German language newspapers were obliged to provide translated copy to a government censor. The Post Office refused to carry newspapers and other publications that officials interpreted as opposed to the war. School and other books in German were burned. Across the country, librarians removed from the shelves books by German authors and even music by composers such as Bach, Handel, and Beethoven. Pacifist and labor literature might also be labeled unpatriotic. In Wisconsin, the WFLC directed libraries to be vigilant in withdrawing "suspicious" literature on the one hand, and disseminating patriotic literature on

64 Wiegand, *Active Instrument*, 9–11.
65 Quoted in ibid., 28.

the other. Wrote Commission Secretary Matthew Dudgeon in a circular letter to all Wisconsin public librarians, "The library, supported by public funds, is a part of the government which is at war with Germany and Austria and has necessarily taken sides. It is, in fact, itself in this war against Germany. To be neutral now is to be disloyal." Dudgeon identified which books were to be suppressed and which encouraged in a bibliography that instructed librarians to remove all biographies of Bismarck, Frederick the Great, and Wilhelm II, unless they expressed an especially critical view of their subject.[66]

In addition to stimulating librarians to identify and remove "disloyal" books and magazines, the war also affected their Americanization program. The flow of immigrants from Europe fell off dramatically with the onset of war in 1914, but at the same time, those immigrants already living in America came under increased pressure to learn English and adopt Anglo-American values, customs, and lifestyles. In 1917 the U.S. Bureau of Education distributed to public libraries a pamphlet titled "Suggested Americanization Program of Work for Public Libraries for Community Service to Immigrants." The document's closing bibliography listed resources like a pamphlet titled "How to Become an American Citizen," by the National Americanization Committee of New York City, a "Citizenship Syllabus" for evening school classes, and a series of circulars, "For better Citizenship."[67]

The end of the war brought no end to anxieties about dangerous literature. Government-sponsored wartime propaganda efforts might have terminated, but the era of commercial propaganda was taking off.[68] The new field of "public relations" was drawing on psychological theories in efforts to mold or even manipulate "public opinion" on behalf of political parties as well as commercial enterprises. Advertising became increasingly professional, relying on statistics, charts, and other scientific techniques employed by "market researchers."[69] In the

---

66 Ibid., 33, 51–52, 89, 90–91, 93, 103, 105–6.

67 Ibid., 117–20.

68 Schudson, *Good Citizen*, 194.

69 Jackson Lears, *Fables of Abundance: A Cultural History of Advertising in America* (New York: Basic Books, 1994), 225–26.

political arena, peace brought little sense of tranquility, as fear of German militarism had quickly been replaced by fear of Russian Communism when the Bolshevik revolution of 1917 sparked a "red scare." Racial unrest mounted, too, as all over the country millions of white Americans joined the Ku Klux Klan. In the south Klansmen and other white supremacist groups stepped up their campaign of terror against African Americans. Thousands of African Americans responded by moving north seeking industrial jobs, a migration that employers encouraged in the face of labor shortages caused by the halt to European immigration. Tensions rose in northern cities; in Chicago, race riots broke out in the summer of 1919, leaving dozens dead and hundreds wounded. Communism and the fight for civil rights became entwined in many people's minds, as the Communist Party took up the quest for racial equality, fighting cases like that of the Scottsboro Boys (1931) and ensuring that they remained in the public eye.[70]

Censorship became more blatant, as in Boston a period ended in which booksellers, the Watch and Ward Society, the Catholic Church, and Brahmins (Boston's leading families) had collaborated to quietly suppress controversial literature. What followed were much more active attempts to ban major works by notable writers such as Sinclair Lewis, Theodore Dreiser, and Warwick Deeping, and even works like Nathaniel Hawthorne's *Scarlet Letter*, George Eliot's *Adam Bede*, and Thomas Hardy's *Tess of the d'Urbervilles*. These backfired, though, spurring the eruption of an anticensorship campaign in Massachusetts that spread to other cities.[71] In some cases it was the library board that took a principled stand. In Chicago, Mayor William J. Thompson criticized one of ALA's adult education "Reading With a Purpose" booklists as containing pro-British propaganda. His representative, V. H. Herrman, removed from the Chicago Public Library four titles from the booklist

---

70 In March 1931, an all-white jury in Scottsboro, Alabama, convicted nine young black men, aged thirteen to twenty, of raping two white women on the freight train on which they had all hitched a ride in search of work, and sentenced eight of them to death, all in the space of sixteen days. But for the interventions of the Communist Party and the National Association for the Advancement of Colored People (NAACP), the case would probably have disappeared quickly from the headlines, but as it was, the "Scottsboro boys" took on a national significance.

71 Geller, *Forbidden Books*, 134–35.

that the Patriot's League had condemned.[72] Chicago Public Library's Carl Roden (who had succeeded Henry Legler as CPL director in 1916) responded in a conciliatory manner, offering to remove the books from circulation rather than from the collection. However, the CPL Board, which held ultimate authority over the collection, defended both ALA and the library, on the grounds that "This exchange of freedom of thought we consider the primary function of a library and in keeping with the American idea of a free press. Any other course would lead to an arbitrary censorship as detrimental to American political liberty as to academic thought."[73] Librarians were abandoning censorship as a professional value.

By the 1930s, some of librarians' organizational procedures for controlling what people borrowed were also disappearing. "The period of years is short since one volume each of fiction and non-fiction was considered a fair and liberal portion for a borrower," wrote librarian Jennie Flexner in 1927. "A reasonable number of books, fiction or non-fiction, is usually allowed on any borrower's card."[74] Open access to shelves was also now the norm in public libraries.[75] Instead, libraries were offering expert advice that readers could choose to consult through a service known as "Readers' Advisory." Between 1922 and 1927, several urban public libraries opened departments designed to promote informal adult education through reading. One of these was the Milwaukee Public Library's Adult Education Department, which opened in 1923 with the aim of giving "personal advice on reading to individuals desirous of continuing their education through private study," as well as providing services to adults registered for classes "in recognized edu-

---

72 According to Geller, the titles were *The American Nation* by Alfred Bushnell Hart (published in 1907), *The Story of American Democracy* by Willis M. West, and two books by Claude H. Van Tyne that "interpreted the American Revolution as a civil war between competing factions" (ibid.).

73 Quoted in ibid.

74 Jennie M. Flexner, *Circulation Work in Public Libraries* (Chicago: American Library Association, 1927), 99.

75 In 1910 former A.L.A. president Arthur E. Bostwick reported, "Open access, though a suspected and doubted experiment fifteen years ago, is now practically universal in America in all but large city libraries." See Bostwick, *The American Public Library* (New York: D. Appleton, 1910), 38–39.

cational institutions."[76] The idea spread. In 1928 the number of libraries offering readers' advisory service was up to twenty-five, and by
1935 it had increased to forty-four.[77] By this time, the service had
developed into a routine for library staff. As a guide to employees, the
1935 *Enoch Pratt Free Library Staff Instruction Book* described a Readers'
Adviser as one who "interviews the patron seeking individual help in
directed reading and study, and attempts to stimulate continuity and
purpose in his reading, whether for cultural, recreational or practical
needs."[78] At the same time, while public libraries were employing professional Readers' Advisers to help patrons develop their own reading
programs along approved lines at no charge, business ventures like the
Book-of-the-Month Club and the Modern Library were helping to construct the "middlebrow" reader by distributing "expert" advice to an
expanded group of book buyers on a commercial basis.[79] Middlebrow
books—neither "trash" nor, for the most part, "literature"—came to be
a staple of public library collections in the middle of the century.

   The rise of fascism in Europe, accompanied by well-publicized book
burnings, helped propel librarians slowly toward a stance of not simply
rejecting censorship but actively embracing intellectual freedom. The
success of Nazi campaigns in manipulating German public opinion
underlined in librarians' minds the need for vigilance against the effects
of propaganda. At ALA's 1934 annual conference in Montreal, Lyman
Bryson exhorted librarians to see themselves as "custodians of the public
mind" by ensuring access to all points of view. Libraries were the "inven-
tion of modern democracy," he proclaimed, and should act as a defense

---

76 *Libraries and Adult Education: Report of a Study Made by the American Library Association* (Chicago, American Library Association, 1926), 240. Others were Chicago, Cincinnati, Cleveland,
Detroit, and Portland, Oregon.

77 Robert Ellis Lee, *Continuing Education for Adults through the American Public Library, 1833–1964*
(Chicago: American Library Association, 1966), 58.

78 *Enoch Pratt Free Library, Staff Instruction Book: Methods and Practices Concerning the Staff and the
Service in the Various Departments and Branches* (Baltimore: Enoch Pratt Free Library, 1 November
1935), 632.

79 Joan Shelley Rubin, *The Making of Middlebrow Culture* (Chapel Hill: University of North
Carolina Press, 1992); Janice A. Radway, *A Feeling for Books: The Book-of-the-Month Club, Literary
Taste, and Middle-Class Desire* (Chapel Hill: University of North Carolina Press, 1997); Jay Sat-
terfield, *The World's Best Books: Taste, Culture, and the Modern Library* (Amherst: University of
Massachusetts Press, 2002).

against totalitarianism. Leon Carnovsky, a GLS faculty member, reported in *Library Journal* on a recent visit to Germany, where all Communist literature and non-Nazi newspapers were banned and access to potentially controversial research severely restricted material.[80] By 1935, many librarians were rejecting their previous accommodationist stance of avoiding controversy, and instead promoting support of freedom of speech and freedom to read. It would be four more years, however, before ALA was ready to exercise leadership on the subject.

The Library Bill of Rights

An awareness of similarities between injustice at home and the rise of fascism abroad prompted librarians to take an explicit stand against censorship in the late 1930s. Sometimes it was the board of trustees that took the lead. In Chicago, local Polish and Russian groups mounted a challenge to works acquired by the Chicago Public Library's Foreign Department, on the grounds that they were too "communistic." The Polish group also complained about "pornographic" materials. Upon investigation, however, the Committee on Library of the CPL Board of Trustees found no reason to remove the offending Communist books, or to limit "the contents of the foreign sections, or of any other department of the Library, to works dealing only with one side of controversial subjects to the exclusion of any or all other sides." Moreover, they commented in response to the Polish objection, "While the books in question are admittedly of varying degrees of literary quality, and often concern themselves with social problems, theories or situations regarding which there is much difference of opinion, it has not been shown, so far, that they or any of them are unfit for general use by adult readers." The CPL Board of Trustees went on to issue a formal intellectual policy statement in 1937 that was probably the first of any library in the United States. "The Public Library asserts its right and duty to keep on its shelves a representative selection of books on all subjects of interest to its readers and not prohibited by law, including

---

80 Geller, *Forbidden Books*, 156–57.

books on all sides of controversial questions," the policy stated. It went on, "The Public Library has no right to emphasize one subject at the expense of another, or one side of a subject without regard to the other side. It must carry the important books on all sides and all subjects."[81]

Other librarians were aghast at the state of "race relations" in America as well fearful of the spread of totalitarianism. By and large, African Americans were excluded from most public libraries either by explicit policy or by collections that were at best irrelevant and at worst insulting. Services were often denied to blacks in the North as well as the South, and collections reflected the prejudices of the white majority. A few significant exceptions existed, however. In New York, (white) librarian Ernestine Rose aimed to make the New York Public Library's 135th Street branch "an integral part" of the African American community.[82] In Chicago in 1932, Vivian Harsh (Chicago's first black director of a branch library) built up a Special Negro Collection of books and other materials "by and about Negroes" that made the Hall Branch a cultural center of the Chicago Renaissance. In Des Moines, Iowa, the public library's progressive director, Forrest Spaulding, undertook a more modest effort to encouraged black and white readers to understand how racism systematically structured American society, through the publication of appropriate bibliographies of books "By and About Negroes."[83] The efforts of public librarians like Rose, Harsh, and Spaulding to encourage more attention to African American history and culture found little counterpart in the standard collecting guides librarians routinely consulted, such as the H. W. Wilson Company's *Standard Catalog* and *Fiction Catalog*, or the *A.L.A. Catalog*. The 1926 edition of *A.L.A. Catalog* clustered a mere fifteen titles under the general heading "Negroes," a further four under "Negro Songs," and two more under "Negro Poetry."

By the late 1920s and 1930s, librarians' views about what counted as

---

81 Joyce M. Latham, "White Collar Read: The American Public Library and the Left-Led CIO: A Case Study of the Chicago Public Library, 1929–1952" (Ph.D. Diss., University of Illinois at Urbana-Champaign, 2007), 2–3.

82 Betty L. Jenkins, "A White Librarian in Black Harlem," *Library Quarterly* 60, no. 3 (1990): 220.

83 Two surviving lists can be found in Box 20 of the collection of the YWCA of Greater Des Moines, Iowa.

worthy materials for collection were changing. The 1926 *A.L.A Catalog* included authors who had previously been deliberately excluded, such as Ovid, Rousseau, Voltaire, Flaubert, Anatole France, and Oscar Wilde. On the other hand, nothing by James Joyce, F. Scott Fitzgerald, André Gide, or Marcel Proust made the list. Emile Zola's *Germinal*, *Nana*, and *La Terre* were missing. Such yawning gaps were becoming a matter of professional concern. The proposed 1929–1930 code of ethics advised librarians that books "should represent all phases of opinion and interest rather than the personal tastes of librarian or board members." Moreover, the code stated, "In an official capacity, the librarian and members of the staff should not express personal opinions on controversial questions, as political, religious, economic issues, especially those of a local nature." Moreover, "no distinctions of race, color, creed or condition should influence the attitude of the staff, and no favoritism should be tolerated." In the library literature, Stanley Kunitz, editor of the *Wilson Bulletin for Librarians*, raised issues of censorship most explicitly.[84]

Further concrete steps toward a policy promoting intellectual freedom in libraries took place in 1938, when, perhaps influenced by Ernestine Rose (with whom he served on ALA's Adult Education Committee,) Forrest Spaulding crafted a document that he titled "The Library's Bill of Rights," which was to have far-reaching consequences for librarianship.[85] On November 21, 1938, the Public Library of Des Moines (PLDM) Board of Trustees adopted this document, which proclaimed, "Now, when indications in many parts of the world point to growing intolerance, suppression of free speech and censorship, affecting the rights of minorities and individuals, the Board of Trustees of the Des Moines Public Library reaffirms these basic policies governing a free public library to serve the best interests of Des Moines and its citizens." The Library Bill of Rights was undoubtedly a response to the growing threat of fascism in Europe, but racism in America must also have been on Spaulding's mind when he drafted the first article to read,

---

84 Geller, *Forbidden Books*, 141, 143, 147–48; "Suggested Code of Library Ethics," *Library Journal* 55, no. 4 (1930): 165.

85 Attaching a constitutional label to this document fitted the times, in which, Michael Schudson comments, constitutionalism had "acquired the trappings of a religious cult" (Schudson, *The Good Citizen*, 202).

"Books and other reading matter selected for purchase from public funds shall be chosen from the standpoint of value and interest to the people of Des Moines and in no case shall selection be based on the race or nationality, political or religious views of the writers."[86] In June of the following year, the PLDM's Library Bill of Rights became the blueprint for a similar document that Ernestine Rose presented for adoption by the American Library Association's Council at ALA's 1939 convention in San Francisco.[87] Following the Council's acceptance, John Chancellor distributed broadsides of the new policy to state library agencies throughout the country, offering each "several hundred copies."[88] ALA's adoption of the Library's Bill of Rights hardly translated into an instant transformation of library practice, however. Librarians were often unwilling to confront their boards of trustees or other prominent community members, and when calls to ban John Steinbeck's *Grapes of Wrath* multiplied in 1939, many librarians complied.[89]

Combating Censorship

In 1948, ALA reaffirmed its commitment to intellectual freedom by adopting a revised version of the Library Bill of Rights that strengthened the profession's commitment to aggressively combating censorship.[90] Yet its stance put librarians at odds with what seemed to be the opinion of the majority of Americans, many of whom saw Communism as a peril and censorship of left-leaning materials as justifiable. Library leaders complained in their professional literature about "Book-banning and Witch-hunts," and protested efforts "to purge all libraries,

---

86 "The Library's Bill of Rights," *Library Bill of Rights 50th Anniversary Folder 1988*, PLDM Archives.

87 *ALA Bulletin* 33, no. 11 (1939): 60. Although it has since gone through a number of revisions, the Library Bill of Rights remains the cornerstone of American librarians' defense of intellectual freedom.

88 Latham, "White Collar Read," 6; Louise S. Robbins, *Censorship and the American Library: The American Library Association's Response to Threats to Intellectual Freedom, 1939–1969* (Westport, Conn.: Greenwood, 1997), 11–13.

89 Robbins, *Censorship and the American Library*, 14. The name "Library's Bill of Rights" was subsequently changed to "Library Bill of Rights."

90 Ibid., 35–36.

schools, and book stores of 'subversive' books."[91] By 1950 and 1951 groups like the American Legion and the Sons of the American Revolution had escalated their attacks on books and films that they considered dangerous.[92] Yet little practical support in terms of suggestions for institutional procedures and educational initiatives was forthcoming from ALA despite its brave policy statement. Gradually during the years 1952–1960, ALA members began to evolve a set of effective strategies for promoting intellectual freedom, but it was not until the mid-1960s that the organization opened its Office of Intellectual Freedom, devoted to helping librarians and others withstand censorship, while educating the public about the right to read.[93]

In the absence of national resources, Wisconsin's librarians often appealed to the WFLC for help. To clarify the Commission's position, John Chancellor (by now its vice-chairman) drafted a public statement in 1950. "Some Wisconsin public libraries have been approached to remove from their collections books on specific lists," he wrote. "Librarians know from past experience that such requests are not uncommon in times of insecurity and fear and that they sometimes come from sincere and well intentioned citizens as well as from those who knowingly use these waves of popular fear to further their own points-of-view ... The public library is an institution uniquely American in that it was created on the premise that only an informed electorate can maintain a democracy, and that completely free inquiry is not only a safe principle to extend to *all* the people but also an essential one."[94]

Issuing this statement hardly solved the problem for small-town librarians, however, as Botsford admitted to another Commission member, Ella Veslak (librarian of Shawano Public Library). "There have been no objections to the statement except that it does not attack the problem faced by most librarians in the small communities; viz., that in the very act of selecting books the average librarian is excluding

---

91 David K. Berninghausen, "Book-banning and Witch-hunts," *American Library Association Bulletin* 42, no. 5 (1948): 204; "Current Attacks on Books," *American Library Association Bulletin* 42, no. 5 (1948): 58.

92 Robbins, *Censorship and the American Library,* 50.

93 Ibid., especially chapters 3 and 4.

94 John Chancellor to Walter Botsford, 5 July 1950, Series 1967, WHS Archives.

from her collection any books that are at all controversial in nature . . . The defense of the average librarian is that she has too small a book budget to buy books for the very few persons in her community who would be interested in controversial books, and at the same time she is subjecting herself to criticism for spending her money in such a manner." Overall, Botsford took a gloomy view about the international crisis; "We are approaching a total war situation with all of its attendant evils and I believed that an institution such as ours should take a stand on this matter of freedom of inquiry at such a time. I think that if the commission does this it will help to keep sanity."[95]

Replied Veslak, "I discussed [the Chancellor letter] last evening with members of my board . . . They agree that the library must provide information as nearly as possible on controversial matters. However, they do sound a real note of warning on so called "isms"— fearing propaganda . . . [T]he reading public should be able to trust the public library to present books in such a way that we know they are the truth—or, only 'part truth,' which ever the case may be. You see, Walter, a small town librarian has a very real responsibility." So far, she went on, Shawano had experienced no calls for censorship. "I suppose I have been careful to present anything we buy through the papers and over the radio in such a way that people know we are seeking to provide them with *information*, not with something that is sensational and flag-waving." On the other hand she recognized the need to tread carefully. "Our American Legion Post would be the first to question me if they thought we were out of line; I believe they have complete confidence in what we are doing."[96]

Although librarians carefully walked a tightrope of impartiality, over the next two or three years the linking of anticommunism to calls for censorship only accelerated, while the Commission maintained its opposition to book challenges. However, it was difficult to assess the extent of the problem. In November 1951, a patron of the Arabel Ludlow Memorial Library in Monroe, Wisconsin, complained about "another new Book on Asia written by Lawrence Rossinger and

---

95 Walter Botsford to Ella Veslak, 24 July 1950, Series 1967, WHS Archives.
96 Ella Veslak to Walter Botsford, 26 July 1950, Series 1967, WHS Archives.

Associates." One such associate, he considered, was Owen Lattimore. In 1950, McCarthy had accused Owen Lattimore, a scholar of Far Eastern affairs and consultant of the U.S. State Department, of being "the top Soviet espionage agent in the United States."[97] Lattimore not only fought back and eventually succeeded in having his name completely cleared, but in 1950 published an indignant book about his experiences, titled *Ordeal by Slander*, that quickly became a standard item in library collections. On the Door Peninsula, for instance, *Ordeal by Slander* was part of the Demonstration collection, and was charged out by at least one reader. In 1951 a student at the Wisconsin Library School circularized all Wisconsin libraries in towns of 2,000 or more population (a total of 115), asking whether or not they had withdrawn any of Lattimore's books. Of these, ninety-seven (84.7 percent) replied. About two-thirds (sixty-seven) owned at least one Lattimore book, but only three librarians replied that they had actually withdrawn one or more, two apparently in response to pressure. Another replied that she had resisted calls to remove *Ordeal by Slander*.[98]

It was hard to assess the accuracy of this picture, though. WFLC officials had the impression, Botsford wrote to Library School assistant professor Howard W. Winger, that "there is widespread censorship on the part of townspeople and sometimes by the librarian, but neither the library board nor the librarian is anxious to make it a public issue" because they felt that such censorship was not likely to have "permanent effects."[99] The Monroe case provided a good example. The librarian, Nellie W. Kohli, reported that she had found a way to deal quietly with the complaint against Rossinger's book. "I had a talk with two legion members," she wrote to Botsford. "Neither of the men questioned our buying and understand the type of person who has caused the present difficulty." Instead of the matter being raised at a (public) regular meeting of the Board of Education, the librarians planned to make a report at a committee meeting. "I believe," Kohli assured

---

97 "Owen Lattimore, Far East Scholar Accused by McCarthy, Dies at 88," *New York Times*, 1 June 1989.

98 Howard W. Winger to Walter S. Botsford, 9 January 1952, Series 1967, WHS Archives. Winger was assistant professor at the Library School.

99 Walter S. Botsford to Howard W. Winger, 3 January 1952, Series 1967, WHS Archives.

Botsford, "that this will be satisfactory to all concerned and there will be no publicity."[100]

Another key issue for public library advocates continued to be the provision of the "right" reading. Researchers and policy-makers criticized popular reading materials as lacking literary or educational quality and emphasized the importance of encouraging library patrons to engage with reading matter that conformed more closely to their own cultural ideals. In 1949, Robert D. Leigh, a political scientist at the University of Chicago, headed a team of social scientists to produce the Public Library Inquiry (PLI), a seven-volume study of American public librarianship, commissioned by ALA and funded by the Carnegie Corporation.[101] The PLI attempted to both justify and also cast doubt on the validity of the library faith. It focused on a number of different areas of librarianship, but explicitly excluded children's services. Argues the historian Christine Jenkins, "The P.L.I. was merely the latest and most public representation of the way in which youth services librarianship was viewed within the profession and within American society as a whole." While on the one hand children's services were often described as "'the classic success of the public library,'" at the same time, "salaries and collection budgets for children's and young people's librarians were notoriously low, and neither young library users nor those who served them were seen as meriting serious attention."[102]

By contrast, adult patrons merited an entire volume, titled *The Library's Public*, by communications researcher and former librarian Bernard Berelson. It reported the results of a 1947 national survey of public library users, along with a summary of all studies of library book use and users published since 1930.[103] "Although no one knows exactly just how to define 'quality' in popular reading," Berelson con-

---

100 Nellie W. Kohli to Walter S. Botsford, 4 December 1951, Series 1967, WHS Archives.

101 The seven volumes included *The Library's Public*, by Bernard Berelson; *The Public Librarian*, by Alice Bryan; *The Public Library in the Political Process*, by Oliver Garceau, studies on government publications, the book industry, and the information film, and *The Public Library in the United States*, by Robert D. Leigh.

102 Jenkins, "The Strength of the Inconspicuous," 364, 366.

103 Berelson, *The Library's Public*, 137. For an analysis of the PLI, see Douglas Raber, *Librarianship and Legitimacy: The Ideology of the Public Library Inquiry* (Westport. Conn: Greenwood, 1997).

tended, "everyone acknowledges that the public library circulates many titles which would not qualify as 'good' by any generally accepted literary standard." Not-so-good titles included "Mystery and detective stories, love and romance fiction, adventure and western stories, recent novels widely publicized but of little literary distinction, popularizations of current affairs characterized by sensationalism and easy dogmatism rather than by dispassionate and qualified analysis—these and similar books are widely circulated by the public library." For Berelson, as for other library leaders steeped the values of the social sciences, good reading consisted of works of what cultural authorities judged to be of "literary distinction," as well as the unemotional pronouncements of experts. Skeptical of librarians' faith in reading per se as a vehicle of improvement for all Americans, and believing that a result of their policy of trying to serve everyone was a dangerous dilution of standards, Berelson argued that since the principal users of the public library were actually middle-class and well-educated "opinion leaders," libraries should focus resources on serving this influential segment of the public, and set aside their goal of reaching all Americans directly.[104]

However, many practicing librarians reacted with outrage at what they saw as an abandonment of a democratic belief in an informed citizenry. Berelson's phrase "opinion leaders" became a code for what some argued was an elitist approach to library service. A 1951 *Wisconsin Library Bulletin* editorial issued a sharp rejoinder; "Those who may not be the 'opinion leaders' in the community [still] enjoy the atmosphere of the public library that is transported in the bookmobile to the smallest village or community center."[105] The WFLC's Door-Kewaunee Regional Library, with its determination to include all community members, implicitly rejected Berelson's advice. Librarians stocked the library with plenty of fiction titles that he would have disparaged, and moreover they were most keen to serve the one population that the PLI ignored: children.

An innovative aspect of the Door-Kewaunee Regional Library was not only that it provided state finance to the communities involved, but

---

104 Berelson, *The Library's Public*, 127–28; 130.
105 *Wisconsin Library Bulletin* 47, no. 2 (1951): 40.

also that local librarians and state officials found ways to work closely and harmoniously together. Librarians took advantage of the resources made available to them through WFLC field workers like Anne Farrington. But they relied, too, on the insider knowledge of staff members like Olivia Traven and Andy Kroeger. Local library staff consisted mostly of women—both professionally trained and untrained—who found that the Regional Library project provided expanded opportunities for organizing, interacting with each other and with the public, and political activities. A topic that had the potential to be contentious was that of choosing the books for the library. By the 1940s, the library profession and its commercial associates like the H. W. Wilson Company had developed a large range of selection guides, and the WFLC encouraged librarians to make use of these. On the other hand, Jane Livingston was keen to tap into the knowledge and experience of local staff members. Because local librarians and central officials were careful to maintain good working relationships, these different approaches appear not to have created difficulties.

A greater source of anxiety for library staff and WFLC officials were the book challenges that library opponents mounted as a vehicle for expressing their displeasure. By the 1940s the library profession was on record as opposing censorship, but could draw on only a few years' experience at taking this stand. Much longer was the history of librarians' consciously excluding materials on moral grounds and, as recently as World War I, on political grounds. Members of the public could be excused if they found librarians' relatively recent espousal of the principle of intellectual freedom confusing. On the conservative Door Peninsula, where the Catholic or Lutheran churches tended to occupy the center of closely knit ethnic community life, for the library to make widely available controversial books like *The Grapes of Wrath* must have been hard to comprehend. Small wonder, then, that challenging such books proved a successful strategy for convincing voters to reject the experiment.

5
Children, Teachers, and the Rural School

Teaching in the one room rural school is a strenuous and difficult
task. The multitude of classes, the janitorial work expected of the
teacher and the difficulty in securing desirable living conditions
had made rural teaching unappealing to many prospective students of teaching . . . Institutions of higher learning recruit far
more of their students from the immediate territory about them
than from more remote territory.

Fifty-Three Years of Progress in Teacher Education: Wisconsin's
County Normal Schools

On a cold winter's day in the early years of the twentieth century, a
hired hand at four-year-old Hazel P.'s southern Door County farm
taught the little girl to read. The two sat on the kitchen floor while the
young man wrote out the letters of the alphabet, and Hazel repeated
them after him. Lacking paper and a pencil, he improvised with a bar
of Bon Ami soap and the black surface of the kitchen range.

To those raised in a culture where paper is a disposable commodity
and pens and pencils are readily to hand, it is hard to imagine a situation in which even a scrap of paper and a pencil stub were hard to come
by. At that time, though, such scarcity was commonplace. Hazel's family was far from wealthy, but neither did they live in poverty. Since the
income from eight cows was not enough to feed a growing family, her
father took a job hauling milk with a horse-drawn cart to make ends
meet. Hazel remembered that during the winter the roads were often
blocked with snow, making her father's job all the more difficult. When
she started to attend her local one-room school, the winter snow drifts
created more problems. "I can remember more than once my father
came to meet me with a blanket and carried me home," she recalled.
Despite her struggles to get there and back, Hazel loved school and
developed a burning desire to be a schoolteacher. Her parents understood her ambition, but saw obstacles. "They knew it required educa-

tion, but money was hard to get in those days," she recalled some seventy years later.

Hazel eventually realized her ambition by attending the Door-Kewaunee County Normal School in Algoma and going on to teach in the very area where she grew up. Women like Hazel were the backbone of the rural school system. Familiar with the complicated organization of one-room classrooms that might contain children from as many as eight grades, and with an intimate knowledge of the students and their families, they represented the stability and reassurance of continuing traditions. In particular, they helped maintain children's access to a pool of reading materials that hardly changed from one generation to the next, and that reflected literary standards about which there was little disagreement. When changes came in the 1950s and 1960s, though, the teachers were eager to take advantage of them, both for their own sake and for that of their students.

The Rural School System

For rural people, the common school has long constituted a site of extra-familial, secular sociability with the potential for cutting across lines of class, ethnicity, and gender, just as early reformers intended. At the end of the nineteenth century the public school system in many parts of the country consisted of small, independent schoolhouses scattered over vast rural tracts. Wisconsin made a constitutional provision for free public education when it achieved statehood in 1848, and immediately followed this up with a law to implement the provision.[1] Neighborhood education followed a general pattern in midwestern states that divided each township into approximately nine school districts, each two miles square, resulting in a schoolhouse at alternate crossroads, and in theory leaving no child further than two miles from the neighborhood school. Within each district, local farmers elected a school board, constructed and maintained the schoolhouse, hired a teacher, chose textbooks, and decided whether they would pay for them

1 Wayne E. Fuller, *The Old Country School: The Story of Rural Education in the Middle West* (Chicago: University of Chicago Press, 1982), 41.

out of tax funds. "The exercise in participatory democracy that followed in this smallest self-governing political division in the nation
showed how thoroughly the farmers controlled the most important
aspects of their children's education," comments historian Wayne
Fuller. "So complete was the mid-western farmers' control over their
school system that they determined not only the number of months
they would have school beyond that required by the state, but also the
dates when the school terms would start and finish."[2] But these isolated
units were beginning to develop connections that would eventually
weld them into interdependent county and state systems. Toward the
end of the century, the county superintendent's oversight began to
compromise the school district's autonomy. His—or, increasingly,
her—attempt to control the schools' curriculum imposed some degree
of centralization and standardization on what was otherwise a dispersed and even chaotic situation.[3] Farmers resisted this rationalization, however, seeing it as an attempt not only to take away local control, but also to impose changes that could prove costly.[4]

Since the schoolhouse was often the only public building in the
neighborhood, it served as a social center for the community—as a
church on Sunday, a polling place at election time, and a public hall for
entertainment, spelling bees, or debate. Despite the apparent homoge-
neity of the district, Wisconsin native Ben Logan remembered his rural
elementary school in the 1920s as a place where children encountered
difference. "Part of the richness of that one-room school was in the
variety of children," he wrote in his autobiography. "Everyone was
from a farm, but each family represented a separate world. There were
different ways of speaking, different clothes, different religions, beliefs,
and superstitions." There were class differences, too. "Some children
always had all the pencils and paper they needed. For some, the loss of
a penny pencil sent them away in tears at the end of the day to a home
where there were no more pencils and maybe no more pennies either.

---

2 Ibid., 47. Fuller notes that school districts were not always as regular as the grid theory supposed: "Schoolhouses were not always at alternate crossroads, and although there might be
more than nine schools in a heavily populated township, usually there were fewer" (44–45).

3 Ibid., 153.

4 Hal S. Barron, *Mixed Harvest: The Second Great Transformation in the Rural North, 1870–1930*
(Chapel Hill: University of North Carolina Press, 1997), 49.

Some children came with nothing. Teacher quietly supplied them, probably paying for the things herself."[5]

School was also a channel for the distribution of print, and served as an acculturating institution, especially for those children who came from homes where books, magazines, and newspapers were scarce or even nonexistent. Teaching methods emphasized reading skills above all, but in the mid-nineteenth century a shortage of classroom reading materials meant that it was mostly the teacher reading out loud who practiced active and sustained reading, while students tended to be relegated to the role of listening.[6] What books existed in the classroom was largely a matter of chance rather than planning. Gradually, though, county superintendents in concert with textbook publishers encouraged the adoption of standardized texts, so that teachers could count on the children at least working from the same books in class.

For children starting elementary school in the late nineteenth and early twentieth century, learning to read was the most important priority. Some, like little Hazel P., had already made progress before starting school. Others had learned to value books, although they might still be unable to decode them. Otto J. Shipla grew up in his grandparents' home in rural central Wisconsin in the 1920s and 1930s, along with two aunts not much older than himself. Before he was old enough for school, he usually waited by the window for the girls to come home at the end of the day, "because they often brought me books to look at." His immigrant grandparents owned few books themselves, but Otto begged his aunts to read to him from books they brought from school, including "The Sun Bonnet Babies" and "Old Mrs. Wiggs in the Cabbage Patch." Shipla admitted that he wept when the girls had to take the books back to school with them.[7]

In 1927, Otto entered first grade, where he discovered that "memo-

---

5 Ben Logan, *The Land Remembers: The Story of a Farm and Its People* (Minnetonka, Minn.: North-Word Press, 1999), 200.

6 Ronald J. Zboray and Mary Saracino Zboray, *Literary Dollars and Social Sense: A People's History of the Mass Market Book* (New York: Routledge, 2005), 157.

7 Otto J. Shipla, *One-Room School Days: An Autobiography of Life as Pupil, Teacher, Teacher-Trainer in a One-Room School* (New York: Carlton Press, 1995), 17. "Sun Bonnet Babies" was probably *The Sunbonnet Babies Primer*, by Eulalie Osgood Grover, published in 1902. *Mrs Wiggs of the Cabbage Patch*, by Alice Hegan Rice, was a best seller, also in 1902.

rization was the method of learning in those days . . . It seemed that we had to memorize everything." But he also had to learn to read. With no access to workbooks or reading books other than a basic reader, it was no easy task, but by the end of first grade Otto had achieved this feat, and was able to move steadily on up through the remaining grades with little difficulty. At each level, the study of reading and language took up much of the day. Pupils studied poems and stories that the state prescribed in official manuals. At the time Otto attended seventh grade in 1932–1933, these included "several classics," all by American or British writers, including *The Legend of Sleepy Hollow* by Washington Irving, *The Vision of Sir Launfal* by James Russell Lowell, *The Great Stone Face* by Nathaniel Hawthorne, and *The Courtship of Miles Standish* by Henry Wadsworth Longfellow. Shipla records that the poems for that year were "Sheridan's Ride" by Thomas B. Read, "Columbus" by Joaquin Miller, "The Arrow and the Song" by Henry Wadsworth Longfellow, "The Bugle Song" by Alfred, Lord Tennyson, "O Captain! My Captain!" by Walt Whitman, "Recessional," by Rudyard Kipling, "The Star-Spangled Banner" by Frances Scott Key, and "Hark, Hark the Lark" (from *Cymbeline*) and "Wolsey's Farewell to His Greatness" (from *Henry VIII*) by William Shakespeare. Books continued to be a rarity in Shipla's home as well as at school. A gift of two books (Horatio Alger's *Strong and Steady*, and Spencer Davenport's *Rushton Boys in the Saddle*) for Christmas in 1933—"very appropriate for my age level" from an aunt "who seldom gave gifts to anybody"—was an unusual piece of luck.[8]

By the middle of the twentieth century in many rural areas the one-room school had faded into memory, as school districts consolidated within counties to create larger graded elementary schools. In 1935, Iowa still had over nine thousand one-room schools, but only just over a quarter of the state's elementary schoolchildren attended them. In Illinois, with nearly ten thousand one-room schools, the population attending them was lower still—just over 13 percent.[9] Wisconsin had passed a law giving state aid for the construction of consolidated schools in 1913, but one-room schools remained the norm for many

8 Shipla, *One-Room School Days*, 21, 57, 74.
9 Fuller, *The Old Country School*, 245.

years after.[10] On the Door Peninsula, even at the end of the 1940s, consolidation was still several years away, and school facilities in the two counties followed the old patterns. Most of the area's rural children attended their local country school for all eight grades. Of a total of 114 schools in 1950, 75 were rural one-room schools, and another 22 were rural graded schools. Four parochial schools, both Catholic and Lutheran, also served rural areas.[11] According to expert opinion, rural children's school performance persistently failed to match that of their urban counterparts. Even rural children who attended urban schools were less likely to succeed in the eighth grade than urban children, claimed rural sociologist Gene Rector.[12] Door County women enjoyed the best opportunities for education; 43 percent had some high school education. But for women in Kewaunee County, and for men in both counties, this figure was only about 30 percent. Teachers were often young women who had themselves been pupils in a similar school before going on to high school and preparation for teaching through the county normal school. At the age of twenty or even younger, they might find themselves in charge of as many as forty children in all eight grades.

In the classroom, former teachers remembered, children sat in columns according to their grade (the youngest nearest the window so that they did not block the light for older and taller students in these days before electric power), and studied on their own for long stretches. Lessons targeted specifically at their grade typically lasted no longer than ten minutes. Teachers struggled to maintain the high degree of organization required to satisfy the needs of such a wide range of ages, so that older children often found themselves helping younger students. It was hard work, remembered Emily H., especially when classes were large. The year before she retired from rural school teaching she had thirty-nine students in all eight grades. "We learned how to make lesson plans, of course," she said. "Our lessons were always done . . . for a whole week and I had to be very organized right down to the minute, because

---

10 Barron, *Mixed Harvest*, 65, 73.

11 Franklin Eugene Rector, "Social Correlates of Eighth Grade Attainment in Two Wisconsin Counties" (Ph.D. Diss., University of Wisconsin–Madison, 1954), 21–22.

12 Ibid., 42.

we only had ten minute classes. But one of the advantages in that type of school was that the older children helped the younger children . . . and then the younger children who were bright and had the time would watch the older classes and probably some of them were advanced just from watching the older classes." Every night Emily took home a big cardboard box of papers to grade, a schedule that left her very little time for any other activities. "We had no time," she told me repeatedly.

Although younger farm children could walk less than two miles to the nearest elementary school, high schools were only to be found in town, and distance often created a barrier to rural students' participation in school events. For some students there was a convenient bus, while others learned to drive, or caught rides with friends. Kewaunee County resident Doris C. remembered the first time she drove her father's car. "I graduated in 1942 from Casco High School," she said. "And I was in the band. We had music lessons all summer . . . I had to go four miles with my saxophone on the handlebar of my bicycle. And there was a big hill to go up. And that was some peddling, to go up that hill." Cycling took time as well as energy—assets that Doris could ill afford. "One bright day, we had lots of hay to make, and my dad wanted me home. My mother was dead—she died when I was six. So I was pretty important. My dad wanted me home. And I said, 'But I've got band lessons.' He said, 'You take the car.' So I was like"—Doris mimicked her own scared voice—"'I have to drive the car? But I've never driven a car before.' He said, 'Well . . . if it don't go ahead it'll go backwards.' So I went, and I'm driving ever since. You know, I never had a driver's license for so long." The still new technology of the automobile helped Doris negotiate the tension between the demands of school and her responsibilities to her family. Ruth W. recalled sharing rides with a relative; "My cousin drove the year before I did—there were four or five of us she drove. I walked a mile to catch the ride at her house. Two of them were across the road from her, and then she drove around and picked up two others." The rides to school reinforced the social experience of school in ways that overlaid the academic experience in these former students' memories. It was fun, Ruth said, especially when her cousin "had the Nash. That was her dad's car, the Nash . . . When we get reminiscing, we always say, 'Oh, the Nash!'"

For other high school students, economic circumstances rather than distance dictated how they spent their hours out of school. Clarice F., who went to high school in Sturgeon Bay during the 1930s, remembered working for her weekly room and board in the city. "The majority of the people in the area I come from didn't even go to high school," said Clarice. "I stayed during the week in Sturgeon Bay with a family and took care of the children, wiped up floors and did the dishes. That's the way my older sister and my younger sister, and my younger brother [managed]. We all went to high school in Sturgeon Bay by working for our room and board." Nobody had any money in those days, she said. "It's hard to believe now. And yet, none of us thought we were poor. Everyone was the same." Because money was short for food, let alone clothes, Clarice learned to sew "real young . . . And we could always cut a dress and make a blouse or something. We could always make a skirt out of some things. We were dressed o.k. for high school." Although divided by ethnicity and religion, rural schoolchildren experienced similar lives in other respects. In the 1930s and 1940s, a chronic shortage of money was a feature of everyone's life.

Teaching

Following high school, a few young people on the Door Peninsula went on to university or one of the state colleges, but for most this was not an option. Clarice F. recalled that she "always wanted to be an American history teacher—a high school teacher," but during the Depression, attending college or university was out of the question for her. A more affordable alternative was the local county normal school. From the 1870s onward, calls for the professionalization of teaching resulted in the establishment of summer training institutes, normal schools, and education departments in universities.[13] In 1866 Wisconsin passed a law establishing state normal schools with the purpose of instructing and training "persons, both male and female, in the art of teaching and in all the various branches that pertain to a good common education; also to give instruction in agriculture, chemistry, in the arts of hus-

---

13 Fuller, *The Old Country School*, 158–59.

bandry, the mechanic arts, the fundamental laws of the United States and of this state, and what regards the rights and duties of citizens."[14] As a consequence of this law, Wisconsin set up five normal schools, which along with the University of Wisconsin provided teacher education for the state as a whole. Yet by end of the nineteenth century, rural educators were complaining that the state normal schools focused too heavily on preparing high school teachers, while paying little attention to the rural schools that most children attended. To fill the gap, two counties—Manitowoc and Marathon—proposed establishing schools specifically to train rural school teachers. In 1899, the state legislature passed enabling legislation and set aside funds for the partial support of two such schools. Over the following decades more and more counties followed suit, so that by the middle of the twentieth century, Wisconsin had twenty-five county normal schools, nineteen of them owned by the counties in which they were located. Not only did the county normal schools increase the supply of trained teachers to rural schools, but they also provided opportunities for higher education to young people to whom it would otherwise have been denied. Touting themselves as "colleges of the common man's children," they were, because of their low operating costs, relatively short programs of study, and distribution across the entire state, within the reach of many more rural high school graduates than the state university system.[15]

Still, criticisms of the quality of rural education persisted. In 1900, a committee that studied the Wisconsin rural schools reported, "Poor teachers, in so great a proportion to the whole number are the bane of the rural school."[16] The Country Life Commission also fastened onto deficiencies in rural education as a major cause of the flight to the cities.[17] Although the county normal schools had increased the number of trained teachers in the rural schools, shortages persisted. One problem was that rural youth often saw their education as providing a highway to the city,

---

14 *Fifty-Three Years of Progress in Teacher Education: Wisconsin's County Normal Schools* (County Normal School Boards' Association and the County Normal Principals' Association of the State of Wisconsin, n.d.), 15.

15 Ibid., 19.

16 Fuller, *The Old Country School*, 159.

17 U.S. Country Life Commission, *Report of the Country Life Commission* (Washington: Government Printing Office, 1909), 53–54; Fuller, *The Old Country School*, 220.

and taught in their home area only as long as they were required to. Another was that the maintenance of so many small schools required the employment of at least as many schoolteachers, creating a dispersed, isolated, and transient workforce. Although the county education system provided a standard and reliable employment avenue during the first half of the twentieth century, because young women were generally required to give up teaching once they married—and certainly if they became pregnant—the teaching body needed constant replenishment.

On the Door Peninsula young people provided a steady stream of recruits to teaching at least partly because they had few alternatives. For girls entering the work force in the late 1940s and early 1950s, career opportunities other than the traditional nursing or teaching were expanding (although they still fell into recognizably feminized categories). In 1946, Madison's *Capital Times* reported that the University of Wisconsin had hosted a conference that featured "Specialized Fields" for women. Among the speakers were an editor of *Glamour* magazine, a home economist with an advertising agency, a personnel officer, a fashion designer, a theater director, a child psychologist, and a commercial artist. A representative from Oak Ridge, Tennessee, emphasized work in recreation, while another from the Federal Bureau of Public Assistance talked about welfare work. The final speaker talked about "marriage as a career," however. For women, work outside the home was still considered anomalous. On another page of the same issue, the newspaper reported an educational and social experiment, as "Boys Turn to Cooking, Girls to Manual Arts" at Wisconsin High School on the campus of the University of Wisconsin. "Boys . . . spend a required number of hours . . . in the home economics kitchen, a brand new, spic and span room, complete with the latest devices to aid the housewife," the article reported. In the "manual training department," on the other hand, girls could be found "with squares, boards, saws and planes, as they make household articles, learn how to join a severed cord, and become familiar with the operations of a lawn mower and the kitchen faucet."[18]

Such innovations as these, newsworthy even in Wisconsin's capital, were still a distant dream for the boys and girls of the more remote Door

---

18 *Capital Times*, 17 November 1946.

Peninsula, whose career aspirations ran along strictly gendered lines. Teaching was one of the few occupations open to both sexes. The most attainable goal for young people wishing to continue their education after high school in the 1930s, '40s, and '50s, and especially for girls, was the Door-Kewaunee County Normal School in Algoma.[19] In the 1940s and 1950s, for a few dollars a year in tuition and a promise to work within the county on graduation, the "DK Normal" offered a one-year (later expanded to two-year) course that trained teachers to work in the rural schools. Now housing the Algoma Public Library, in the early 1950s the buildings of the DK Normal included a women's dormitory (men students who could not live at home boarded with a family in Algoma) and a rural model school, in addition to classrooms for the student teachers.

Most students planned to enter DK Normal during their final year in high school, but Janice L. entered the school in 1951 on the spur of the moment. "Actually I came to DK the day that school was starting," she said. "I'd never felt like I was coming here at all. I thought I was going to the school of nursing, but my parents didn't think they could afford it. So the day school started I quit my job at the telephone company in Green Bay and came here . . . I was at the telephone company working during the summer to get a little money ahead . . . So then I came home and I said, 'I've quit the job and I'm coming to school here.' I taught thirty-five years after that." Her year's tuition, Janice said, was twenty dollars. "When I was a baby," she related, "my parents bought a Prudential insurance plan . . . When I came to DK, my twenty dollars was the money that my parents had given me in that policy . . . That was my tuition."

Some entered teaching not because they wanted to contribute to rural life but because they wanted to escape it. Often this strategy worked. "When I graduated," said Anita S., "they were heading for the Milwaukee area. They'd start here for two years, and then when they'd gotten enough experience they'd head down there." Apart from the attraction of city life, pay was often better elsewhere. "In the southern part of the state, they were paying more than they were paying in this

---

19 The school's official titled varied over the sixty-four years of its existence. From 1908 to 1922 it was known as the County Training School, from 1923 to 1926 as the County Rural Normal School, from 1927 to 1954 as the County Normal School, and from 1955 to 1972 as the County Teachers College. See C. Lamal, E. R. Olson and L. H. Timm, *Monograph of Door-Kewaunee County Teachers College* (Algoma, Wis: Door-Kewaunee County Teachers College, 1972), iii.

area, so it gave an incentive," commented former teacher Gerald G. "A lot of people left this area, who graduated from this area and went to teach in the Milwaukee area . . . They'd come back and . . . we'd ask them what they made, and oh my!" At other times, however, the strategy backfired. Another DK Normal alumna, Sylvia N., grew up on Washington Island. With her friend Marian, Sylvia departed for the Normal in the 1930s, hoping that college would provide her with a way to leave the island for good. On graduating, the two young women thought of themselves as having been "out in the world" and felt "maybe it would be fun to go somewhere else." But the county superintendent had other ideas. "When we graduated, do you know what they did?" Sylvia said with a laugh. "Sent us back to Washington Island to teach the two rural schools." Sylvia spent her whole career teaching on the island, an outcome that she seemed not to regret. Alumni of the DK Normal formed a network that started while they were still students. "I lived in the dormitory," said Anita S. "Made a lot of friends." Normal school graduates thought of themselves as members of a special community. Many years after the normal school closed, a conversation with one former student inevitably brought up names of many others, sometimes known personally, sometimes by reputation. Decades later, this network persisted.

When Otto Shipla graduated from high school in 1939, like other Depression-era teenagers he found his options were limited. Although he had registered for the University of Wisconsin at Madison, he was unable to raise the tuition money. Instead, following a friend's advice, he enrolled in the Central State Teachers College at Stevens Point to take the two-year course to become a teacher in a one-room school. He entered college only to discover that although many courses filled the curriculum, most of these involved memorization, just like his own elementary education. And when he started teaching in rural Adams County in 1940, Shipla realized that the curriculum had changed little since he himself was a pupil in a one-room school in 1934. "I was to find out in the fall of 1940," he admitted, "that the [university] courses did not help me too much in my teaching. I too often found myself doing things the way my teacher had done them at Fordham."[20] State manuals set out "prescribed poems" and "pre-

20 Shipla, *One-Room School Days*, 78–79.

scribed stories." Poems Shipla taught in seventh and eighth grades were identical to those he himself had learned as a child: "Sheridan's Ride," "Columbus," "The Arrow and the Song," "Bugle Song," "O Captain! My Captain!" "Recessional," "The Star-Spangled Banner," "Breathes There the Man" (from Walter Scott's "The Lay of the Last Minstrel"), "Wolsey's Farewell to His Greatness," and "Hark, Hark the Lark." In their reading class, these grades also read "classics" that Shipla found familiar: *The Great Stone Face, The Courtship of Miles Standish, The Legend of Sleepy Hollow,* and *The Vision of Sir Launfal.* The standard curriculum changed little from year to year, creating not only a small pool of texts but a limited reservoir in rural communities of knowledge about books and reading. Looking back on her schooldays in the Jacksonport School (Door County) during the 1940s, Carol Birschein, too, remembered learning a lot of poetry. "Those were the days when you read [Longfellow's] 'Evangeline,' [Edgar Allan Poe's] 'The Gold Bug,' and [Washington Irving's] 'The Legend of Sleepy Hollow,'" she wrote later. "Poetry like Christina Rossetti's 'The Wind' . . . Oliver Wendell Holmes' 'Old Ironsides' . . . Walt Whitman's 'O Captain! My Captain!'. . . Whittier's 'The Barefoot Boy'. . . James Russell Lowell's 'The First Snowfall.' There was Longfellow's 'The Children's Hour.'" These "classic" poems became the basis of the children's own literary efforts. "We made and illustrated a booklet for almost every poem and picture we studied, and entered it at the Door County Fair, hoping for a prize," Birschein recalled.[21] All across America, such poetry constituted a virtually national school curriculum during the 1920s, '30s, and '40s, one that laid down for schoolchildren a common set of experiences in terms of both the texts studied and the methods of studying them. Children learned not only to read, but also to declaim in public and from memory, since it was believed that participation in the political and social life of the nation required public eloquence, an ability to speak clearly and to make oneself heard. Moreover, the sentiments and moral values that such works conveyed buttressed the moral uplift and Protestant values of hard work and service to others that the public schools attempted to instill.[22]

---

21 Jacksonport Historical Society, *Jacksonport through the Generations*, vol. 3 (N.p.: J.E. Publishing, 2000), 77.

22 Joan Shelley Rubin, *Songs of Ourselves: The Uses of Poetry in America* (Cambridge, Mass.: Belknap, 2007), 120–21, 115, 113.

In 1950, Shipla joined the faculty of the Door-Kewaunee County Normal School, where he found he needed to be a "jack-of-all-trades." Other teaching faculty included the school's principal, three additional instructors, and a part-time music teacher, as well as a matron who took charge of the women students' dormitory, and a teacher who ran the model rural school attached to the facility. Together, the five instructors covered all the main aspects of the curriculum set out by the Wisconsin Department of Public Instruction: reading methods and language arts, history, art, science and mathematics, sociology and psychology.[23] In addition to the seventeen required credits taken each term (trimester), students were also required to take not-for-credit courses in physical education, chorus, dramatics, and library science.[24]

Students used the model or "Demonstration" school for school observation and practice teaching. In the months of November and March, they traveled to one-room schools in the region. Because the aspiring teachers had attended similar schools and experienced virtually the same curriculum, they found they slotted easily into the real-life teaching situations, even though the time for preparation was short. Clarice F., who entered the DK Normal in the mid-1930s, recalled that even after one year students could function effectively in their first teaching position. "It's surprising what we learned in one year," she told me. "But I also think the reason that it came to us so easily was that we were in these rural schools to start with . . . We knew the routine." Janice L. agreed. "We had very good training. We really learned to teach," she said. Still, there were drawbacks to such a very brief program. "We didn't have the academic background that the kids get in college," Janice went on. "We didn't go into depth with all of the history and geography, and things like that. It was assumed that we had enough of the academics getting up through high school, and here then we got the basics of teaching. When I think maybe in college they give you a lot of the academic and don't go into the actual procedure to teach something this way or that." New ideas were unlikely to penetrate this closed circular system in which rural school students evolved into teachers, perpetuating the knowledge and skills that they them-

23 Shipla, *One-Room School Days*, 123, 115.
24 *Fifty-Three Years of Progress*, 37.

selves had learned as children. During their normal school training, student teachers had little leeway to experiment. They had to prepare detailed lesson plans and were under the constant supervision of their instructors. Moreover, the DK Normal principal "made out a rigid schedule to be followed by all college students, of exact times when each subject in the one-room school was to be taught and what subjects the practice teacher would teach each week," Shipla commented.[25]

The county normal schools were firmly embedded in a local institutional network that included the county extension system, library service, and voluntary organizations like the Scouting movement. They maintained libraries and loaned out books to rural teachers and county education staff.[26] The buildings that housed the county normal schools represented a considerable capital outlay for the areas concerned, and often doubled as meeting spaces for county and home demonstration agents, farmers' groups, Scouts, and university extension classes. County normal faculty and even rural teachers provided a source of educated talent that local groups drew upon for radio broadcasts, judging contests, and speaking at events. Counseled Shipla in a mimeographed handout for his students, "Teaching, even in a one-room school, is not a process in which teacher and pupils are absorbed in academic materials and isolated from society. The teacher must be a leader not only of pupils in the school, but a leader in the community." As part of a list of twenty different ways that could help achieve this goal, he suggested, "Be interested in all youth and adult education in your community. Cooperate with 4-H Club leaders, Scout organizations, etc. Participate in community surveys to find community resources and needs." He also advocated taking to the airwaves: "Attempt to present a program on the local radio station (Sturgeon Bay or Green Bay). The radio has been eager to present programs in the public interest and for the public welfare."[27] In these ways rural teachers occupied the center of a web of officially sanctioned activities, spreading their influence systematically across the county, reaching

25 Shipla, *One-Room School Days*, 128.

26 *Fifty-Three Years of Progress*, 8.

27 Otto Shipla, "Public Relations Suggestions for Teachers of Rural One-Room Schools," mimeograph, August 1951, Otto Shipla Papers, author's collection.

every rural home with school-age children as well as many of those without.

Access to Books

For the many thousands of children who attended Wisconsin's rural schools in the 1930s and 1940s, reading at school consisted largely of reading prescribed texts that formed part of the literary canon. Reading books for pleasure, especially books written for children, was a rare event. A provision in the Wisconsin constitution (1848) had encouraged the establishment of school libraries, and Wisconsin's first school law made it possible for township officers to establish library funds. But no legislation could force districts to buy books. In 1878 the state superintendent of schools wrote that only 328 Wisconsin school districts reported having libraries that year.[28] As a beginning teacher in the Milwaukee public schools in the 1890s, Lutie Stearns found herself in charge of seventy-two children, most of whose parents were German immigrants. The only book in the room was a single reader, and the school had no library. Stearns met the need in two ways. First, she made a class library out of soapboxes filled with donated books and magazines, and raised seventy-five dollars by giving stereopticon lectures on Germany, using the money to buy periodicals. But she also tapped into city resources that included the Milwaukee Public Library. On Thursday evenings, accompanied by three boys each carrying two market baskets, she took the "horse car" to the library, where she borrowed two books for each child in her class.[29]

For teachers in rural schools, however ingenious and energetic they might be, isolation, lack of transportation, and poor roads made such a collaborative remedy more difficult. Still, some teachers did combine to improve the book supply. At Otto Shipla's one-room school in Adams County, every pupil was expected to read some library books. "Our library was small with few books, but the County Superintendent's

---

28 Fuller, *The Old Country School*, 78.
29 Lutie E. Stearns, "My Seventy-five Years: Part I, 1866–1914," *Wisconsin Magazine of History* 42, no. 4 (1959): 215.

office had a system of moving red boxes of library books every month from one school to another," Shipla recorded. On the other hand, the school's own library "was a mess with many old books needing repair." Since the county superintendent offered prizes for schools that improved their libraries, Shipla spent "many hours after school and on weekends mending library books" that winter. At the end of the school year, his effort was rewarded when the school received a new set of encyclopedias.[30]

Reading conditions and facilities varied from county to county, and even from school to school. In the 1940s, Door Peninsula rural class-rooms still contained little physical equipment beyond basic furniture. A shelf of well-worn books at the back of the room might provide the only reading materials apart from the district-designated textbooks. Much depended on the generosity of the local school board. "We had very few library books in our school . . . and we [had] probably read all those books at our school already," former student Eileen R. recalled. Clarice F. had similar memories of her own southern Door County schoolroom; "When I was in fifth grade, we had two cabinets built into the wall . . . One was all fiction, and one was all research. By the time I got out of the eighth grade, I had read all of the fiction books—most of them two or three times." On the other hand, Lucille K. remembered that in the northern Door County school where she herself was a student, "between the two classrooms [which were] for grades one to four and five to eight, there was a kitchen library. It served as a kitchen and as a library. [There were] those old fashioned shelves that you'd have to turn this little knob to get into this glass case and then we would always sit there reading books. That was the extent of our books . . . They didn't [change often]. But I know that we had to make a library list every year and update that, so through the district we got a few books every year." Lucille remem-bered going to Worley's bookstore in Sturgeon Bay to buy books "if we didn't have enough of that one subject. We would buy extra books and then hand the bill to the school board."

By the mid-twentieth century, the county superintendent was select-ing the textbooks for the rural schools, and standardization prevailed.

---

30 Shipla, *One-Room School Days*, 94–97.

Reading series were known by the names of their chief protagonists—
Dick and Jane, Alice and Jerry. Former teachers recalled that textbooks varied little from generation to generation. "Basically, what I
read when I went to grade school was the same ones I taught out of,"
commented Anita S. Doris C. remembered that she both learned and
taught from "Dick and Jane," and that shortage of funds played a big
part in this conservatism. "There was no buying a new book when [the
old ones] were good," she pointed out. Although teachers exercised little influence over textbook choice, some remembered that they had
more control over other classroom reading materials. Anita S. recalled
a system by which some Kewaunee County teachers informally passed
around a box of books from school to school; "We had it for maybe six
weeks or two months . . . We took that box of books and transported
them to the next school. And then somebody had a box of books and
they would bring it to your school." For Doris C., the demise of the
Door-Kewaunee Regional Library provided her Kewaunee County
rural school with an unexpected windfall when the library books allocated to Kewaunee County were distributed among the schools, and as
a young teacher she was asked to go and choose books for her class.

Lucille K., who taught in Sister Bay, remembered going to the
Sturgeon Bay Public Library "many times and just drawing out books
because we didn't . . . have a nice library up here." Eventually Lucille
was able to obtain books from the Sister Bay library, but in earlier
years, she would drive down to Sturgeon Bay "and pick up a group of
books and then bring them back for the school—some for my own use
and some for the children to read." Children who lived in the city could
also take advantage of the facilities of the Sturgeon Bay Public Library.
Even rural children who traveled to the city to attend high school could
perhaps fit in a visit to the library on their way home. In this way, the
public library provided a way for school students to exercise independence as well as to expand their reading opportunities.[31] The Sturgeon
Bay High School had a library, but Clarice F. had difficulty using it

31 The link between library use and children's independence is made by Alistair Black in "The
Past Public Library Observed: User Perceptions and Recollections of the Twentieth-Century
British Public Library Recorded in the Mass-Observation Archive," *Library Quarterly* 76, no. 4
(2006): 450.

since the open hours were very restricted. But she had to pass the public library on her way to and from school. "Every night after school I stopped in for a book, and I would stay up until two o'clock in the morning and read it. I don't know why I wasn't tired the next day, but I wasn't." She loved history and historical novels in particular, but "I read just about anything I could get my hands on, to tell you the truth . . . I used to read all the time."

In the early 1950s, for teachers and students alike, regular visits from the two county bookmobiles transformed rural classroom reading opportunities. For the first time, rural teachers had regular access to an educational resource that simply arrived on their doorstep. "If it hadn't been for that bookmobile I suppose those children wouldn't have had the opportunity to read many books," pointed out former rural teacher Emily H., "because I don't think any of them had a library . . . Well there wasn't a local library. You would have had to drive to a library and most of those people didn't have time to do that." Children in both counties eagerly anticipated the bookmobile's arrival, whether at their schools or at a crossroads near their homes. "We could go down to the village in Jacksonport and get books to read," said Eileen R., "I know that my parents were really excited about that. And I know it . . . not only came to the schools, but it came to smaller communities like . . . Jacksonport, West Jacksonport . . . It came every week or two but at first it didn't stay for very long. I think we only had like a half an hour or an hour to get [the books] because they had so many stops to make and there was only one bookmobile."

In 1951, officials collected circulation statistics for the rural schools that the bookmobiles visited in the two counties.[32] Overall, they calculated, 3,321 children were enrolled in the schools. On average, each child borrowed 23.3 books during the year. When the figures were broken down into district, though, some variation emerged. Confirming local residents' understanding of the geography of reading, the children of Brussels borrowed the fewest books (13.4 per child). But Brussels was followed by northern Ephraim Village (16.9 per child), confounding local expectations. Still, Ephraim had its own village

32 See Appendix 1, Table 4.

library, as did some other Door County communities. As already noted, rural Kewaunee County and southern Door County had no permanent village libraries, so southern Peninsula children were entirely dependent on bookmobile visits, unless their parents drove them into Algoma or Kewaunee. Perhaps this accounts for the fact that, contrary to the geography of reading, children in the south borrowed more books at school than those in the north, on average. By far the highest number borrowed in the two counties was in the southernmost Kewaunee County town of Franklin, where on average the children borrowed over forty books each, followed by those of the nextdoor town of Carlton with over thirty. The children of Red River (reputedly not a reading community) borrowed an average of over twenty-nine books each. Even the children of Montpelier borrowed an average of 22.4 per child.

Officials and teachers marveled at the bookmobiles' success in areas that local opinion categorized as uninterested in books and reading. On the day when the bookmobile visited the schools, "[We were] very *very* excited . . . I'm sure we were hard to contain for the teacher," said Eileen R., "because it was such an event for us to think that they were bringing books out to us." Eileen remembered that the van "was painted red and green. And we entered the bookmobile from the back end." The books were arranged "by grade level. There were encyclopedias way on the top shelf and then they went on down with the lower grades on the bottom so they could reach them and see them." She also called to mind the "warm, cozy" feeling of the bookmobile and the smell—"I don't know, it was a good—yeah it was—there was just something about it that I liked the way the bookmobile smelled." Lucille K. remembered that "there were shelves on one side—I think it was six layers, all just like a library set up, and then on the other side there was another six shelves or seven . . . and the books were there. Some of them would be on the table—there was a middle table, right in the middle and that's where we would take them to the bookmobile driver and he would check them out for us." To remind them of the due date of the books they borrowed, "the children got little—they called them T-cards," said Lucille, "a little green card and it told when you would have to have the book back. If they did not bring the book back on that day—if they had forgotten, they could take it to . . . a store in Ellison Bay."

Although some teachers limited the number of books children could choose, others encouraged children to pick as many books as they could carry away. Some organized a secondary circulating system so that children had access to a constantly changing collection of books chosen by their classmates. As books came into the classroom, the teacher would record on library-provided cards which child had borrowed what title. She would then designate a special shelf where a book could be placed when the child who had chosen it had finished reading it, and from there, other children could borrow the books. As the months went by and the novelty wore off, teachers and children became accustomed to the bookmobiles' regular appearances. Teachers could count on a supply of print materials to enhance their classroom activities. They also appreciated the adult help. "It was a nice quiet atmosphere, it was just a very enjoyable time," said Lucille K. "Well, you know when you're out in the rural school and you do all your own Phy. Ed. and you do your art and you do your music with no other help—it was a break."

Eileen R. remembered that the librarian encouraged the schoolchildren to check out books for their parents, in an act of role reversal. "Our parents would have a book that they specifically wanted to read and so then they would ask us to bring that one home for them," said Eileen. The library provided other incentives, too. "We'd always get a free bookmark, always get a bookmark. I'm sure that was always a special thing too, you know, you got a bookmark." For Door Peninsula children in the early 1950s, to receive even a bookmark was an event to be remembered. "And I know that we were always asking for more books, to bring more books. If there was a particular book, like maybe we were studying a specific subject, or our teacher had spoken about a certain author or books . . . if they didn't have it on the bookmobile, they would get it for us and then bring it the next time." But for the children of the two counties, along with their parents and teachers, the most amazing feature of the library was the number of books available to read for sheer pleasure. For teachers, most of whom had grown up in the restricted print culture of the Door Peninsula, as well as for their students, the library collection opened up a world of print that must have seemed boundless.

As the November 1952 referendum approached, teachers became

increasingly anxious about the library's survival. While passage of the referendum seemed likely in Door County, in Kewaunee County criticism of the experiment had always been more vocal, and as time went on this opposition showed no signs of abating. In September, fifty-eight Kewaunee County rural teachers (almost all women) issued a notice "To Voters of Kewaunee County" in the local newspapers; "Do you know that the part of your tax dollar which was spend for the Bookmobile has been a great factor in aiding and broadening of the education of the Kewaunee County rural children? We, the rural Teachers of Kewaunee County wish to thank you through this publication and sincerely hope you continue such a fine program at the Referendum vote in November."[33] Through this unusual collective action, however mildly expressed, the teachers were enlisting an informal network that normally operated out of sight. Perhaps it was this organizing experience that encouraged some teachers to take a bolder step after the referendum suffered defeat in Kewaunee County. The Door County supervisors, following their referendum mandate, had quickly designated $30,000 to establish a Door County Regional Library. In the wake of the library's defeat in the south, the *Algoma Record-Herald*, perhaps hoping to reverse the Kewaunee County supervisors' failure to do likewise, reported on low educational attainment in Kewaunee County; "We blush as we write this. Kewaunee county residents over 25 years of age have the lowest education median in the state with half having completed 8.4 years."[34] A few days later, teachers formed a delegation to try to reverse the supervisors' decision, arguing fruitlessly for two hours in favor of some kind of rural library service in Kewaunee County.[35]

Within a few years, the rural school system too had come to an end in both Kewaunee and Door counties, as school districts consolidated and rural children took the bus to larger schools that eventually each acquired its own well-stocked library. The Door-Kewaunee Normal— by then called the County Teachers College—closed its doors in 1972. But the end of the normal school system did not see the end of social

33 *Luxemburg News*, 18 September 1952.
34 *Algoma Record-Herald*, 4 December 1952.
35 *Algoma Record-Herald*, 18 December 1952.

and professional networking among teachers. In 1963, the state of Wisconsin made a bachelor's degree a requirement for holding a teaching certificate.[36] Normal school graduates began to attend college part-time to update their qualifications. Clarice F. banded together with other women to drive the hundred-mile round trip from Algoma to college. Clarice saw a notice about the opportunity to update her qualifications in the paper. "I mentioned it to a friend of mine, and she said, 'Can I ride with you?'" Clarice suggested that they take turns driving. "It was every Monday night . . . from seven until 9:30." Despite the grueling nature of this weekly schedule, other women were eager to join them. "As people heard about this, the group got bigger and bigger. Pretty soon we had a full carload. Five in the car, and we took turns driving. Then in the summertime, we thought, 'Now we can go and take six credits.'" Just as they had driven themselves to high school in the 1930s and 1940s, in the 1960s and '70s these normal school alumnae continued to collaborate in producing and reproducing the print culture infrastructure of rural Wisconsin, while at the same time providing themselves with opportunities for career advancement through the school system. "I know we have a picture of six of us girls riding in a car," said Clarice, "and we took a picture for the newspaper because . . . had we driven separately, we would have driven over—what was it? Six thousand miles."

Interviews with former rural schoolteachers reveal that teaching was an important route of upward social mobility for young people on the Door Peninsula. The County Normal School provided post–high school education at minimal cost to hundreds of young men and women for whom college or university was out of reach. Once certified, these new teachers found themselves simultaneously part of an extended print network that channeled specific texts to generations of school students, and at the same time often in sole charge of a geographically isolated schoolhouse, with potential for the exercise of individual choice and discretion. For other young people, reading began and ended with

---

36 In 1971 the state of Wisconsin budget eliminated funding for the four county colleges still in existence (Dodge, Sheboygan Falls, Outagamie, and Door-Kewaunee), and in July 1972 they all closed. See Lamal et al., *Monograph of Door-Kewaunee County Teachers College*, 4

school. For many farm children on the Door Peninsula, limited reading opportunities in the schoolroom were unlikely to be extended at home, and library services were often inaccessible, especially in the rural south.

The advent of the bookmobile radically changed this situation, however. Despite the Wisconsin Free Library Commission's efforts to focus on adult readers, children constituted by far the largest category of patron. Young people joined adult readers in the upgraded village libraries and at rural bookmobile stops, but the greatest access was provided to children through the graded and one-room schools. The bookmobiles made regular stops at both public and parochial schools, greatly expanding the reading opportunities of both students and teachers. In the rural schoolroom, the library and the school systems intersected as members of the two organizations came into contact with each other, reinforcing each other's values.

6
What to Read: Children's Choices

> Teachers and 92% of all rural students have used the [Regional
> Library] services to enrich school programs and for personal use.
> Standard achievement tests showed rural children gained two
> and one-half years in grade level during the two years, from
> March 1950 to March 1952, or one-half year more than normal
> progress. It was felt that this gain was largely due to the wider
> range of books and materials available.
>
> Luxemburg News, *October 30, 1951*

The Regional Library was refreshing the stagnant pool of print resources on the Door Peninsula in an unprecedented fashion. Suddenly, residents were awash in reading possibilities, as never before. Moving so rapidly from a situation of print scarcity to print abundance raised questions of choice that teachers and children had rarely confronted before. Among the aims of the Demonstration was to bring "good" reading—reading that not only extended their mechanical abilities but also introduced principles of literary taste and the organization of information—to the children of the two counties. To what extent were children free to select books that appealed to them, and what in fact did they choose? Circulation records not only reveal borrowing patterns, but also provide the only indication that survives of the range of books that the library provided for children.[1] *People like to read about themselves* had remarked reading experts Douglas Waples and Ralph Tyler in their large-scale study of adult reading preferences.[2] To what extent did Door and Kewaunee children read about themselves?

---

1 It is impossible to tell how adequate a representation the books checked out by this unscientific sample of readers is of the collection as a whole.

2 Douglas Waples and Ralph Tyler, *What People Want to Read About: A Study of Group Interests and a Survey of Problems in Adult Reading* (Chicago: American Library Association and University of Chicago Press, 1931), xxiii. Emphasis original.

Approved Reading

The library's organization of space and personnel was designed to point children in certain directions. Eileen R. remembered that there was always a librarian on the bookmobile. "The librarian would be there," she said, "and they'd help us pick out books—especially the younger kids—to see if they could read them or if it was in their abilities to read, and then also helped the younger kids fill out their cards to check them out." In addition to the librarian as reader's adviser, the bookmobile and libraries were physically organized to steer children toward materials considered appropriate for their age. Books were organized by grade level, and the librarian encouraged the children to check out their own grade-level section, or perhaps a level or two above. There was always a catalog on the bookmobile. "In fact, that is where I learned to use the card catalog system—on the bookmobile," said Eileen. "I needed to fill out the numbers and the cards and everything and know exactly where they were. But we also had the freedom to just go and browse also and look for books. And if we were looking for a specific subject or a specific author, that's where I learned how to use the card catalog. It was an educational tool, yes."

Librarians were eager to intervene in what they saw as the circumscribed lives of the children—especially those living on farms—on the Door Peninsula. They believed that acquiring the habit of reading could lead children to a better-informed and richer existence, but recognized that this belief was not necessarily shared by the children's own families. Most children came from families where education, by and large, was limited to the rural school. Few adults—barely one-quarter in Door County and only 18 percent in Kewaunee County—had more than an eighth-grade education.[3] Ethnicity and religion could also combine to dissuade children (especially boys) from embracing a wide variety of print materials. In both counties, children saw "nationality" and religious affiliation as the basis of social identity and believed that together they accounted for differences in rural social customs. "When you're out in the country, you'd better make sure that whoever

---

3 "Characteristics of the Population, Part 49: Wisconsin," in *Census of Population: 1950*, vol. 2 (Washington: Government Printing Office, 1952), 49–122.

you were going to make friends with was your nationality," commented Doris C. "And also your religion," added Anita S. "The Germans were the Lutherans and the Czechs were the Catholics. You drew that black line. Oh, yes."

On the Door Peninsula in the 1950s, to be Catholic was to be different, to the extent that in 1951 the Religious Information Bureau of the Knights of Columbus (a Catholic fraternal organization) had taken out an advertisement in the *Algoma Record-Herald*. In "A Letter to Our NON-CATHOLIC Neighbors," the organization attempted to combat "false ideas about Catholics and the Catholic Church," and regretted "lack of understanding" and "absence of good will" among those who live in common neighborhoods. The *Record-Herald's* editors endorsed the advertisement, arguing that "Understanding is Important," and that "understanding and consideration of the rights of others are vital ingredients in the true democracy for which we all strive." At the same time, all ethnic groups shared certain basic values. That men and women occupied separate positions in the social order was unquestioned by most. In the same issue of the *Algoma Record-Herald*, the patriarchal quality of life was underscored by an advertisement for Father's Day—"another 'family' day with Father's name on it! Thoughtful families will shower all manner of gifts on that Happy Man who is familiarly known everywhere as 'the Head of the House.'" [4]

Although they came from a variety of ethnic and religious backgrounds, most of the children living on the Door Peninsula were descended from relatively recent European immigrants. The children of migrant workers who came to pick fruit in Door County's famous cherry orchards every summer constituted an exception, however. These Hispanic families of Mexican origin lived in camps, largely isolated from the resident community, except when they came to Sturgeon Bay on Saturday afternoons to shop. From her vantage point in the city's Carnegie Library, Jane Livingston watched the cherry pickers drive "in truckloads in the back of big pickup trucks." It was "a very interesting time and I'm glad that I was here to see it," Livingston remembered, "because they worked so hard during the day but . . . it

---

4 "A Letter to our NON-CATHOLIC Neighbors"; "Understanding is Important"; "The Head of the House," *Algoma Record-Herald*, 28 June 1951.

was come Saturday afternoon they took off, and they didn't have very good living quarters in those days . . . [but] I wish you could have seen the spit and polish of those children. They dressed them up . . . their little petticoats were starched as could be and they were dressed to the T." The workers would start picking cherries in the southern part of the county and work their way north as the fruit gradually ripened over a period of about six weeks. "Then they'd go hire for something else. They had a regular route that they traveled." The Door County bookmobile included the migrant camps in its schedule during cherry-picking season, and the library ran programs for migrants and their families. "We got a special grant from some place, and we brought books—children's books," said Livingston. "They had some social services programs for the children too. But we went into the camps with story hours and things like that. Of course, that was a short season . . . I think that [later] some of the school districts set up programs because those kids weren't getting much education and they had some summer classes for them too."[5]

The librarians made strenuous efforts to reach all the children of the region, and to influence young people's choice of reading materials. The bookmobile's layout and procedures presented children with an impression of freedom within well-understood limits. Out of sight of the library borrowers, undergirding this system lay a mesh of controls designed to ensure that some materials found their way onto the shelves, while others were firmly excluded. Librarians understood that when it came to making books available to young people, they were treading on political eggshells. After all, one of the most successful strategies adopted by the library's opponents was to challenge the suitability of the reading materials it provided. Of concern to the officials at the library commission was that children read books of literary quality. To give guidance to teachers and librarians, in 1949 the Wisconsin Free Library Commission published a pamphlet that included "A Partial List of Series Not Circulated by Standard Libraries."[6] This list was

---

5 *The Idea in Action: A Report on the Door-Kewaunee Regional Library Demonstration, 1950–1952* (Madison: Wisconsin Free Library Commission, 1953), 23.

6 *Weeding the Library: Suggestions for the Guidance of Librarians of Small Libraries* (Madison: Wisconsin Free Library Commission, 1949), 9.

copied from the *Bulletin* of the New Hampshire libraries, with some additions by the New York and Michigan State Libraries. Titles on the list represented "the type of book not approved for purchase with library funds nor for placing on the shelves of any public or school library in Wisconsin." The list contained some of the nineteenth century's most popular authors for children—including Horatio Alger, Oliver Optic, and Pansy—as well as twentieth-century series books: the Bobbsey Twins, the Oz books, and Nancy Drew.[7]

Although authorities on children's reading like Anne Carroll Moore had long frowned on these and other series books and discouraged librarians from selecting them, children themselves found them hard to resist. Former bookmobile patron Marlene and her sister Delores of Door County remembered loving the series books about girl detectives Nancy Drew and Trixie Belden, although, conforming to the WFLC standards, the Regional Library appears not to have carried these. Kewaunee City resident Al B. read "a whole series" of Tom Swift books. "Boys would read Tom Swift, and girls would read the Bobbsey Twins," he told me. Tom Swift was on the WFLC's disapproved list, though, and the library did not stock them. "My mother would buy books," said Al, "or I would exchange them with some of my friends." The nearest store that might have carried them was in Green Bay.

Al's mother was happy for him to read the Tom Swift books, and his family had the means to enable him to do so, but children well recognized that some kinds of print were more likely to receive adult approval than others. Ben Logan confessed to illicitly reading Western magazines during his central Wisconsin childhood in the 1920s. Climbing "high up into a pine tree in the front yard" with a magazine in his pocket, Ben "became a silent Western hero . . . riding into a troubled

---

7 L. Frank Baum created the Oz series, though others contributed to it. Multiple authors employed by the Stratemeyer Syndicate wrote the Bobbsey Twins and Nancy Drew series, under the pseudonyms Laura Lee Hope and Carolyn Keene. Iowa writer Mildred A. Wirt Benson authored the early Nancy Drew books. The first, *The Secret of the Old Clock*, appeared in 1930. Trixie Belden mysteries appeared between 1948 and 1986. New York author Julie Campbell wrote the first six books, and subsequent titles were written under the pseudonym "Kathryn Kenny" by several in-house writers at Western Publishing. Iowa writer Nicolete Meredith Stack was the earliest of these. For more on girls' series books, see Sherrie A. Inness, ed., *Nancy Drew and Company: Culture, Gender, and Girls' Series* (Bowling Green, Ohio: Bowling Green State University Press, 1997).

land to set things right, then riding on again at the end."[8] Marlene and Delores remembered that they read comic books as children in the 1950s. This was a time when comic books were the subject of great concern and controversy. Psychiatrist Frederic Wertham even led a crusade against the genre, claiming that reading comics led to juvenile delinquency.[9] "Our neighbors across the street . . . were from Chicago," recounted Delores. "[T]heir father was a janitor in the Chicago apartments, and he would collect all the comic books . . . [T]hose boys had boxes and boxes full . . . [W]e would read the comic books all the time. Not that we could ever buy any because we didn't have any money to buy them, but we sure got to read them from Ed and Joe." The children understood perfectly that teachers, librarians, and even their parents considered this reading "inferior." Were there comic books on the bookmobile? "Oh, no," said Delores emphatically, and "Oh, definitely not," said Marlene.

As well as creating lists of books to be excluded from library shelves, leading children's librarians had devised systems for clearly identifying books that they especially approved. One was by means of two awards made through the American Library Association. The older of the two, the Newbery Medal (named for the eighteenth-century English bookseller John Newbery), first awarded in 1922, is the oldest children's book award in the world and goes to the most distinguished American children's book published the previous year. The Caldecott Medal (dating from 1938 and in honor of the nineteenth-century English illustrator Randolph J. Caldecott) is awarded to the artist of the most distinguished American picture book for children published in the United States during the preceding year.[10] Another means of stressing quality was through the use of published selection guides. Since the second half of the nineteenth century, librarians had recognized that children's ability and inclination to read would increase if they had available a variety of pleasurable materials. In response to the

---

8 Ben Logan, *The Land Remembers: The Story of a Farm and Its People* (Minnetonka, Minn.: North-Word Press, 1999), 170.

9 Frederic Wertham, *Seduction of the Innocent* (New York: Rinehart, 1954), 10.

10 Until 1970, other books cited as worthy of attention were listed as Newbery or Caldecott "runners-up." Since 1971, these have been referred to as Newbery or Caldecott Honor Books.

movement to increase the range of children's books, in 1909 the publisher H. W. Wilson began *Children's Catalog*, a series of selection guides for librarians that quickly became a standard tool for those building collections for children. Since *Children's Catalog* was one of the guides that the Wisconsin Free Library Commission staff used to make their recommendations for purchase, it is likely that Door-Kewaunee library staff, too, drew on both the seventh edition (1946) and the eighth (1951) in deciding what to buy for the Demonstration project.[11]

A major feature of the Wilson guides was their reliance on the recommendations of practicing librarians, so that, the editors claimed, "the selection is based on the votes of children's librarians and school librarians who carefully checked the sixth edition, the supplements from 1941 to 1945 and list of several hundred new books, considering each title for inclusion or omission. The final selection . . . represents the composite opinion of a large and varied number of librarians in actual public library or school library work." *Children's Catalog* included a star system to recommend particular books for purchase. Especially recommended books received a double star. In the seventh edition, of the 4,200 titles listed, about a quarter (1,100) were starred for first purchase, of which five hundred received two stars. These books, the editors wrote, were, "on the whole, the books of lasting merit which ought to be made available to all children. The titles marked with a single star, about 600 in all, are books which have been found to be most generally useful in libraries and which have wide appeal to children . . . Librarians of small libraries who purchase the starred books and second-hand copies of out of print books will have the beginning of a basic collection." Another evaluative device was a system that designated books as appropriate for particular grades at school. However, the editors cautioned, "Grading must never be taken too seriously."[12]

---

11 The copy of the seventh edition of *Children's Catalog* (1946) now in the Children's Cooperative Book Center in Madison, Wisconsin, is stamped "Book Selection Department, Wisconsin Free Library Commission, State Office Building, Madison."

12 *Children's Catalog*, 7th ed. (New York: H. W. Wilson 1946), v, vi.

What to Read?

To what extent did children's library choices conform to the librarians' efforts to shape their young patrons' reading?[13] The circulation records in the D-K database suggest that girls checked out books in larger numbers than boys. Of the children identifiable as girls or boys, girls constituted just over 62 percent, boys nearly 38 percent.[14] The circulation slips provide no information about the borrowers' ages or grade levels, however, and it is hard to tell whether children in all grades took equal advantage of the bookmobile. At the same time, it is possible to infer from a list of the children's most popular choices that children in all the elementary grades made extensive use of the library.[15] *Children's Catalog* graded the four most popular titles (Ariane's *Lively Little Rabbit*, Alvin Tresselt's *White Snow, Bright Snow*, Margery Clark's *Poppy Seed Cakes*, and Helen Bannerman's *Little Black Sambo*) that circulated as intended for kindergarten or grades one to three. But of the remaining thirteen books, only three were intended for younger children. The rest were mostly aimed at the middle grades—suggesting that children aged ten and older were taking substantial advantage of the bookmobiles' offerings. Of course, the children were given little choice: when the bookmobile showed up at their school, all were expected to take advantage of it. But for older boys, especially those from "non-reading" communities, being surrounded by books on the library van must have been an unusual experience.

Among the seventeen most popular titles that received eight or more charges, four books had won either a Newbery or Caldecott award. Girls and boys both made charges of award-winning books, though boys were more likely to pick Caldecott winners than Newbery winners, possibly because picture books were designed to appeal to younger readers, and older boys were perhaps less likely to take advan-

---

13 Using the names recorded on the circulation slips it is possible to estimate the number of girls and boys checking out books. Not all children filled in their names, probably because the younger ones were unable to do so. The name of the school was always filled in, however. Probably the bookmobile staff helped fill out the slips, but lacked the time to fill them out completely.

14 See Appendix 2, Table 3, Girls' and Boys' Charges.

15 See Appendix 2, Table 4, Most Popular Titles.

tage of the library. Altogether, 109 children charged out Caldecott Medal and Honor Books, 116 Newbery books. Among the most popular was Alvin Tresselt's *White Snow, Bright Snow*, illustrated by Roger Duvoisin, a Caldecott Medal winner in 1948. The two most favored Newbery winners were Marguerite Henry's *Misty of Chincoteague* (1948) and Lois Lenski's *Strawberry Girl* (1946). A handful of adults, too, picked award-winning books for children. Mrs. J.B. of Luxemburg, for instance, charged out four Caldecott titles.[16] As a proportion of the total number of charges, award winners constituted only 4.5 percent, but still, librarians and teachers must have been gratified to see the books judged to be of high quality circulate among young people whose access to books of any kind was previously so limited.

Not surprisingly, in this list of seventeen titles, fiction predominated, accounting for all the books except one.[17] These well-liked titles mostly received official sanction from *Children's Catalog*; only two of the books failed to appear in the selection guide, and ten received one or two stars. The single most popular title charged out by children was *Lively Little Rabbit*, by "Ariane" (pseudonym for Georges Duplaix, and published in 1943). This was neither starred nor an award winner, but of the next seven most popular titles (Alvin Tresselt's *White Snow, Bright Snow*; *Poppy Seed Cakes* by Margery Clark—actually two librarians named Mary E. Clark and Margery Quigley; Helen Bannerman's *Little Black Sambo*; Katherine Grey's *Rolling Wheels*; Eric Knight's *Lassie Come Home*; Marguerite Henry's *Misty of Chincoteague;* and Lois Lenski's *Strawberry Girl*), all but one (*Rolling Wheels*) received double stars from *Children's Catalog*, and three were award winners.[18]

In terms of author popularity too, fiction considerably outweighed other genres.[19] Far out in front was the prolific Lois Lenski, Ohio-born author and illustrator of over a hundred books for children, many of them with a regional theme. Explained Lenski in the foreword to

---

16 See Appendix 2, Table 5, Charges of Caldecott and Newbery Books.

17 See Appendix 2, Table 4, Most Popular Titles. The presence of *Little Black Sambo* would be astonishing to twenty-first-century librarians, in view of its controversial history. See the discussion later in this chapter.

18 See Appendix 2, Table 4, Most Popular Titles.

19 See Appendix 2, Table 6, Most Popular Authors.

Strawberry Girl (a Door-Kewaunee favorite), "I am trying to present vivid, sympathetic pictures of the real life of different localities. We need to know our country better: to know and understand people different from ourselves; so that we can say, 'This then is the way these people live. Because I understand it, I admire and love them.' Is this not a rich heritage for our American children?"[20] In *Strawberry Girl*, the Boyers—a family of "Anglo-Saxons" with roots in South Carolina— settle in Florida with the intention of prospering though cultivating market crops like sweet potatoes, peanuts, and strawberries. In the early twentieth century, Lenski explains, Florida was still new territory, "aside from the early Indian and Spanish settlements." Since these two groups figure not at all in the story, Lenski apparently felt they had little significance to Florida's history. The Boyers are poor but hard-working, and intent on improving their lot through better agriculture and education. Like other Crackers (so-called from the cracking of Floridian cowboys' whips), the Boyers use "flavorsome" speech, represented in the story by use of dialect words and spellings—"pore" for poor, "shore" for sure, and "purty" for pretty. The characters are all white; African Americans appear only incidentally as part of the background, much like the alligators and palmetto trees that supply colorful and exotic imagery to Lenski's implied white, northern readers.

The Boyers' nearest neighbors are the Slaters, an even poorer family that relies on traditional free-range farming of cattle and hogs. In addition to their adherence to what Lenski casts as outmoded farm practices, the Slaters are held back by illiteracy, compounded by a scorn for reading and school. Worst of all, Mr. Slater periodically gets drunk, throwing away what little cash he earns on gambling and alcohol, while his wife and children go hungry and ill clad. Sometimes he goes on terrifying rampages, shooting the heads off his wife's chickens, depriving his family of eggs and cash. Naturally the two families clash, as the Slaters' cows and hogs trample the newly planted strawberry fields and munch on the tender shoots in the Boyers' orange grove, leading to hostility and outright violence. Despite these family tensions, the "strawberry girl"—nine-year-old Birdie Boyer—carries on an ambiva-

---

20 Lois Lenski, *Strawberry Girl* (New York: Dell, 1974), xi.

lent friendship with Jefferson Davis "Shoestring" Slater (a boy of about her own age), and with his little sisters, while Mrs. Boyer persists in attempts to assist the down-trodden Mrs. Slater. In the end, Mr. Slater sees the errors of his ways through the good offices of an itinerant preacher. Converted to Christianity, he turns his back on alcohol and gambling, and encourages Shoestring and his other children to attend the nearby one-room school. There the teacher immediately sets to work to rid Shoestring and Birdie of their regional dialect. "'Any' trouble, not 'no' trouble, Jefferson. And 'if,' not 'iffen.' 'Teach' me, not 'larn' me," says the young, pretty Miss Dunnaway.[21]

The prevailing messages of *Strawberry Girl*—that new farming methods and technologies were desirable, that education was a way out of poverty, and that middle-class customs and speech were superior, reinforced the prevailing meta-text about the making of America. Many of the children of the Door Peninsula, whose grandparents and great-grandparents had immigrated to America from Belgium, "Bohemia," Poland, Germany, Norway, and Iceland, and some of whom still spoke the languages of those countries at home, would have failed to recognize themselves and their families in the pages of the books provided for them by the library. Perhaps they did not expect to see themselves so depicted, but accepted without question that the official reading provided by the school and the library would be about children whose lifestyles were presented as American, whom they themselves were (perhaps implicitly) expected to emulate.

Others on the list of authors who had written award-winning books and were popular with Door-Kewaunee children, were Stephen W. Meader (Newbery), and Margaret Wise Brown, Maud and Miska Petersham, and Berta Hader (Caldecott). On the other hand, some frequently read authors wrote books that were absent from the pages of *Children's Catalog*, including books with a "Disney" theme and Zane Grey's westerns. Failure to appear in *Children's Catalog* was not necessarily a sign of dubious moral or educational values on the part of the author. Both boys and girls frequently picked Frank Lee Beals's books about "heroes" of the American West, such as Kit Carson, Davy

---

21 Ibid., 190.

Crockett, Chief Black Hawk, and Buffalo Bill, even though they perhaps did not meet professional librarians' literary standards. Beals was a veteran of the Spanish American War and World War I, and in the 1940s he was a superintendent for the Chicago Board of Education. One of the reasons that books by Beals were missing from *Children's Catalog* may have been their possible status as textbooks. Part of the American Adventure Series published by the Wheeler Publishing Company, the books themselves appeared similar to other stories designated for young readers. However, one giveaway was the inclusion of comprehension questions at the end of every three or four chapters. Another was a "Word List" with pronunciation guidelines (though no definition) at the end of each book. In *Buffalo Bill*, for example, students learned to pronounce "Sioux," for instance, as "Soo" or "Sooz."[22] The writing was also self-consciously pedagogic. In *Buffalo Bill*, Beals described settlers' wagon trains as "made up of thirty-five wagons. Each wagon was pulled by three yoke (pairs) of oxen. Oxen were used because they could stand the long, hard trip of two thousand miles far better than horses or mules." Beals described the wagons in detail, as "turned up at the ends like boats" and watertight. "They were built this way to protect the supplies when crossing the rivers and streams which had to be forded," he instructed his young readers. "Their shape also kept the heavy loads from sliding back and forth as the wagons were pulled up or down hill." Later, to test their attentiveness, readers were asked, "Give a brief description of a wagon train."[23] Though full of useful information, the books were short on literary distinction. Characters lacked development, and perhaps in keeping with their pedagogic purpose, the books employed a restricted vocabulary. Still, although lacking high literary quality of the type achieved by award-winners and starred titles, these books were morally acceptable by the standards of the day and also achieved the librarians' aim of engaging children's interest and stimulating in them a desire to read. This, after all, was their principal aim. The messages of these books also did nothing to disturb official values for a literacy that supported the standard account

---

22 Frank Lee Beals, *Buffalo Bill* (Chicago: Wheeler, 1943), 252.
23 Ibid, 14–15, 37.

of America dominated by English-speaking white men of northern European descent.

Even more clearly marked as intended to instruct, another category of popular books consisted of stories that publishers specifically marketed as "readers," often in series, and often written by reading specialists and other well-known educators. This category (which received an astounding 718 charges—14 percent of the total of children's charges), included books in series like Scott, Foresman's famous "Dick and Jane" (by William H. Elson and William S. Gray, published from 1930 on). The most popular of these writers was Miriam Blanton Huber, but others included Arthur Gates, Mabel O'Donnell (author of the "Alice and Jerry" reading series that Row, Peterson published from 1938 on), Myrtle Banks Quinlan, Horace Mann Buckley, Gertrude Hildreth, and Nila Banton Smith. Most of these authors did not appear in *Children's Catalog*, probably because the selection guides had a policy of not including reading textbooks for children past the third grade.

Nila Banton Smith was a distinguished educator who taught in the Detroit public schools, went on to hold positions at a number of universities that included Greensboro College, Whittier College, the University of Southern California, and New York University, and also served as president of the International Reading Association. She wrote many books about teaching and learning to read, as well as reading series that included "The Unit-Activity Reading" (multiple books published by Silver Burdett in the late 1930s and early 1940s), "Learning to Read" (six books published by Silver Burdett in 1945) and "Be a Better Reader" (published by Prentice-Hall in several editions from the late 1950s through the 1970s). Door-Kewaunee children checked out twenty-one Smith titles: five charges from "The Unit-Activity Reading" series and all the rest from "Learning to Read." The most popular individual titles were *Down the Road* (six charges), *Bill and Susan*, and *In New Places* (five charges each). Gertrude Hildreth specialized in early learning and teaching gifted children. For twenty years she was staff psychologist and teacher at the Lincoln School of Columbia Teachers College, before moving to Brooklyn College as a professor. In addition to scholarly texts on teaching and learning, she also produced reading series for children. In Door and Kewaunee counties, children chose titles from her series "Easy Growth in

Reading" like *Mac and Muff* (six charges), *Going to School* (four charges), and *At Play* (three charges).

Several of the authors were connected to Columbia University's Teachers College. Miriam Blanton Huber, whose series "The Wonder-Story Books" and the less enticingly titled "Core-Vocabulary Readers" were very popular with children in Door and Kewaunee counties, also wrote *The Influence of Intelligence upon Children's Reading Interests*, which Teachers College published in 1928. A report of an experiment Huber carried out with groups of "bright," "average," and "dull" nine-year-olds in the New York City schools, *The Influence of Intelligence* concluded that all children (no matter what their "intelligence" level) preferred to read poems and stories that experts rated as of high quality. Presumably designed to provide high-quality reading material to readers of all levels of ability, Huber's Wonder-Story Books and Core-Vocabulary Readers together were charged out forty times by Door-Kewaunee patrons in the sample.

Arthur Irving Gates was one of the most prominent and prolific reading specialists of the twentieth century. A professor at Teachers College, he wrote a great many scholarly texts, as well as books for children, and collaborated with other reading authorities in the production of reading series. In 1930–1931, with William S. Gray, Gates was responsible for introducing the idea of the basal reader in American education. Gates and Huber collaborated with a third author, Frank Seely Salisbury, on a series published by Macmillan from 1945 on called "Today's Work-Play Books," which children checked out from the Regional Library in large numbers. Girls and boys chose books like *Good Times on Our Street*, and *Friends and Workers* (six charges each), which carried these experts' reading pedagogy into Door and Kewaunee County homes. Although teachers and librarians drew a distinction between story or picture books and books designed to teach children to read, imagining, perhaps that the latter would be less vivid or entertaining, evidently the children of the Door Peninsula read them with enjoyment, returning to them again and again.

Gender, Race, and Ethnicity

As Kewaunee resident Al B. had noted, girls and boys displayed some distinct preferences.[24] Lists of most popular titles and authors give an indication of boys' most popular books.[25] Lois Lenski was again the front-runner, but the next two most popular were Glenn Blough's science titles, and books by Sanford Tousey, who wrote stories with a western theme. Not far behind were Frank Lee Beals and Zane Grey, who also wrote books about the west, while further down the list (in ninth place) was science writer Bertha Morris Parker. A graduate of the University of Chicago and a former science teacher, Parker wrote a large number of science textbooks during the 1940s and early 1950s, many of them part of the "Basic Science Education" series mostly published by Row, Peterson. With titles like *Six-Legged Neighbors*, *Birds in Your Backyard* and *Winter Is Here*, these texts proved especially popular with boys, who made at least fifteen of the thirty charges of Parker titles (compared with seven by children identified as girls). Parker coauthored some of her books with Glen Blough, whose own titles were even more sought after in the library. In the late 1940s and early 1950s, Blough, a native of Michigan, was employed by U.S. Department of Health, Education, and Welfare as a specialist for elementary science, and he went on to become a professor of education at the University of Maryland. Like Parker, he wrote many science books for children published by Row, Peterson in the 1940s, as well as a series of textbooks for the middle grades published by Scott, Foresman. Books produced through the WPA's Writers Program were also popular with boys. These had titles like *Birds of the World*, *Lightning and Electricity*, and *Legends of the Mighty Sioux*, and perhaps appealed to young male readers in the same way as the science titles.[26] Librarians must have been pleased to see the popularity among boys of these nonfiction works

---

24 In his study of the reading preferences of fifty thousand New York school students, George Norvell, too found significant differences in the interests of boys and girls. See *Reading Interests of Young People* (Boston: Heath, 1950), especially chapter 9.

25 See Appendix 2, Table 7, Girls' Favorite Authors, Table 8, Girls' Favorite Titles, Table 9, Boys' Favorite Authors, and Table 10, Boys' Favorite Titles.

26 See Appendix, Table 9, Boys' Favorite Authors.

that their professional training taught them to value so much more highly than fiction.

The numbers of charges in the D-K database are too small to draw definitive conclusions, but they do point to some possible, and perhaps unremarkable trends. Girls seemed to like stories about families. Boys picked books about animals. But both boys and girls liked books with a western theme, and although relatively more boys than girls chose science books, these were popular with both groups. Both boys and girls seemed to enjoy the nonfiction books published through the WPA Writers Program. Both liked the Disney books about characters like Mickey Mouse and Donald Duck, made popular through movies and cartoon strips from the late 1920s on. Did Door Peninsula children *"read about themselves"*? In the two counties, children indeed seemed to veer toward reading about characters in roles that they perhaps could identify themselves playing. Yet if ethnicity was a defining group characteristic, the collections of the local library and schools would have done little to help either migrant or resident children recognize their own ethnic group or broaden their knowledge and understanding of each other's cultures.

The authors most clearly demarcated as preferred by girls were fiction-writers Mabel Leigh Hunt, Louisa May Alcott, Elizabeth Orton Jones, and Eleanor Thomas. Mabel Leigh Hunt was both a children's librarian and the author of about thirty books for children that revolved around a domestic theme, with a historical setting. Louisa May Alcott, too, was famous for her novels, written in the second half of the nineteenth century, about middle-class family life in New England. Elizabeth Orton Jones, on the other hand, was well known as an author-illustrator of books for young children, while Eleanor Thomas wrote reader-type books with titles like *Your Town and Mine*, and *Stories About Sally*. No children identified as boys checked out *Little Women*, or, indeed, any title by Louisa May Alcott (these included *Eight Cousins*, *Jack and Jill*, *Little Men*, *Old Fashioned Girl*, *Rose in Bloom*, and *Under the Lilacs*).

Books about families presented women in traditional roles as wives, mothers, carers, and housekeepers, mirroring and reinforcing Door Peninsula girls' own experiences of patriarchy. Books that explicitly offered girls a choice about the course of their adult lives included career fiction, usually with a romantic theme. Twenty-four young people (but no adults) made charges of seventeen separate titles that fell into this category. Not surprisingly, twenty of the borrowers were identifiable as girls, none as boys. Although some, like *Sky Hostess* by Betty Peckham and *Cecily Drake, Movie Editor* by Elisabeth Lansing, pointed young women in innovative directions, the subjects of these novels generally adopted careers traditionally deemed suitable for women, like teaching and nursing. Door Peninsula girls were already well aware of these options, but perhaps appreciated the realistic depictions of the heroines' training and work experiences and sympathized with their hopes and anxieties.

In *Sue Barton, Student Nurse* (borrowed by a Sister Bay reader), for instance, Sue travels alone by train to the hospital which she will enter as a probationary trainee. Despite the fact that her father is a doctor, Sue had received little encouragement to become a nurse from other friends and family members, who had assured her that she would be "doomed to a life of bread and water and scrubbing floors."[27] Sue finds this implausible, though. "Who takes care of the patients?" she asks, skeptically. "Elijah's ravens?" The hospital is situated in a city "on the edge of the slums," where "swarms of dark-skinned, poorly clad children . . . were shouting and playing in the streets."[28] Most, but not all of Sue's fellow probationers are from comfortable homes, and some are even described as rich. All are implied to be white. Race is never made explicit, but Sue freezes out an attempt by one Grace Holton to comment on class distinctions. Such topics are off limits, she indicates. Throughout the book, the excluded Grace is depicted as fat, giggly, clumsy, and unsophisticated, in contrast to Katherine (with her slight English accent) and the millionaire's daughter Constance, both of whom become Sue's special friends. Thus readers learn that it is not acceptable to comment on social difference, and are encouraged to identify with the graceful and poised representatives of the upper and middle classes.

Senior nurses cut authority figures who occasionally treat the probationers with kindness, more often with impatience. At the hospital, Sue has to contend with "Miss Cameron," a fearsome instructor. A

---

27 Helen Dore Boylston, *Sue Barton, Student Nurse* (Boston: Little, Brown, 1938), 4.
28 Ibid., 5.

stock figure in career novels for girls, older single women like Miss Cameron represent dedication, competence, and expertise. These formidable women know better than the novices what is good for them, and are not afraid to say so. Their juniors may complain at their treatment, but in their hearts they accept their authority, recognizing it as justified. Patients, on the other hand, are objects of concern, the usually grateful recipients of the nurses' skilled attention. Often they are immigrants, with heavy Italian or Irish accents. The ethnically other also appear as low-level workers, like the Irish Nellie, the elderly but invaluable maid in the Out-Patient Department, whose long-standing feud with another maid, Maggie, is resolved through Sue's mediations.

In Sue Barton's world, people are largely defined by their class, ethnicity, and gender. Most nurses are white, middle class, and Anglophone. Patients are also white, but are often marginalized by their "foreignness." All the nurses are female, and Sue Barton encounters only male doctors, one of whom, Dr. Barry, provides the story with romantic interest. However, in another nursing career story, *The Organdy Cupcakes* (chosen by an Algoma reader), the author Mary Stoltz explicitly challenges these gender expectations. "Organdy cupcakes" are the caps that students earn when they graduate to become nurses. Far from seeing these hats as ridiculous relics, the young women eagerly look forward to acquiring the right to wear them, and sport them proudly. One of their instructors is Dr. Bradley who—surprise!—turns out to be a woman. Praised by the students for her ability, she was also admired for being "one of the most successful pediatricians in town" and for her "beautiful clothes."[29] Career women don't have to be dowdy, the book implies. In her lecture to the student nurses, Dr. Bradley addresses her choice of specialization. "Some of you," she tells them, " . . . feel that women who become doctors elect Pediatrics because it's the field most open to them." There is some truth to this, she admits, "though the picture changes daily." Her own choice was based on principle, she says. "I'm in Pediatrics because it's where I want to be, because I believe that children are the most important people in the world, and the pleasure, the privilege, of knowing and helping them is not replaceable."[30]

---

29 Mary Stoltz, *The Organdy Cupcakes* (New York: Harper Bros., 1951), 14.
30 Ibid., 16.

Although Dr. Bradley's marital status is not made clear, we assume that she is single. What, one of the student nurses idly wonders, would Dr. Bradley be doing "had she not chosen to be Dr. Bradley"? Marriage presents itself as the only answer: "Seeing a properly elegant husband off on a late commuter train, dropping a couple of sturdy children at a private school, whisking off to the club for nine holes before luncheon." The student, Gretchen (herself from an affluent home), finds the picture appealing. "For a moment, only a moment, Gretchen pitied the doctor for the woman she might have been."[31] While readers are nevertheless encouraged to interpret Dr. Bradley's decision as the right one for her, another "working woman," a night nurse named Mrs. Peder, cuts a less enviable figure. Student nurse Rosemary wonders why Mrs. Peder, the mother of two little boys, worked such hours. "Only one night a week to bathe those bouncy boys' bodies herself, one night to read a drowzy [*sic*] story, to open a window and firmly tuck the healthy rebels against sleep into their own low beds. She must miss them terribly," Rosemary speculates. "Will I be like that?" she asks herself. "Or perhaps she wouldn't be married at all. Would she, then, be like Miss Merkle, the stern, middle-aged Director of Nurses, with only her pathetic dog Dollar for company in her lonely evenings?"[32] At the end of the book, Stoltz leaves the marriage question unresolved. Of her three chief characters, only Gretchen appears to follow the traditional path of marrying the tall, handsome Dr. Whitney. This will not be the end of her nursing career, though. She plans to go back to college and then into Public Health nursing. Nelle and archaeology-obsessed Wally seem attracted to each other, but graduation means the start of a nursing career rather than marriage for Nelle, too. Rosemary chooses to become an Army nurse, and the prospect of an ongoing relationship with Dr. Kenneth Grafton is left open.

Adèle de Leeuw's *With a High Heart* (borrowed by a reader at Maple Grove School near Fish Creek) is about librarianship.[33] A second-year

---

31 Ibid., 15.

32 Ibid., 65.

33 Adèle de Leeuw, *With a High Heart* (New York: Macmillan, 1947). Thanks to Derek Attig for drawing my attention to this book in his paper "Mobilizing Body and Mind: Reading the Bookmobile in Mid-Century America," given at the conference "The Culture of Print in Science, Technology, Engineering, and Medicine (STEM)," held in Madison Wisconsin, on September 13, 2007.

library student, the attractive and talented Anne McLane, is sure that her summer practicum will involve a plum position at the well-appointed Claremont Library. To her shock, the indomitable Miss Pruitt assigns her instead to the struggling and understaffed Kenyon County Library, where an accident to the head librarian soon forces Anne to drive the county bookmobile. A breakdown on her very first trip brings help in the form of Matt English, a young farmer with "a lean and friendly face."[34] Since Matt borrows from the library the scientific books he needs to improve his farming techniques, their friendship develops. Gradually, Anne learns to love her job as well as Matt, as she comes into contact with a series of needy library patrons, all of whom she is able to help. There is Willem Harmsma, a blind ex-engineer, whose miserable life is transformed by talking book records. Anne's old dolls' house and a handloom made by her father brighten the days of Berta Polachek, the disabled child of Polish immigrants. Anne secures help from the terrifying but wealthy Mrs. Twining for Cissy O'Connell, the eldest of an Irish family's thirteen children, to go to college and study bacteriology. In the end, Anne and Matt agree to spend their lives together in a future that by implication includes both librarianship and scientific farming.

These career novels featured young women from educated, middle-class, Anglophone families, whose driving force in their chosen careers was fed by an underlying passion to give service to the less fortunate. These needy individuals tended to be members of ethnic minorities, often Irish or Italian. As students, the young women suffer under the tutelage of awe-inspiring older single women, who have put aside domesticity to devote themselves to the education of a new generation. Education and service are important, but not everything to these young women, however. Romance, too, has its place. Still, attraction to— always—the opposite sex does not deflect the girls from their career goals, at least not immediately. Most Door Peninsula readers would have been unlikely to recognize their own families in the depictions of the central characters' prosperous and educated backgrounds. At the same time, though, they probably did not see themselves in the impov-

34 De Leeuw, *With a High Heart*, 34.

erished objects of the heroines' worthy intentions. Rather, they were encouraged to identify with Sue, Anne, Gretchen, and Rosemary and, in so doing, to develop a vision of women as active promoters of the public good in the world outside the home. Personal choice, determination, learning from experience as well as from books: all these blended with an ethos of public service to draw on both Yankee and Progressive traditions of community uplift and moral self-development.

The career books for girls had no counterpart for boys. Rather, boys were drawn to books about manly heroes such as cowboys, military men, and sportsmen. Girls did check out books by authors identified as "male" like Frank Lee Beals, albeit in small numbers. Of the five titles by Beals—*Buffalo Bill*, *Chief Black Hawk*, *Davy Crockett*, *Kit Carson*, and *Rush for Gold*—the only one not checked out by any girls at all was *Kit Carson*. Similarly, four girls checked out books by Sanford Tousey (compared with fifteen boys). Ten girls and twelve boys chose books by Zane Grey. Perhaps on the Door Peninsula as elsewhere in twentieth-century America, less stigma attached to girls reading books intended for boys than the reverse. Authors most clearly preferred by boys were Hamilton Williamson, Virginia Lee Burton, Sanford Tousey, and Joseph Wharton Lippincott. Hamilton Williamson wrote animal stories, too, but for younger readers. Four boys (but no girls) chose his *Baby Bear*, although two boys and two girls picked *Lion Cub, A Jungle Tale*. Virginia Lee Burton's picture books, also designed for younger children, included stories about machinery that were not popular with girls. No girls chose *Katy and the Big Snow* (about a tractor), although one did pick *Mike Mulligan and His Steam Shovel*, and another *The Little House*.

Targeted at children in the middle grades, Joseph Wharton Lippincott's single most popular title was *Wilderness Champion: The Story of a Great Hound*, set in Alberta, Wyoming, and the Florida Everglades, and chosen by seven boys (six from Kewaunee County) and one Kewaunee County girl. The Wilderness Champion is Reddy, a reddish-colored hound who is adopted as a puppy by an old but still powerful wolf. The wolf rears him for a year and teaches him to hunt and to defend himself. Eventually, Reddy's owner, a ranger called Johnny, reclaims him and the two form an impressive team. The high points of the book are the fast-paced descriptions of Reddy's successful hunting exploits, in which he takes on a fearsome mountain lion, a pack of coyotes, and even timber wolves. Readers are encouraged to appreciate Reddy's strength, skill, and bravery, as well as his loyalty and intelligence.

Similar characteristics are celebrated in Stephen W. Meader's *River of the Wolves*, chosen by four Kewaunee County boys (but no girls). This captivity tale of the eighteenth-century French and Indian Wars recounts the adventures of Dave, a boy from Dover, New Hampshire, after he is taken prisoner in an Indian raid and forced to travel north into Canada with other captives. On the journey, Dave distinguishes himself by his strength, quick-wittedness, and bravery and the Indian "savages" accept him as their blood brother. Dave becomes fluent in Abenaki and learns to live like his captors, but secretly nurses plans to escape. Sight of a map from a missionary priest gives him hope that he can find his way home by following a river. When his captors become hopelessly drunk on a barrel of French brandy, Dave and Nancy (an equally "spunky" young captive) slip away in a stolen canoe. Skills learned from the Indians save them on their hair-raising river journey, and they make it to Fredericton, where they board a schooner to Portsmouth. "Gee," Dave murmurs at the very end, "don't things turn out fine if you just stick to it long enough?"[35]

Native Americans appear in books about the west as objects of curiosity and fear, and also some ambivalence. In *River of the Wolves*, Dave survives capture because an Indian boy befriends him, and also because Dave himself is open to developing such a friendship. Yet he has no compunction about tricking the Indians in order to escape, or about stealing a canoe from them. In Sanford Tousey's *Kit Carson: American Scout*, Kit develops a symbiotic relationship with Native Americans and marries an Arapaho woman. His knowledge of Indian languages and customs makes him much in demand as a negotiator. Still, the reader is assumed to side with the settlers. After Carson settles down in New Mexico, he "did not lead an altogether quiet life on the ranch, for redskins continued to annoy the white settlers and traders," Tousey asserts. "Whenever there was a very hard scouting job, Kit was sent for. He knew best how to handle the Indians." [36] Like

---

35 Stephen W. Meader, *River of the Wolves* (New York: Harcourt, Brace, 1948), 249.
36 Sanford Tousey, *Kit Carson: American Scout* (Chicago: Albert Whitman, 1949), 45.

horses, the book suggests, Indians needed skilled, knowledgeable, and firm treatment.

In the popular books by Frank Lee Beals, Native Americans fall into stereotyped categories of good and bad Indians. In *Buffalo Bill*, the young Billy Cody befriends several young Sioux boys and defends them as "good Indians" when warned to be on his guard against them.[37] Still, the Indians are the generalized enemy. Bill Cody kills "his first Indian" at Plum Creek at the age of twelve, rather as he might have killed his first bear. [38] Beals has Kit Carson express the dilemma. "We whites belong to another civilization," Carson explains to Bill. "We are builders. The Indians are content to live as they have always lived. They had tried time and again to stop our march of progress, but they cannot do it. This uprising will be put down, but that will not end the trouble with the Indians." Eventually, though, Carson says, "the day will come when the Indians and the white men will live in peace. Then we will all be Americans."[39]

Seven children (five boys, one girl, one unidentified) borrowed *Buffalo Bill* in the D-K database sample. Four (one boy, one girl, two unidentified) borrowed *Chief Black Hawk*, a story set closer to home for these Wisconsin children. In an introduction to this tale of calamity for the region's Native Americans, Beals sets out his theory of their history in more detail. "The story of the American Indians is a record of a brave, proud, people," he asserts. "The struggle to preserve their own way of life against the advancing civilization of the white man is tragic, but it is filled with deeds of high courage and patriotism . . . It is hoped that this story of Black Hawk will help to bring back something of our early pioneer life and a better understanding of our American Indians."[40] In recounting the events of the war that opened Wisconsin to white settlement, Beals casts Black Hawk as a hero, an honest and proud leader who stands up to President Andrew Jackson and in doing so earns his respect, despite the fact that, as Beals understates it, "President

---

37 Beals, *Buffalo Bill*, 53.

38 Bill laughingly describes Plum Creek as "the place where I killed my first Indian." Ibid., 174.

39 Ibid., 214–15.

40 Frank Lee Beals, *Chief Black Hawk* (Chicago: Wheeler, 1943), n.p.

Jackson did not like Indians."[41] Beals endows Black Hawk with the qualities that his implied young, white, readers should emulate. Black Hawk is fearless, of course, but he is also proud and dignified, yet simple. He stands straight; he stands by his word, and he refuses to kill women and children. In Beals's sanitized account, Black Hawk wins freedom for his people and is content to be moved across the Mississippi and settled on fertile lands in Iowa. Beals fails to mention that subsequent pressure from white settlement pursued the Sauk and Fox Indians even on the far side of the river, and that the story of their forced westward migration hardly ended with the conclusion of the Black Hawk wars in 1832.

Still, Beals's account of Black Hawk was relatively sympathetic, and was perhaps even considered progressive in its day. In the 1940s and 1950s, multicultural children's literature had yet to become a standard feature of classrooms and children's library collections. It was 1965 before Nancy Larrick, the International Reading Association's former president, drew national attention to the "All-White World of Children's Books."[42] But even ahead of the publication of this landmark article, some librarians and educators recognized a need for a multicultural approach to providing children's services and collections. An early subject of dispute was Helen Bannerman's *Little Black Sambo*, a title that received ten charges (the fourth most popular) in the sample of circulation records. In 1945, Helen Trager of the Bureau of Intercultural Education took issue with *Little Black Sambo* (first published in 1899 in London, to instant acclaim). The Scottish Bannerman had written the story while living in India with her husband, a physician. In the story, written for Bannerman's own small children, a little Indian boy outwits savage tigers by fobbing them off with his brand-new clothes. In the end, tigers competing for Sambo's finery chase themselves around a tree so fast that they turn into ghee (butter). Little Black Sambo's mother then uses the ghee to make a stack of delicious pancakes, so that instead of the tigers eating the boy, the boy eats the tigers. The published book became immensely popular, but because Bannerman

---

41 Ibid., 242.

42 Nancy Larrick, "The All-White World of Children's Books," *Saturday Review* (September 11, 1965): 63–85.

immediately lost the copyright (and a fortune) to her London publishers, she also lost control of what happened to subsequent editions, including those printed in America. In the United States, many different editions appeared in which the book's Indian setting became overlaid with racial connotations that interpreted the heroic Sambo as a negatively stereotyped African American.[43] Trager's critique and the controversy it spurred resonated with such children's librarians as Charlemae Hill Rollins, a colleague and close collaborator of Vivian Harsh at the George Cleveland Hall branch of the Chicago Public Library. Rollins's lifelong goal was to encourage children's literature free of racial slurs. In the 1930s she had protested against derogatory portrayals of black children in books for the young, and began a seven-year project at the request of the National Council of Teachers of English that resulted in her ground-breaking annotated bibliography *We Build Together: A Reader's Guide to Negro Life and Literature for Elementary and High School Use*.[44] Although *Little Black Sambo* had appeared in the first edition of *We Build Together* (for want of alternatives), Rollins now joined the effort to remove the book from lists of recommended books for children.[45] On the Door Peninsula librarians, teachers, and children alike were probably unaware that one of their favorite books was under dispute. From the mid-1960s and 1970s on, a great push for multicultural inclusiveness in children's literature ensured that attention to diversity now constitutes a standard element in university courses on children's and young adult literature.[46] *Little Black Sambo* eventually disappeared from recommended lists.

Although most of the children's literature that the Door-Kewaunee library made available largely served to promote an ongoing Americanization project, this was not entirely true of all the books. Non-American

43 Barbara Bader, "Sambo, Babaji, and Sam," *Horn Book Magazine* 72, no. 5 (September–October 1996): 537.

44 Charlemae Hill Rollins, *We Build Together: A Reader's Guide to Negro Life and Literature for Elementary and High School Use* (Chicago: National Council of Teachers of English, 1941).

45 Bader, "Sambo, Babaji, and Sam," 539–40.

46 Kay E. Vandergrift, "Female Advocacy and Harmonious Voices: A History of Public Library Services and Publishing for Children in the United States," *Library Trends* 44, no. 4 (Spring 1996): 693; Merri V. Lindgren, ed., *The Multicolored Mirror: Cultural Substance in Literature for Children and Young Adults* (Fort Atkinson, Wis.: Highsmith Press, 1991).

authors were responsible for some of the titles that children frequently checked out. Maj Lindeman, for example, was a Swedish author who wrote humorous stories for younger readers about children in sets of three—the boys Snipp, Snapp, and Snurr, and the girls Flicka, Ricka, and Dicka. Lindmann's books were favorites of both girls and boys. Then there were stories written by American authors, but depicting other cultures, like the novels of Pearl Buck and Eleanor Lattimore and the short stories of Harold Courlander and George Herzog. A handful of books represented black Americans seriously and even tackled racism directly. Arna Bontemps's *The Story of the Negro* (a Newbery honor book of 1949) circulated three times. Six children made charges of *Tobe*, by Stella Sharpe, a story of the day-to-day life of a North Carolina black farm family in easy-to-read language, and accompanied by photographs of real children. Door Peninsula farm children might easily have identified with these boys and girls through the pictures of them working in the fields, feeding animals, and gathering honey.[47] John R. Tunis wrote stories about sports and sports players. His *All-American* (published in 1942, seven charges) tackled the issue of racism in high school football in an explicit way that most writers at this time preferred to avoid. In *All-American*, the white captain of a high school football team protests against the exclusion of an African American player from a game in the South. Despite accusations of "Bolshevism" in the local newspapers and threats against his father, the captain is able to reverse the team's decision to travel and play in the South.[48]

Books that disrupted the official picture of a homogeneous white America were few, however. Whether they were boys or girls, the children of the Door Peninsula during the early 1950s read books that by and large imparted a consistent message about what it meant to be an American. The reading series—whether the textbooks that teachers used in the classroom, or the "readers" written by reading experts that

---

47 Barbara Bader, *American Picturebooks from Noah's Ark to the Beast Within* (New York: Macmillan, 1976), 375.

48 William Jay Jacobs, "John R. Tunis: A Commitment to Values," in *Authors and Illustrators of Children's Books: Writings on Their Lives and Works*, ed. Miriam Hoffman and Eva Samuels (New York: R. R. Bowker, 1972), 397.

children checked out from the library—featured white children in middle-class suburban settings. The picture books and stories that the bookmobile and libraries stocked so amply also told a standard tale about the production of America as a nation. Books about families showed women and girls in domestic settings. Books with a historical theme presented stories of white conquest and white settlement as national achievement. Even the stunningly popular books of Lois Lenski, which made a particular effort to depict difference in regional and historical terms, contrived to depict diversity in only a superficial manner.[49] Yet for many of the children on the Door Peninsula, even the stories of middle-class children living comfortable suburban lives in English-speaking families must have provided a glimpse into another world—one far removed from the reality of their own tradition-based farm families. In that sense, then, the librarians achieved their aim of broadening their young patrons' outlooks, and perhaps of stirring in them a desire to turn away from their rural backgrounds. Far from shoring up the rural way of life, reading may even have accelerated the flight from it. Small wonder that the taxpayers of Montpelier and other conservative townships saw little reason to support this subversive influence.

Library circulation records show that students were overwhelmingly interested in reading stories, and there was nothing wrong with that, local librarians felt, if it meant that students read more often. To teachers and librarians, simply encouraging reading as a habit was more important that maintaining the distinction between good and bad reading that library authorities like Bernard Berelson tried to promote. In this philosophy, providing what borrowers wanted to read took precedence over providing what experts considered good for them. Marlene and Delores, erstwhile comic book *aficionadas*, agreed. "Some people's philosophy was if [the children] were reading a comic book they were reading junk," said Delores. "But I let them read that book.

---

49 "Although they were widely praised and do show differences in ways of life in different parts of the United States, the plots and characters are very similar, and they are about children who strive for the conventional values of the educated middle class," commented the compilers of an authoritative reference book several decades later (*Dictionary of American Children's Fiction, 1859–1959: Books of Recognized Merit*, ed. Alethea K. Helbig and Agnes Regan Perkins [Westport, Conn.: Greenwood, 1985], 290).

If you were learning to read, what difference . . . if it's a comic book, because that might get you interested in reading something else." And in Door County especially, librarians believed that the new service had a lasting effect on the region's print culture. "On the bookmobile, we really raised a generation of readers," said Jane Livingston proudly, many decades later.

7
Women, Print, and Domesticity

Flo never went to bed without setting the lamp carefully
on a chair beside her and laying at least six cumbersome volumes
where she could reach them. She might read only one, but
she would not run the risk of finishing that one and
finding herself bookless.

Kathleen Norris, *The Venables*

If for Door Peninsula schoolchildren, the bookmobile's visits generated
a party-like atmosphere, their mothers, too, found visiting the library
could be the high spot of the week. Not only did it provide them with a
constantly changing supply of books and magazines to take home, but it
gave them an opportunity to socialize with neighbors as well. A bookmobile stop could last anywhere from a half hour to two hours, and during
that time neighbors might greet each other for the first time since the
previous library visit. "In the wintertime [it] was nothing for Mrs. Jones
to pick up Mrs. Smith: 'Oh we'll all go to the library.' They all went in
one car — car pooled it," remembered former bookmobile driver Bob H.
Women's charges account for over 90 percent of the surviving adult
reading records, and over two-thirds of these women patrons were rural
residents who either used the bookmobile service at its crossroad, school,
or village stops or borrowed from the small village libraries. Probably
their lives conformed to what seems still to have been a common pattern
for rural married women at the time: an endless series of farm and domestic chores that included child care, gardening, cooking, cleaning, perhaps
still caring for poultry and milking, and laundry — though some, it seems,
drew the line at making soap.[1] Women's experiences of the library inter-

---

1 Interview with Hazel P., Door County, 24 May 2001.

sected with their experiences of other institutions that promoted read-ing, especially the women's and homemakers' clubs that constituted women's primary secular social organizations in the postwar period.

Women's and Homemakers' Clubs

Northern Door County had cultural experiences and aspirations, interviewees told me, that were foreign to the "practical" south. The north's reputation as a region of readers was confirmed by the fact that in addition to the Sturgeon Bay Public Library (housed in its purpose-built Carnegie building), several other Door County communities had small libraries of their own. Kewaunee County, by contrast had only two—in the cities of Algoma and Kewaunee. Some of the Door County village libraries had been founded by local women's clubs, and during the period before they joined the Door-Kewaunee Regional Library were what Jane Livingston dubbed "token libraries"—libraries with limited opening hours, limited collections, and run by volunteers or untrained staff. Still, they were much better than nothing, Livingston felt, and represented considerable effort on the part of their organizers, many of whom were women's club members.

Women's clubs were a northern phenomenon, according to Livingston. "They don't have women's clubs down in southern Door, they just have [extension service] Homemakers—practical," she said, implying a class difference between the north and the south. Unlike southern women, whose lives were circumscribed by domestic expectations and obliga-tions, northern women were less likely to be confined to their homes and could engage with the community in significant ways, especially through their women's clubs. In Sister Bay, the largest village in the north of Door County, Livingston said, "the women's club . . . collected books from anyone who wanted to contribute. They had a library in a room at the side of their village hall. These village halls were pretty good-sized, they had an auditorium." In Ephraim, summer visitors spurred the founding of the library. "There were . . . dynamic people in Ephraim and these people all met and talked with each other," remembered Lee Traven, son of librarian Olivia Traven. Summer visitors donated books to the Ephraim library, which were kept in the village hall in the summer and in the barber's shop in the winter. In the village of Bailey's Harbor, on the other hand, philanthropy played a key role in establishing a library. A local benefactor, Michael McCardle, who was chief executive officer of the Sunbeam Corporation, left money to build a village hall, one room of which was to be a local library. "This man [McCardle] worked . . . with the Rockefeller Foundation," Lee Traven related, "and he and another woman . . . got that library going."

On Washington Island with its population of Icelanders, the library emerged from a combination of local activism and philanthropy. Former schoolteacher Sylvia N. told me the story. "On Detroit Harbor Road was a little cottage. It belonged to the Detroit Harbor Ladies Aid—one of our first ladies' organizations on the island. They had a kitchen and a meeting room and some rooms upstairs for sailors to rent out. And [a wealthy] family from Milwaukee . . . used to come up the shore in yachts and buy property. And when the last . . . died, they sent all their books to the island." However, the donation was a mixed blessing to the islanders. "What were we going to do with them?" Sylvia asked, shaking her head. The Detroit Harbor Ladies Aid came to the rescue with the offer of the use of their clubroom. In 1940, Sylvia went on, a thousand books arrived in "massive boxes . . . A very handy man offered to take these real book boxes and make us book cases." Unfortunately the books came in no particular order, presenting the volunteers with a problem. "Do you know what we did with some of [the books], because they were such a mess?" said Sylvia. "We had to sort." Moreover, not all the books were judged suitable for the library. "And so we put them in a box. And because my husband was a commercial fisherman, so nobody would see them at the dump, he took them and dumped them out in Lake Michigan!" Sylvia laughed heartily at the memory. Still, she recognized that not everyone would have found the story so funny. Consigning books to the depths of the lake would have seemed like sacrilege to some, and a waste of resources to others. At the very least it might have deterred other potential donors from giving books to the library.

For Bailey's Harbor librarian Olivia Traven, membership in the local women's club helped provide an entry into the library profession. Although Traven had grown up and gone to high school in Milwaukee, she spent her summers in Door County. "My grandfather was a marine engineer on the lakes," explained Lee Traven, "and my grandmother's

mother lived here, so she brought her daughters here every summer
. . . My great great grandfather . . . came to Bailey's Harbor in 1860 . . .
He built the first pier and a dry goods store . . . His house was where
the town hall is, where the library is now." It was in Door County that
Olivia met her future husband, who was then in the Coast Guard.
After the Traven family moved permanently to Bailey's Harbor in 1937,
Olivia Traven became active in the women's club and a founder of a
private wildlife sanctuary. In the mid-1940s, the Bailey's Harbor
librarian decided to leave, and the village asked Traven to take over. "It
was the greatest day in my mother's life when she was asked to be the
librarian because she loved books and reading, and the story hours
with the children especially were precious to her," recalled Lee Traven.
"Some of those children that are adults now mention that they [appre-
ciated] the story hour." Traven was a fervent advocate for the library,
and not afraid to express her views in public. "She was always very
almost outspoken about what she believed. My grandmother used to
say that she got that from her Yankee father," said Lee Traven. "She
was articulate, she could stand up and speak, so she was active in the
woman's club in the state—the Federation of Woman's Clubs." Her
Yankee roots and prominence in the local community gave her a confidence to take on a public role that other women must have envied. And
as with other Door Peninsula librarians, trained and untrained,
Traven's heart lay with children's work.

Although they valued what the women's clubs could achieve for
libraries, some professional librarians were ambivalent about them. At
least part of their lack of enthusiasm arose from an awareness of class
distinctions. "I have some wonderful tales about the women's club in
Sturgeon Bay," Livingston admitted. "When I came here the women's
club was meeting in the basement area [of the library] . . . and they
were a thorn in our sides. They were very noisy, and those were the
days where you at least tried to keep the kids a little quiet." The
Sturgeon Bay library was a typical Carnegie building; on entering
through the front door, visitors were faced with a choice of going
upstairs or downstairs. "Well, they would loiter in the whole hallway,
yakking," said Livingston. "They were always dressed up spit and polish with hat, white gloves . . . and then they'd go downstairs, and they
had the furnace room where they made their coffee. Well, that building

wasn't wired for too much electric use, and they were always blowing the fuses . . . But they'd bring stronger fuses and put them in, so every time after they'd left I'd have to go down and check out the safety." Finally the club members got the message that the library staff was not happy with their presence. "I wanted the meeting room that they had downstairs. That was their private property they'd started to think. I was using it for story hours and the two didn't mix very well." Eventually the women's club moved elsewhere—to the courthouse, perhaps, Livingston conjectured. "But the ladies were—you couldn't be too hard on them because they were the ones that were promoting the library, so you had to tippy toe."

Women's clubs were rarer in the southern part of the Door Peninsula to some extent because midwestern women's clubs tended to be an urban (or at least village) phenomenon. In Iowa's Open Country during the early part of the twentieth century, Deborah Fink found, women who lived in town, or who could travel there easily, formed associations such as "the Friendship Club, the Lucky Thirteen . . . the Music Club, the Study Club, and the Community Club." Farmwomen, by contrast, were less likely to join clubs. "What clubs they had frequently used work as the pretext for organizing . . . for example . . . The Cheerful Workers, whose members gathered to quilt and sew rags for rugs."[2] In the late 1940s, the city of Algoma was home to a women's club that included the public library among its causes, but in the rural areas farmwomen were more likely to belong to homemakers' clubs sponsored by the county extension agency. These organizations provided not only a social venue in which rural women met regularly as a group, but a means of expanding their learning opportunities and organizational abilities. Extension workers used homemakers' clubs to help farmwomen adjust to structural changes resulting from an accelerating industrialization of agriculture and to introduce changing technologies to farm homes. They also used them to transmit a very specific set of beliefs about domesticity.

When settlers migrated to the Midwest from northeastern and mid-Atlantic states in the middle and second half of the nineteenth century, they brought with them cultural expectations that, among other things,

---

2 Deborah Fink, *Open Country Iowa: Rural Women, Tradition, and Change* (Albany: State University of New York Press, 1986), 94–95.

idealized married women as "naturally" suited to presiding over a sanctified home and simultaneously unfit for labor in the fields. This ideology persisted in the culture that Yankees established in the newly settled agricultural communities of the Midwest and became incorporated into the agricultural institutions that formed in the second half of the nineteenth century. The system that agricultural experts envisaged as transforming the countryside was organized along similarly pastoral gendered lines. According to the division of labor devised by the extension service, men's work, directed by a male agent, was defined as "agricultural," while women's work, directed by a female agent, was seen as "domestic."

Although all farm families of European origin also organized themselves along gendered lines, these did not necessarily conform to the extension service's Anglo-American cultural norms. Whereas for women to work in the fields was taboo for white Anglophones of "Yankee" descent, for instance, for Germans, Norwegians, and other European immigrants it was a normal practice. At the same time, traditional German families were intensely patriarchal in ways that also contravened extension notions of appropriate family structure and practices. Although the men of German households were free to socialize in the community, women's lives were far more strictly circumscribed. Beyond service to the church and socializing with kin, women were supposed to be at home, looking after the children and the house, or "helping out" on the farm.[3] Restrictions such as these ran counter to the extension service's aim to provide more opportunities for women's education, community action, and sociability.

Technological Change and Family Life

By the middle years of the twentieth century, changes in domestic technology were slowly transforming Wisconsin farmhouses. Although

---

3 Sonya Salamon, *Prairie Patrimony: Family, Farming, and Community in the Midwest* (Chapel Hill: University of North Carolina Press, 1992), 22–23, 183–85; Jon Gjerde, *From Peasants to Farmers: The Migration from Balestrand, Norway, to the Upper Middle West* (Cambridge: Cambridge University Press, 1985), 194–98.

most urban dwellers enjoyed centrally generated household electricity from the 1920s on, rural dwellers found themselves left behind, and electrification constituted a sharp contrast between city and country. Some farmers generated their own power, and central station power was available to a few farms situated close to towns, but mostly power companies argued that it was too expensive to wire widely scattered farmsteads. "The absence of electrical power did not mean only that people had to depend on gas or kerosene for illumination," writes historian David Danbom. "It also meant that they beat rugs, heated flatirons on wood or coal stoves, and cooled food in dripping iceboxes . . . And it meant that a device like a radio could not simply be plugged in but had to be hooked up to cumbersome batteries that needed frequent recharging."[4] By the late 1940s most Wisconsin farms were electrified, though many still lacked indoor plumbing, as did many village homes of the period. With rural electrification, farm and village women joined city dwellers as potential consumers of such household machines as refrigerators, freezers, stoves, and water heaters. Farm journals like *Wallace's Farmer* published photos and news items about farmwomen buying the new household equipment, thus reinforcing the messages of the extension service and of nationally distributed publications like *Ladies Home Journal* and *Good Housekeeping.* Farm journals joined a steadily developing mainstream in employing the theme of sex appeal to advertise "household products which had no obvious or direct connection to sex," writes Fink. "While advertisements in *Wallace's Farmer* were still directing women to buy poultry feed and equipment, some of the new advertisements showed thin and glamorous women in ecstasy over household products."[5]

In the era before electric light and central heating made it possible to read in all rooms of the house (even in the bathroom and even in winter), evening reading was likely to take place in the company of others. Kerosene lamps were standard in rural homes well into the twentieth century, and their use could be confined to a single room— often the dining-room, where all the family members would gather around the table every evening to share the limited light supply. One

---

4 David B. Danbom, *Born in the Country: A History of Rural America* (Baltimore: Johns Hopkins University Press, 1995), 220–21.

5 Fink, *Open Country Iowa*, 128–29.

day in the Logan household, Ben Logan relates, his father "brought home a new lamp for the dining-room table, an Aladdin with a cone-shaped mantle." Hazel P., too, remembered that acquiring a mantle lamp was a landmark event. "My father's brother lived out in the state of Washington. He didn't have any kids so he had a little bit more money to play with than my dad did," she said. "And every Christmas he'd send us a check, I think it was ten dollars, which was a lot of money at that time, and I remember one year Pa took that money and he spent six dollars of it to buy a mantle gas lamp. Boy, did we think we were ritzy!" Technological improvements meant that the light it gave "was white, like the light from a bare electric bulb in a store," wrote Ben Logan. The additional light changed the pattern of family sociability, though. The new lamp opened up the corners of the dining room, allowing the family to "scatter away from the little circle we'd always formed." Not everyone was pleased with the result. "I remember Mother standing in the doorway to the kitchen one night, frowning in at us. 'I'm not sure I like that new lamp . . . Does a new lamp have to change where we sit at night?'" Eventually everyone came out of their corners and gathered again round the table. "Mother sat down with us and nodded. 'That's better.'"[6]

For the Logans as for other rural residents, reading was often a family affair, with the mother at the center. After the evening chores were done, Ben related, "We came in out of the dark cold of winter and gathered again in the dining room, crowding close to the stove for a few minutes before the lamp pulled us into a circle around the dining-room table." While the children did their homework, their father would be "reading or planning next year's fields, figuring what seeds and how much fertilizer and lime we need, his stubby pencil moving slowly and firmly on his ruled tablet." The Logans were accustomed to sharing their books by reading passages out loud, sometimes with unexpected consequences. When one of the family would start chuckling, the others would urge, "'What's so funny?'. . . Soon the whole room was filled with laughter. That could start a discussion that ranged over every continent in the world. At school the next day a written report on

6 Ben Logan, *The Land Remembers: The Story of a Farm and Its People* (Minnetonka, Minn.: North-Word Press, 1999), 235.

Chicago might, for some unexplainable reason, turn out to have a kangaroo in it." At the same time, their mother would be performing a seeming miracle: simultaneously reading and mending clothes. "When we asked how she could do that, she said, 'I read something that has a lot of thinking between the sentences.' Usually it was the Bible or a book of poetry."[7]

The link between sewing and reading had been firmly established in antebellum New England. Before the advent of industrial garment making, hand sewing and mending filled much of women's time, and many sought to mitigate the tedium by working in groups, often while one of their number read aloud. Husbands, too, might read to their wives in the evening, while the latter sewed or mended. Once sewing machines, with their noisy clatter, became popular in the late nineteenth century, this link was weakened. Still, sewing machines speeded up only the stitching process. Other forms of handwork, or indeed housework, proceeded quietly, allowing women to listen while others read to them. Like Ben Logan's mother, other women also learned to read and sew simultaneously. Knitting while reading from a book propped open was a common trick, one that some women learned from older friends and relatives. Women also took advantage of the long hours spent sewing to memorize poetry.[8] Joan Shelley Rubin describes such reading as "women's work," the fitting in of reading, copying, and other literary activities between their domestic obligations. Some cookbooks even reprinted poetry in among the recipes, enabling women "to sneak a moment of reading between chores."[9]

Technological change affected farms in a multitude of ways. New kinds of machinery, and especially the use of chemical fertilizers, pesticides, and hybrid seeds required new skills and knowledge on the part of men. No comparable skill and knowledge were thought necessary for women, however. A 1948 *Wallace's Farmer* article titled "What Education Do Farmers Need?" pointed to the increasingly "scientific"

---

7 Ibid., 232.

8 Ronald J. Zboray and Mary Saracino Zboray, *Everyday Ideas: Socioliterary Experience among Antebellum New Englanders* (Knoxville: University of Tennessee Press, 2006), 132–34, 180–81.

9 Joan Shelley Rubin, *Songs of Ourselves: The Uses of Poetry in America* (Cambridge, Mass.: Belknap, 2007), 292, 245.

nature of farming and found that successful farmers valued two years of agricultural training in college. But although land grant institutions also maintained major programs in home economics, few farmers stressed these as important to their farms' success. "While a good wife was an asset on the farm (farming was, after all, becoming a complicated and intricate operation)," concludes Fink, "she was strictly an assistant."[10] On the one hand, the mechanization and concentration of some traditional spheres of women's farming, like poultry and egg production, meant relinquishing this activity to men. On the other, mechanization of fieldwork made it possible for women to "help out" in activities formerly reserved for men, and shortage of hired male labor made it increasingly likely that they would spend more time in the fields. But farmwomen were not exempt from the domestic ideology of the 1950s, and fieldwork was contrasted unfavorably in the dominant Anglophone culture with "homemaking," an activity that was presented not only as natural to women, but also as preferred by them.[11]

Although the period of the 1950s is often depicted as the era when Rosie the Riveter was steered back toward containment in a domestic cage, rather than retreating entirely from the labor force many urban women moved into a feminized sector of the labor market that was already overcrowded and poorly paid, such as typing and clerical work.[12] On the farm, a similar process took place. During World War II, home agents—"the government's voice in rural homes"—encouraged women to produce healthy war workers by preparing balanced meals, nursing their own sick, caring for clothing, managing household accounts, and generally consuming as few resources as possible, just as they had in World War I.[13] In response to a 1943 *Wallace's Farmer* article titled "How Farm Women Help," women wrote letters to the journal stating that they "did more field work, less housework, canned more fruits and vegetables, and took care of older people in their own homes

10 Fink, *Open Country Iowa*, 130.

11 Katherine Jellison, *Entitled to Power: Farm Women and Technology, 1913–1963* (Chapel Hill: University of North Carolina Press, 1993), especially chapter 6.

12 Eugenia Kaledin, *Mothers and More: American Women in the 1950s* (Boston: Twayne, 1984), 61; Fink, *Open Country Iowa*, 106–7.

13 Fink, *Open Country Iowa*, 106–7.

rather than having others do it. They adjusted time spent visiting and meeting in clubs so as not to interfere with farm work, and they sewed sheets and pillow cases from feed sacks."[14] Although women who stayed on the farms expanded and intensified their work as farmers during the war, this ended when the war did. Farmwomen ceased being independent producers and reverted to the role of assistant to their husbands.

In the 1950s, a preoccupation with using household equipment sparingly was gradually replaced by a consumer imperative to do the opposite. Consumerism became an exercise in citizenship through a linkage between the pursuit of individual material goals and the national economic interest.[15] The home became a major focus of spending as suburban communities sprang up, consisting of newly built houses for white families on the outskirts of cities, equipped with up-to-date household appliances and furnishings. Popular magazines, television shows, and advertisements portrayed the model family as focused on the home—raising children and spending time together around the TV or the backyard barbecue. The white, middle-class domestic idyll depended on the presence of a home-based wife and mother whose role was to control the family's operations from the kitchen—now relocated from the back of the house to a central and commanding position.[16]

This tranquil vision would seem to be at odds with the crisis atmosphere of the atomic age and the Cold War. But historians have pointed to the phenomenon of domestic containment as forming an "ideological duality" with the anticommunist hysteria of the late 1940s and early 1950s. "McCarthyism," comments Elaine Tyler May, "was fueled, in large measure, by suspicion of the new secularism, materialism, bureaucratic collectivism, and consumerism that epitomized not only the achievement but the potential 'decadence' of the New Deal liberalism."[17]

---

14 Ibid., 124–25.

15 Lizabeth Cohen, *A Consumers' Republic: The Politics of Mass Consumption in Postwar America* (New York: Vintage, 2003), 8–9.

16 Clifford E. Clark Jr., "Ranch-House Suburbia: Ideals and Realities," in *Recasting America: Culture and Politics in the Age of Cold War*, ed. Lary May (Chicago: University of Chicago Press, 1989).

17 Elaine Tyler May, *Homeward Bound: American Families in the Cold War Era* (New York: Basic Books, 1988), 10–11.

In rural America, organizations like the Farm Bureau, for instance, transmitted conservative political views and included prayers and the Pledge of Allegiance at their meetings. The 4-H program, too, introduced ceremonies designed to foster religion and patriotism.[18] In the eyes of these official and quasi-official organizations, being a proper American depended on a political orientation that stressed collective security over individual independent thought. To be patriotic also meant adhering to cultural norms that construed the nation as home. During World War II, heightened rhetoric linked women and domesticity with patriotism in specific ways. Cookbooks published during the war asserted that "food will win the war," points out Jessamyn Neuhaus, as a "combination of propaganda and marketing barraged the nation with messages about the more-important-than-ever cooking duties of women."[19] As the Cold War gathered momentum in the late 1940s and early 1950s, even stronger adherence to traditional gender roles seemed to provide stability and security against the threat of atomic annihilation.[20]

Pressures on women to conform to this gendered pattern were powerful, but even so, by mid-century they were finding ways to get off the farm. Some had learned to drive, while others depended on their husbands or older children to take them to town or church, visit a neighbor, or attend the monthly meeting of the extension-sponsored homemakers' club. These latter groups focused primarily on domestic skills and activities, and so seemed to reinforce the era's conservative domestic containment message. But at the same time, club activities recognized the double-duty nature of farmwomen's lives, with responsibilities in the fields as well as the home, and represented an effort to reduce the domestic part of this burden. Home agents drew rural women's attention to the new labor-saving devices being commercially produced for the household.[21] As farm journals increasingly featured household consumer products, some editors even suggested that domestic tech-

---

18 Fink, *Open Country Iowa*, 126.

19 Jessamyn Neuhaus, *Manly Meals and Mom's Home Cooking: Cookbooks and Gender in Modern America* (Baltimore: Johns Hopkins University Press, 2003), 117.

20 May, *Homeward Bound*, 21.

21 Ronald E. Kline, "Agents of Modernity: Home Economists and Rural Electrification, 1925–1950," in *Rethinking Home Economics: Women and the History of a Profession*, ed. Sarah Stage and Virginia B. Vincenti (Ithaca, N.Y.: Cornell University Press, 1997), 237–52.

nology might take priority over the purchase of new machinery for the farm.[22] Thus county extension agencies, farm publications, and commercial advertising joined together in urging farm families to mechanize household tasks, just as they were mechanizing other farm work. The idealized world of official printed publications and farmwomen's own educational institutions depicted the domestic lives of rural women as comparable to those of their urban and suburban counterparts, contributing to a suburbanized vision of rural life.

Homemakers' clubs continued to be a major focus of women's sociability and education during the middle decades of the twentieth century. Jane Livingston's mother had been active in the homemakers' movement in the 1930s. The home agent used to come up from Madison on the bus, and since the Livingston home was on the main road, the agent came to their farm to start the round of meetings. Activities could be wide-ranging. In the 1940s, the Freedom Township Women's Club of Palo Alto County, Iowa, participated not only in local meetings but also in programs devised by national extension service and Farm Bureau administrators. They entered statewide competitions, composed poetry, and in public performed plays that they themselves had written.[23]

Growing up in rural Wisconsin's Polk County during the 1950s, author Sara De Luca recalled that her mother belonged to only one organization apart from church: the county extension homemakers' group. The group's monthly meeting was a high spot from which De Luca's mother would return later in the evening, "all coffeed up and too excited to sleep." She was also eager to transmit her newfound knowledge. She brought home mimeographed "lessons" which she sometimes shared with her daughters, De Luca related. "Last night's lesson was all about housecleaning, using the new products to advantage," her mother would say. "You girls are all going to be keeping house some day. And I'm counting on you to help me now as much as you possibly can. You really ought to read this."[24] She proudly saved her ten-year

22 Jellison, *Entitled to Power,* 150–51.

23 Karen Smith, "Extending the Private Sphere: The Freedom Township Women's Club and Extension Service Texts, 1923–1948," unpublished MS, with permission of the author.

24 Sara De Luca, *Dancing the Cows Home: A Wisconsin Girlhood* (St. Paul: Minnesota Historical Society Press, 1996), 157.

membership award—"a framed certificate representing ten years of monthly meetings devoted to lessons in family nutrition, budget-wise shopping, emergency first aid, home nursing, bread baking, party planning, cleaning, canning, vegetable gardening, slipcovering, stain removal, and various other skills demanded by a family in the 1950s." On the back of the certificate was printed the Homemakers' Creed: "We, the Homemakers of Wisconsin, believe in the sanctity of the *home*, the cradle of character, blessed by motherly devotion and guarded by fatherly protection."[25]

Anita S., of rural Kewaunee County, was a lifelong member of a homemakers' club from the 1960s onwards. As a young mother in 1963, she joined a group called the Sunshine Club that had been founded in 1949. For women like Anita, the club provided both a welcome social experience and a unique educational opportunity. Having graduated from the Door-Kewaunee Normal School, Anita was one of the few club members with more than a high school education. All the women lived on farms in the same locality and visited each other's homes in rotation for the monthly meetings. "Some drove, and those that lived close enough together would carpool," she related. "There were three, four neighbors—we would carpool. It was a nice time to be with the neighbors and know what was going on. Just to know families." The social aspect was the most important part, Anita said, but the boundary between sociability and education was not clearly defined. "You talk social, you talk family matters, you talked and you learned from your neighbors. You learned how to take care of your kids. You learned how to do different cooking methods—short cuts. Lots of them." For Anita, it was the highlight of her life when she was asked to join the neighborhood group. "I thought I was the cat's meow. And . . . it was the best thing for me. It was my only time out."

The patriarchal world in which these women lived routinely denigrated their efforts, however. "'Mama's off to her Homewreckers meeting,'" De Luca's father joked, "the only night of the month when Mama could not be found at home."[26] Anita S., too, was familiar with the derogatory term. Although her own family supported her membership,

---

25 Ibid., 156–57.
26 Ibid., 157.

others of her acquaintance would heckle, "Oh, she's going to the Homewreckers meeting!" Even in 2002, Anita said, "I hear that a lot of times . . . You weren't home. How could you be a homemaker and not be home?" Undaunted, Anita adhered to an active philosophy of home-making that indignantly upheld its value; "It's many, many opportuni-ties—occupations. You're the nurse, the caretaker, you've got to know baby talk, you've got to know reading, you've got to know your math. You've got to balance books, read recipes. You have to read. There is no such thing as being 'just a homemaker.'"

Although some homemakers' clubs were still going strong at the end of the twentieth century, already by the end of the 1950s many home-makers were "working out," earning wages outside the home. Shifting away from an ideology that urged women to put their families first, ignoring their own needs, the monthly club lessons began to stress self-fulfillment. Late in 1959, De Luca's mother invited the rest of the fam-ily to attend the Homemakers' Musical Revue; "The star performer was Mary Jane Manson, a young, unmarried home economist, recently employed by the Polk County Extension Office. Mary Jane pranced around the stage, twirling a parasol, singing:

> Single gal, single gal,
> Around the town she flies,
> Married gal, married gal,
> Rocks and cradles and cries.
> So, if you are a single gal,
> Single you should stay.
> Don't become a married gal,
> And dream your life away."

Sixteen-year-old Sara took this advice seriously; "I'd be one of those modern types featured in the Ladies' Home Companion," she promised herself. "I could picture myself already, wearing city suits, high-heeled shoes, and little white gloves, waving at my gleaming appliances as I danced out the door."[27]

---

27 Ibid., 163–64.

Reading and Domesticity

For adults, as well as for children in both Door and Kewaunee counties, but especially for those living in the south, the Regional Library opened up reading possibilities in ways they could probably hardly imagine. Even those in the north of the Peninsula—characterized as "readers" in their own and the popular imagination—must have marveled at the choice and variety of books and periodicals that suddenly appeared in their neighborhoods at no cost to the reader. How did married women living in rural families take advantage of these new possibilities? The sample of library records that has survived provides a unique opportunity for gauging the reading interests of this elusive group—ordinary women readers whose lack of institutional affiliation and elite status made it unlikely that their letters and diaries would survive in archives. The records of their library choices help to reconstitute a picture of their reading practices.

Talking to community members who remembered rural life in the middle of the century provided an important additional dimension to the picture that emerged. The link between gender and reading is almost a cliché among print culture historians, and it was probably to be expected that among adults that it would be women who mainly checked books out of the bookmobile and rural libraries. Yet several interviewees recalled that in their own rural families of the interwar period, it was often their fathers who spent time reading for themselves—who were, in their own words, "readers." Retired schoolteacher Emily H. and former library director Jane Livingston remembered that their farmer fathers read farm magazines. It was her dad, Jane reported, who was the "real reader" of the family, as did Kathy G., the daughter of a former bookmobile driver. Anita S. remembered that after church on Sundays, her family would stop at the police station where they would pick up the Sunday paper, and her father would read the newspaper out loud to everyone. Older residents recalled that their fathers read farm newspapers—*Wisconsin Agriculturist, Hoard's Dairyman*, and *Successful Farmer.* Their mothers, on the other hand, were perceived as usually too busy with domestic and farm work to read much—women who simply lacked time. Jane Livingston recalled, though, that her mother "always read the newspaper." The rural mail carrier brought yesterday's newspaper by noon, and after dinner (a midday event) her mother "would stretch out" on the sofa. Fatigued from the chores of running a large household without indoor plumbing or electricity, Jane's mother took time "off" for her reading after preparing the day's big meal. Recognizing the significance of this practice involves understanding the circumstances of such a woman's life. Probably this was the only time she had to herself in the entire day.

It is likely that these experiences of fathers as devoted readers were unusual on the Door Peninsula. As officials anticipated and research findings predicted, women and girls predominated among the users of the Door-Kewaunee Regional Library. As already noted, among the young, boys were less likely to charge out books than girls, and this pattern only strengthened among adults. Among the surviving charge records, only seventeen men could be identified. In trying to determine which of the library patrons were men and which women, the practice, still common in the early 1950s, for adults to sign themselves Mr., Mrs., or Miss enabled me to draw inferences as to age, sex, and marital status. Fifteen readers clearly identified themselves as adult men in their signature, by the use of the title Mr. Another reader—probably a man—used the title Dr., while yet another styled himself "Rev." This group charged out thirty-four books, accounted for 5 percent of adult records, and for only 2 percent of male records. On the other hand, two hundred women who signed themselves "Mrs." made 593 charges (an average of nearly three each), while a further ten self-styled "Miss" charged out twenty-four titles. Two couples (counting for seven charges) signed themselves "Mr. and Mrs.," and four readers simply signed their initials. Another twenty-five charges were made by unnamed vacation visitors to "Schuller's Cabins," modest holiday homes owned by the Schuller family of Kewaunee County. None of these latter charges seem to have been made by children, judging from the titles selected.

Nearly all the adult male readers lived in Door County. Only two gave addresses in Kewaunee County—one of which was in the city of Algoma. The Door County residents were mainly from the north—the one man who gave a southern Door County address appeared to be a grade school teacher in the Belgian community of Brussels. Not surprisingly, six of the readers came from the city of Sturgeon Bay or its surrounding area, but another five came from Egg Harbor, and the remainder from Bailey's Harbor, Fish Creek, and Ellison Bay. By and large, this group of "northern" men conformed to local expectations about the geography of reading. Of their thirty-four charges, twenty-three (66 percent) consisted of fiction. Mr. R.M. of Sturgeon Bay displayed a preference for mystery novels—Erle Stanley Gardner, Ellery Queen, Margaret Scherf, and George Coxe. Two Egg Harbor residents, Mr. R.D. and Mr. A.B., shared a taste for westerns, including Gregory Jackson's *Powder Smoke on Wandering River*, William Raine McLeod's *Ranger's Luck*, and Peter Field's *Return to Powder Valley*. But a couple of other men charged out novels conventionally associated with women: Josephine Pinckney's *Three O' Clock Dinner* and Jan Struther's *Mrs. Miniver*, a best seller and Book-of-the-Month Club choice in 1940, and another Egg Harbor man chose two 1943 best sellers, Louis Bromfield's *Mrs. Parkington* and Marcia Davenport's *Valley of Decision*.

The remainder of this group's choices consisted mainly of biography and "how-to" books. Unsurprisingly it was the clergyman who selected Roland Bainton's *Here I Stand: A Biography of Martin Luther*. An Ellison Bay reader picked the popular *Kon-Tiki*, by Thor Heyerdahl (a Book-of-the-Month Club choice for 1950). Other nonfiction titles selected included *Log Cabins* by W. E. Swanson, Frank G. Ashbrook's *How to Raise Rabbits for Food* (chosen and renewed by the "doctor"), and Stacy Maney's *It's Fun to Make It Yourself*. The lone rural Kewaunee County male reader evidently had an interest in health and food, charging out Bertha Clark Damon's *Sense of Humus*, and J. I. Rodale's *Healthy Hunzas*. By and large, then, these men conformed to general expectations for public library readers at the time—that they preferred fiction, that men tended to pick westerns and mysteries, and that their nonfiction choices revolved around "masculine" or relatively gender-neutral topics. Although the distribution of male readers supported local theories about the geography and reading, their choices of library books refuted the belief that it was primarily women and children who were interested in fiction. Adult male readers such as these, even if they had been more numerous, would not have contributed to a reading profile of the engaged citizen that state officials were so keen to encourage as the ideal library user.

The two hundred married women borrowers, by contrast, were distributed much more evenly throughout the two counties, complicating the geography of reading.[28] Twenty of the Door County residents used the bookmobile service at its crossroad, school, or village stops. Another thirty-six patronized the small village libraries. In Kewaunee County, thirty-three women used the bookmobile. The remainder—the largest contingent—used the "city" libraries of Sturgeon Bay, Algoma, and Kewaunee. But since even the cities of the Door Peninsula were hardly major conurbations at this time (after all, the largest urban area, Sturgeon Bay, had only just over seven thousand inhabitants in the late 1940s), all the women library users could be considered "rural" by comparison with those inhabiting large industrial cities. A common feature of these towns and villages was the high level of sociability. As Anita S. put it, "That's what makes [the city of] Kewaunee a small town. You can go down the street, and go to the grocery store and get stuck there for two hours getting a gallon of milk."

Ninety-one women residents of Door County accounted for 221 charges (38 percent), while the remaining 110 residents from Kewaunee County were responsible for 364 (62 percent), and a visitor from Chicago borrowed one book (*Unrelenting*, a suspense novel by Constance W. Dodge).[29] Within Door County, residents of its northern part predominated. The most prolific readers there were Mrs. P.H. of Bailey's Harbor (sixteen charges), Mrs. R.S. of Fish Creek (ten charges), and Mrs. R.J. of Sturgeon Bay (eight charges). But southern Door communities also had their share of readers: seven lived in Brussels, two in Maplewood, and nine in Forestville. Collectively, residents of Forestville accounted for twenty-seven charges—more than any other Door County community outside Sturgeon Bay. And Kewaunee County readers from the areas in and around Luxemburg (twelve) and Casco (four), as well in the southernmost regions of Tisch Mills (two) and Denmark (six) also made use of the library in large enough numbers to suggest that the stereotype of the southern part of the Peninsula as lacking an interest in reading was an oversimplification, at least where women were con-

---

28 This distribution may be an artifact of the original intention of WFLC officials to save some circulation data from districts representing the whole Demonstration area.

29 These figures exclude the two married couples from Door County, who together charged out seven books.

cerned. Some of the heaviest library users came from these more rural southern areas. Mrs. E.H., for instance, of Pilsen Garden, charged out eighteen books in a single bookmobile visit in July 1951. Mrs. H.S., whose postal address was a rural route near the city of Kewaunee, charged out fourteen in two visits. Mrs. B.G. of Luxemburg charged out eighteen books in three visits. Mrs. J.B. of Luxemburg Village charged out twelve in two visits, another Luxemburg resident, Mrs. L.R., accounted for ten charges in two visits, and Mrs. G.P., a reader from Tisch Mills (one of the areas considered especially opposed to the library), charged out eight in two visits.

Like readers in other parts of the country (both male and female), these married women were especially interested in fiction. In 1936, Jeannette Howard Foster summarized the findings of five studies of urban reading conducted at the Graduate Library School of the University of Chicago between 1933 and 1934. According to these studies of about twenty thousand readers in the Chicago area in and outside of libraries, 60–75 percent of all reading consisted of fiction. Foster's own study found that "Housewives' interest in novels of family life is among the outstanding preferences . . . more than twice the percentage of married women read these stories," and that "all but two of the writers in the class ["Family"] are women."[30] Among the Door-Kewaunee married women readers, fiction constituted almost half (262 charges, or 46 percent) of all their charges. They particularly liked mysteries, romances, and historical novels, as well as other novels with a domestic theme, though they also charged out a number of westerns. Like their urban counterparts, these women readers liked to read books about family life, written by women. Particular favorites were Kathleen Thompson Norris and Mazo de la Roche. Norris was a prolific novelist of Irish Catholic descent who wrote stories that idealized family life and the role of women as mothers of many children. The seven Norris titles checked out consisted of *An Apple for Eve*, *Beauty's Daughter*, *Lost Sunrise*, *Over at the Crowleys'*, *The World Is Like That*, *Runaway*, and *The Venables*.

In *The Venables* (borrowed by an Ellison Bay reader who charged

---

30 Jeannette Howard Foster, "An Approach to Fiction through the Characteristics of its Readers," *Library Quarterly* 6, no. 2 (April 1936): 124, 160.

out three Norris novels on the same date), Norris interrogates the role of women in the twentieth century. Set in San Francisco in the early 1900s, the story focuses on Flo Venables, the second daughter in a large family that falls on desperately hard times when the father dies unexpectedly. Flo's mother finds herself woefully unprepared to provide for her six young children, not to mention various older hangers-on who include her brother and mother. Still, her husband's death saves her from the inevitability of bearing yet more children (in addition to the six survivors, she has lost four others as infants), a fate she dreads. Flo and her older sister Lily know nothing about sex, right up to the point of Lily's marriage at age eighteen to an older man, a wealthy and controlling lawyer whom Flo suspects of manipulating her family out of an inheritance. Flo gets a job and just barely manages to keep the family afloat. Eventually the inheritance becomes hers, and she is able to go to college. But what of marriage? Flo is not at all sure that she wants this for herself. She has seen her mother go through a succession of exhausting pregnancies and agonizing deliveries. Her sister suffers from an over-controlling husband. She herself would rather be a doctor, she maintains. Eventually, however, she succumbs to love and the book ends in anticipation of her marriage to an older professor. The possibility of a career set aside, the conservative course of action wins, and the status quo for women is reassuringly reasserted.

De la Roche wrote a series of books set in Canada about an upper-class Anglophone family—the Whiteoaks of Jalna. The sixteen "Jalna" books, which appeared between 1927 and 1960, sold over eleven million copies in English language editions. Six Door Peninsula readers checked out five Jalna titles: *Whiteoak Heritage*, *Whiteoaks of Jalna*, *Return to Jalna*, *Mary Wakefield* (twice), and *The Master of Jalna*. Built in the late nineteenth century by the English Captain Philip Whiteoak, the country house of Jalna is proving hard to keep up by the early 1930s as the Whiteoak family descends into genteel poverty. In *The Master of Jalna* (1933), their time is occupied with family romances, rivalries, scandals, and schemes for making ends meet. Despite their impecunious situation, no one does a stroke of what Door Peninsula readers would have recognized as work, except the two Cockney servants and the nursemaid. Family dynamics, always lightly expressed, occupy the entire narrative, which ends inconsequentially, requiring the reader to move on to the next novel in the saga. Farmwomen accustomed to fitting their reading into small spaces between domestic tasks must have found such a pattern of reading unfamiliar. Perhaps they were captivated by the novelty of extending their reading beyond a single title to an entire series of similar books. Perhaps they felt conflicted about the amount of time they found themselves devoting to reading. Or perhaps, like Janice A. Radway's romance readers, they felt empowered to assert their right to read in this extended manner.[31]

Other authors popular with Door Peninsula readers who wrote on domestic or romantic themes were Edna Ferber, Frances Parkinson Keyes, Faith Baldwin, Grace Livingston Hill, and Emilie Loring. Thirteen women readers chose best sellers, predominantly historical fiction. Two chose Thomas Costain's *Black Rose*, another took two weeks to read Franz Werfel's *Song of Bernadette*, while others picked Samuel Shellabarger's *Captain from Castile*, James Hilton's *Random Harvest*, and Sholem Asch's *The Nazarene* (also a Book-of-the-Month Club choice). One reader selected Ernest Hemingway's *For Whom the Bell Tolls*, another A. J. Cronin's *Green Years*, and yet another Elizabeth Goudge's *Green Dolphin Street*. Other Book-of-the-Month Club fiction consisted of Giovanni Guareschi's *Little World of Don Camillo*, John Hersey's *Wall*, and A. B. Guthrie's *Way West*.

The only nonfiction best sellers selected were Betty MacDonald's *The Egg and I* and Ernie Pyle's *Brave Men* (also a Book-of-the-Month Club selection). As a group, the married women charged out 104 books of nonfiction—a higher proportion than that of the group of men readers. Autobiographies and biographies were popular, including *Cheaper by the Dozen*, Frank B. Gilbreth Jr. and Ernestine Gilbreth Carey's story of their engineer parents' large family. Less domestically oriented choices were biographies of Willa Cather, the Marx brothers, and German Field Marshal Ernst Rommel. But two-thirds of the women's nonfiction choices consisted of "how to" books that provided instruction on cooking, sewing, gardening, and crafts like making curtains and drapes and even marionettes. Best-selling cookbooks like Fannie Farmer's *Boston Cooking School Cook Book* were represented, as was *Betty*

---

31 Janice A. Radway, *Reading the Romance: Women, Patriarchy, and Popular Literature* (Chapel Hill: University of North Carolina Press, 1991). See especially 86–118.

Crocker's Picture Cook Book. First published in 1950, the General Mills publication broke records in the first year of its sale, beating other best-sellers like *Kon-Tiki*, and David Riesman's *Lonely Crowd*. By 1951 it had gone through seven printings and sold over two million copies.[32] Readers also chose cookbooks with a regional flavor; one Kewaunee County reader chose Michigan author Della Lutes's *Home Grown* while two others (one from the city of Kewaunee, the other from the southern Door community of Forestville) picked *The Best from Midwest Kitchens*. Two Kewaunee City readers revealed an interest in new household technologies when they picked a book on home freezing.

Books about raising children, marriage, and family were as popular as books about cooking. Two Fish Creek readers chose *Your Baby: The Complete Baby Book for Mothers and Fathers*, a title that suggests that parents should share a more equal role in child-rearing than was common at that time and in that place. Mrs B. of Algoma checked out a number of family-oriented titles, including *Growing Together, It Runs in the Family, Understanding Your Boy, Keeping Your Child Normal*, and *Life with Family, a Perspective on Parenthood*. Mrs. B.'s preoccupation with parenting and family books reflected an application of expert study and recommendations to what in previous eras had been largely a matter of private, individual choice based on class, religion or ethnic tradition.[33]

Periodicals were a frequent choice for the married women who had access to the permanent unit libraries (the bookmobiles did not carry magazines, for lack of space). The periodicals themselves provided short versions of the preferred kinds of reading revealed in the women's library charges. Three women chose *National Geographic*, and another *Popular Mechanics*, but it was the nationally distributed mass-market women's magazines that predominated. *Ladies Home Journal, Good Housekeeping* ("The Magazine America Lives By"), and *House and Garden* (six charges each) were the most frequently selected, while *McCall's, Women's Home Companion, Better Homes and Gardens*, and *Story Parade* were also represented. The women's magazines consisted of a

---

32 Karal Ann Marling, *"Betty Crocker's Picture Cook Book*: The Aesthetics of American Food in the 1950s," in *Prospects: An Annual of American Culture Studies*, vol. 17, ed. Jack Salzman (New York: Cambridge University Press, 1992), 79; Neuhaus, *Manly Meals*, 170–71.

33 May, *Homeward Bound*, 26.

standard repertoire of feature articles, short stories, and serialized fiction, interspersed with heavy doses of advertisements, particularly for household goods.

Along with an emphasis on the family as central to the life of white American women, the magazines attempted to foster the habit of reading (in their own interest, after all) and promoted the reading of domestic novels. The November 1950 issue of *Good Housekeeping* (charged out by two Kewaunee readers) began to serialize Frances Parkinson Keyes's *Joy Street*, the story of an affluent Boston bride who, though Protestant herself, becomes friendly with a large family of Irish-origin Catholics in which the mother is a model of domestic fulfillment. Keyes, a convert to Catholicism, like other authors favored by Door-Kewaunee readers wrote stories about white, upper-class family life. She described her own learning to write as rooted in her domestic surroundings: "I learned to write standing beside my grandmother—the first Frances Parkinson—before I could even read, when she taught me chapters and chapters of the Bible by heart . . . I learned to write from my eldest son, when woefully unprepared, I began to teach him myself because there was no one else at hand to do it for me. I learned from working in the village library, and acting in the village dramatic club, and sewing in the village church guild. In short, I learned as anyone can learn who wishes to—from the persons with whom I was thrown and the surroundings in which I lived."[34] Any woman could write as she herself did, Keyes implied, by drawing on the common experiences of what she suggested was an unremarkable American existence.

The same November 1950 issue of *Good Housekeeping* highlighted the benefits of reading in contrast to the dangers of television, especially for children. "Against the positive benefits of television—the widening of horizons, the many new friends, the sheer entertainment, the sugar-coated educational pills—are arrayed formidable evils," wrote Bianca Bradbury in an article titled "Is Television Mama's Friend or Foe?"[35] "A book has to overcome too much sheer inertia, and rare is the child who will tear himself away from the screen to go off by himself and

34 Quoted in *Good Housekeeping* 131, no. 5 (November 1950): 15.
35 Bianca Bradbury, "Is Television Mama's Friend or Foe?" *Good Housekeeping* 131, no. 5 (1950): 58, 263.

read one. I think that the beautifully illustrated, brightly colored juveniles that flood the market today will have a hard time competing."[36] In 1950, television had yet to appear on the Door Peninsula, but even so, women of the two counties must have been fascinated to read about its perils as well as its attractions. The magazines often advertised books, including books for children, and even published children's books themselves. *The Better Homes and Gardens Story Book*, for instance, advertised its contents as "'Little Black Sambo,' 'Old Mother Hubbard,' 'Brer Rabbit,' 'Peter Pan in Never-Never-Land'—50 carefully selected stories and poems you knew as a child which will start *your* children on the road to literature," all for under three dollars.

For adults, the November 1950 issue of *House and Garden* (also charged out by Kewaunee City readers) listed "Reference Books for the Home" as consisting of *The Complete Book of Flower Arrangement, All About House Plants, Wild Flowers at a Glance, Emily Post's Etiquette, Bartlett's Familiar Quotations, Rand McNally Cosmopolitan World Atlas, Roget's Thesaurus, Complete Stories of the Great Operas,* and *Webster's Dictionary.* No doubt with an eye on the Christmas market, the magazine also reviewed books for adults as well as for children. Most of these fitted the same middlebrow profile as the Door-Kewaunee readers' public library choices. "New Books for Pleasure and Information," listed, among others, *Belles on Their Toes* by Frank B. Gilbreth Jr. and Ernestine Gilbreth Carey (advertised as "Further adventures of the Cheaper by the Dozen family"), A. J. Cronin's *The Spanish Garden* ("A compassionate novel about a vain, possessive father and his neurasthenic son"), Joyce Cary's *A Fearful Joy* ("A bizarrely humorous novel about Mr. Cary's newest fictional English heroine"), and *The Adventurer* by Mika Waltari ("A full-blown historical novel by the author of The Egyptian, set in sixteenth-century Europe"). But it also included *Reprisal* by Arthur Gordon—"A swiftly paced novel about negro vengeance in a southern town, expertly told in taut, steely prose," and *Courtroom,* by Quentin Reynolds: "A behind-the-scenes introduction to Samuel S. Leibowitz, the great criminal lawyer and judge, brilliant defender of the Scottsboro boys."[37]

---

36 Ibid., 64.
37 *House and Garden* (November 1950): 217.

But for the inclusion of these last two books (both by white authors), one would never guess from the magazine selections that the 1940s and 1950s were a period of heightened racial tension in America, or that the United States was inhabited by anyone who was not white and middle-class. Readers interested in what was then termed "race relations" would have found little help in selecting books to review from the pages of these mass-market magazines. But if the magazines' ethnic and racial presumptions matched those of the Door-Kewaunee readers themselves, they also presumed a level of readerly affluence that the Wisconsin women must have found jarring. From the ubiquitous advertisements for twelve-place settings of sterling silver to articles on kitchen remodeling, the magazines presented affluent cities and suburbs as the national norm. They also featured the domestic arrangements of the rich and famous. "You have to work in a kitchen to evaluate just how well it operates," suggested a *House and Garden* article in November 1950. "So when Mr. and Mrs. Adam Gimbel decided to remodel the one in their New York brownstone, they turned the job over to their cook, Catherine Barbas. Her first concern was to allot the work space so that she and her husband George, who is the Gimbels' butler, should have their own spheres of action, intercommunicating but not overlapping."[38]

Door Peninsula newspapers also carried some advertising of consumer products for the home, but for most rural residents these must have seemed hopelessly out of reach, with the price of even a cheaper bedroom suite promoted in the local paper at about half the average monthly wage. Most Door Peninsula families lived in traditional homes unlike the ranch-style houses that dominated the new housing developments springing up around the nation's large cities. And few rural women had managed to escape from an endless round of kitchen and farm chores even during the war years. Yet, despite their focus on domestic concerns, far from reinforcing traditional gender roles, the women's library choices had the potential to open up new worlds, just as cultural authorities believed, though not necessarily in the way that they intended. Nancy A. Walker argues that between 1940 and 1960,

---

38 Ibid., 234.

women's magazines transmitted a "multivocal" rather than a unitary concept of domesticity, often celebrating the ideology of woman as homemaker, but at other times subverting it.[39] Magazines promoted a broad understanding of domestic activity, in common with general cultural understandings that included not only food preparation and housekeeping, but also home-related concerns and activities like child-rearing, family health, and gardening, and also individual and community matters, such as personal appearance and civic engagement.[40]

Instead of choosing to educate themselves in conventional ways as citizens by reading books on current affairs, the women borrowers opted for fiction, instruction manuals, and popular magazines that connected them to the middle-class domestic consumerism preoccupying dwellers of suburbia. But rather than induce a mindless conformity to corporate-generated values, these women's reading experiences may have represented multiple small acts of resistance. For the Door-Kewaunee women, carving out part of the day for the personal pleasure of reading a novel may have constituted a departure from the prescribed domestic ideal.[41] In the patriarchal families that still constituted the norm on the rural Door Peninsula, finding time for emotional "replenishment" must have been a rarity. As Jessamyn Neuhaus points out, paradoxically, the very act of reading domestic instruction manuals prompts a reappraisal of accepted gender roles. By "stating assumptions about women's lives," cookbooks, gardening and sewing books "left room for those 'assumptions' to be questioned." The manuals and magazines introduced women to new ways of homemaking, ways that differed from the practices of their mothers and grandmothers, and that opened up space for the exercise of individual taste and difference.[42]

As part of their role as guardians of culture and of child-rearing, it was mainly Door Peninsula mothers who took responsibility for encouraging the children to read. Former rural school teacher Emily H.'s

---

39 Nancy A. Walker, *Shaping Our Mothers' World: American Women's Magazines* (Jackson: University Press of Mississippi, 2000), ix.

40 Ibid., viii.

41 Radway, *Reading the Romance*, 61–62.

42 Jessamyn Neuhaus, "The Way to a Man's Heart: Gender Roles, Domestic Ideology, and Cookbooks in the 1950s," *Journal of Social History* 32, no. 3, (1999): 529–55.

mother (herself a former teacher) encouraged Emily to read, and drove her to Sturgeon Bay to check out books from the public library. "Oh I loved to read," Emily recalled, "but I remember when I read *Uncle Tom's Cabin* . . . I cried and my mother noticed the tears. She said, 'Emily you put that book down right now! You're reading too long—your eyes are watering,' and I was too embarrassed to tell her that I was crying." Conforming to a tradition of supervising their offspring's literary encounters, this group of women library patrons also charged out materials for their young children. About 30 percent of their charges consisted of children's stories and readers. Evidently mothers wished to pass on to children their own love of reading as a recreational activity. Perhaps, too, they enjoyed reading stories aloud to their younger children, and even peeked into the books that older children brought home from school. Particularly favored by these mothers were books by Swedish author Maj Lindman (nine charges). No other author came close in popularity to Lindman's tales of boys Snipp, Snapp, and Snurr and girls Flicka, Ricka, and Dicka. Among the nineteen charges of children's nonfiction that women made were books about animals, with titles like *Puddle: The Real Story of a Little Hippo*, *Birds in Your Backyard*, and *Insect World*.

Mrs. B.G.—perhaps a schoolteacher in Kewaunee County—charged out *Food or Famine, the Challenge of Erosion*, *It Happened Here: Stories of Wisconsin*, and *The Junior Party Book*. Like the women's choices of nonfiction for themselves, biographies (written for children)—of Davy Crockett and Florence Nightingale—also featured in this list. However Mrs. B.G.—a prolific reader responsible for eighteen charges—also seemed to pick books for her own interests. Apparently a keen gardener, she selected four gardening titles, *Garden Flowers in Color*, *Plant Disease Handbook*, *Weekend Gardener*, and *Grow Your Own Vegetables*. She also chose two books about home decorating: *How to Beautify and Improve Your Home*, and *How to Make Curtains and Drapes*. She was one of a very few readers to choose a book with a Wisconsin theme: Thurine Oleson's *Wisconsin, My Home*, and in picking Julia Weber's *My Country School Diary: An Adventure in Creative Teaching*, she was perhaps reflecting on her own professional practices. However, she also chose novels, presumably for her own relaxation: Shirley Seifert's *Turquoise Trail*, Nelia White's *Pink House*, Noel Streatfeild's *Mothering Sunday*, Samuel Rogers's

Dusk at the Grove, and Elswyth Thane's *Light Heart*. Some other married women who charged out several books made eclectic choices that seemed to reflect their role as selector of reading materials for the whole family. Three charges of novels by Kathleen Norris, for instance, were made by Mrs W. from a rural route near Ellison Bay; she also checked out Elizabeth Seifert's romance *A Certain Dr. French*, Maj Lindman's *Flicka, Ricka, Dicka and the Strawberries*, plus two books of nonfiction: *Concrete Block Houses* and *How to Get the Most House for Your Money*. To be successful in meeting a variety of readers' demands, such selections must have required some careful advance planning as well as a degree of concentration and organization when faced with the actual shelves of the bookmobile and the relatively short time span in which to make the final choices.

For rural residents of the Door Peninsula, for the first time the Regional Library provided all adults with free access to books. But it was mainly women who took advantage of the expanded library services. Unlike Jane Livingston's mother, who could carve out only enough time in the day to read the newspaper as she rested on the sofa, or Ben Logan's mother, who had to combine reading and sewing, these women apparently found more opportunities to engage with books. Few chose to borrow poetry or other works "with a lot of thinking between the sentences." Rather, women library patrons found themselves able to read extensively—not only books of fiction, including mysteries, historical novels, and stories about families, but also books of direct relevance to their own lives, centered as these were on home and the family. Books and magazine articles about cooking, home decorating, health, and childcare provided them with ideas and information about how to carry out their traditional roles in nontraditional ways. The library did not simply filter information and stories down to its patrons. Readers checked out a variety of reading materials among which "stories" predominated, and although these failed to conform to the library leaders' hopes that library use would be a sign of involved citizenship, nevertheless in many other ways the library was indeed a site of citizen action as readers engaged with social and political processes not only during the Demonstration itself but in the following decades.

The stories of reading that emerged from women's experiences with the Door-Kewaunee Demonstration suggest that readers, far from being passive and powerless recipients of decision processes in which they played no part, had a profound influence on the ways in which the organization operated and the extent of its services. Through protest and political activism in Door County, a popular bookmobile service was extended for thirty years. Women's and homemakers' clubs played a direct role in the establishment of branch libraries, from organizing support and fund-raising to soliciting donations of books and furniture, mending books, and painting walls. Local employees with no previous library training—not just "professional" librarians and state officials—collaborated with readers of all ages and ethnic backgrounds to shape library collections in ways that fulfilled readers' own desires.

8
Winners and Losers: The Referendum and Its Aftermath

Those of you who have been here for the "duration" know something of the trials and tribulations, the unforeseen crises, and the element of real tragedy which have gone into this program. Regardless of what happens in November, we know that it has been good—we know that it has been successful even though the many elements constituting that success cannot be measured in dollars and cents.

Anne Farrington, The Idea in Action

How am I going to do this? You know, you don't just go start a library by yourself.

Gayle G. (interview)

True to its determination to make the project a democratically based joint venture between the state and the local residents, the plan for the Regional Library Demonstration provided for voter feedback in the form of a referendum in the fall of 1952. Voters were asked to consider the question, "Shall Kewaunee [or Door] County continue to participate in the Door-Kewaunee Regional library or some similar library?"[1] Although the results would be nonbinding, county supervisors were widely expected to base their decision about the library's future on the referendum as a statement of the people's will. Both before and after the referendum citizens debated their decision, articulating a variety of views about the value of books and reading. Results were different in each county, affecting the distribution of reading materials for decades to come. The project also had an influence beyond the Door Peninsula,

---

1 *Algoma Record-Herald*, 30 October 1952.

in shaping legislation that would radically change the funding structures for public libraries in Wisconsin. In so doing, Wisconsin's libraries joined a movement that was under way across the United States.

Citizen Participation: The Referendum

Recognizing the need to win over potentially reluctant voters and legislators, the WFLC used pamphlets, spots on local radio stations, and articles in newspapers and the state library literature to mount a sustained publicity campaign. The WFLC also sent out an evaluative questionnaire to gauge the reactions of local library boards. Replies seemed positive. A library board member wrote from Washington Island, "I am 100 percent in favor of the regional plan. Prior to it, the library service was extremely limited. We were only able to have our library open one day a week, and during January-February found it necessary to close completely." By contrast, under the regional system, the library could be open three afternoons and evenings the year around.[2]

As the date for the referendum drew near, local newspapers lent their support. Arguing that voting for the library made fiscal sense, library staff wrote articles that spelled out the financial calculations: "An 80 acre farm valued at $8,625 . . . paid $3.66 in taxes. With five individuals in the average family it meant a charge of 73¢ per individual. Considering that a school age child used 27 books and each adult used 2 books, that would mean that 58 books were used per family. Dividing $3.66 by 58 meant that each book cost the family about 6.3 cents. The total value of the books used was $20.00."[3] Newspaper editors were careful not to sound too directive. "We have never felt that it is our job to tell you how to vote," wrote the editors of the *Kewaunee Enterprise*. "It is our job to give you the facts, as clearly and unbiased as we are able to do so, and then it is YOUR job to sift them and determine for yourself what you feel is the right vote for you." However, it was

2 *The Idea in Action: A Report on the Door-Kewaunee Regional Library Demonstration, 1950–1952* (Madison: Wisconsin Free Library Commission, 1953), 19–20.

3 *Luxemburg News*, 30 October 1952.

clear where the newspaper's sympathies lay. "To us, books have always been an important part of living. We would not care to live in a home without books or magazines, or in a town without a library. And we would like to see every child have a book whenever he shows a desire to read one—it is his contact with our country's past, all the wonderful people who have made our country great come to us only through books."[4]

Algoma Record-Herald editors appealed to their readers' civic duty, as well as to their sense of good financial management. "Each of us as intelligent, progressive citizens should look at the proposal from the standpoint of costs . . . and also on the other side of the ledger—just what is the Regional library giving us in return for our hard-earned tax dollars—it's as simple a business proposition as that."[5] On the other hand, some benefits were beyond price; "Consider what good your children of school age, to say nothing of adults, are getting from the bookmobile service. Can it be measured entirely in cold dollars? . . . We think that you should vote 'yes' on this question . . . and we make no bones about it." Local teachers paid for a signed advertisement calling for continuation of the library.[6] The Algoma Woman's Club also voiced its approval of the demonstration in the newspapers, claiming that the Algoma library under the regional plan had "gained everything and lost nothing."[7]

Library opponents used many of the same publicity strategies. "One of the main reasons our Grand Parents came to a 'Land of the Free' is to get away from Gravey [*sic*] Taxes," wrote Clarence Antholt and Gordon Mallien, residents of the Belgian-dominated community of Brussels, in a paid newspaper advertisement. "A 'yes' vote on the Bookmobile issue means favoring the hardships they left." Spelling out the calculations could work against the library, too. "We're already paying heavy school taxes for the information these books are suppose to contain," argued Antholt and Mallien. "During the summer months the Bookmobile makes its regular stops even though its services are not

---

4 *Kewaunee Enterprise*, 30 October 1952.
5 *Algoma Record-Herald*, 9 October 1952.
6 *Luxemburg News*, 18 September 1952.
7 *Algoma Record-Herald*, 9 October 1952.

used to their full extent . . . If every school district spends one half of its bookmobile costs or less in books in a short time we would have all the books necessary to enrich the teaching programs and for the personal use of the people of the district." Disregarding—or perhaps ignorant of—the dollar price of authorship and publishing, the two men argued, "A ton of good paper today sells for $225.00 a ton. Print it into books and loan it to Door County youngsters at $30,000 a year. If that isn't Gravy Taxes what is it?"[8] In Montpelier, Supervisor Nejedlo found it easy to drum up opposition, now that state funding was about to be withdrawn. "It was a year when . . . they were having a hard time balancing the budget," former district attorney George Miller remembered, "so he was able to get a lot of people lined up to turn them down." These opponents found support in official Republican Party campaign literature that called for fiscal stringency. "GREATEST DISAPPEARING ACT ON EARTH" screamed an advertisement in which a cartoon donkey waved a banner of WASTE over a sack of YOUR HARD-EARNED TAX MONEY. "NOW YOU SEE IT AND NOW YOU DON'T!"[9]

Opposition had reached such a pitch that in the heated pre-election atmosphere, some residents took action to thwart the library directly. But although it seemed that some Kewaunee County residents saw sabotaging the bookmobile as a powerful way to express their outrage at the library, others were articulate supporters in print. "Where else can one obtain so much for so little?" wondered a rural Kewaunee County reader in a letter to the *Wisconsin Library Bulletin*. "Children's books—so many, so interesting—adult books—romance, adventure, mystery—fiction of all kinds; cook books, books of manual arts, science, biography—name it and you can have it . . . Perhaps one reason I am so enthusiastic over the Bookmobile service is because books are so expensive. Very few of us can buy all the books we want to read, and there are so very many books to which one only wants to refer."[10] Supporters gained small victories that not only made them feel good at the time but held vivid memories fifty years later. Virginia J. recalled with pride

---

8 *Sturgeon Bay Advocate*, 30 October 1952.

9 *Luxemburg News*, 16 October 1952.

10 Mrs. John Marnard, "From a Bookmobile Patron," *Wisconsin Library Bulletin* 47, no. 2 (1951): 45.

accompanying her mother, former rural schoolteacher Clarice F., to a community meeting to discuss the library. "One man said that his father never had a bookmobile," she recounted, "so he didn't need one either." To this Clarice had a quick reply. "Your father didn't have a car either," she retorted, "but that didn't stop you getting one."

Although library staff worked hard to overcome opposition, they had a premonition that things were not going well, especially in Kewaunee County. "We just didn't have enough friends in Kewaunee County," recalled Shirley J. "We didn't convert enough people. That was . . . a very bad fall for all of us. We spent a lot of evenings running around Door and Kewaunee Counties giving talks that fall of '52. And it didn't work." Former district attorney George Miller felt that, despite the moralistic rhetoric and the appeal to conservative values, the underlying problem was an unwillingness to pay taxes. "As the opposition started to build up," he commented, "then they were going to be turning in the state share of it, then they had the more solid argument, because it was going to have to be put in the budget then."

On November 4, 1952, the nation went to the polls. The big question confronting voters was the presidential race. Who would be the new president to replace Harry S. Truman: Republican Dwight D. Eisenhower or Democrat Adlai Stevenson? In Door and Kewaunee counties, the result surprised no one when 81 percent of Door County and 77 percent of Kewaunee County electors voted for Eisenhower. Senator Joseph McCarthy also received strong endorsement in both counties.[11] "A whopping all-time record-breaking vote was recorded Tuesday as Kewaunee county joined the Republican parade . . . The county voted Republican right down the line," proclaimed the *Algoma Record-Herald* two days later.[12] But despite a virtually foregone conclusion that the two counties would support the Republican Party, the Regional Library issue was far from predictable. On the evening of the 4th, as the ballots were being tallied, library staff and supporters anx-

---

11 In Door County, McCarthy received 7,513 votes as opposed to 1,902 votes received by his opponent, Democrat Thomas R. Fairchild. In Kewaunee, the vote was 6,412 to 1,941. See James R. Donoghue, *How Wisconsin Voted, 1848–1960* (Madison.: Bureau of Government, University Extension Division, University of Wisconsin, 1962), 97, 57.

12 *Algoma Record-Herald*, 6 November 1952.

iously awaited the referendum's outcome. Despite the Republican clean sweep, it was possible that the referendum result might still bring good news to library supporters.

Indeed, in the final result, Door County voters voted in favor, contributing to an overall majority in both counties of 910. However, for the Regional Library to continue, the referendum needed a majority in each county. As the evening wore on and votes were tallied, it became obvious to the library staff that their pessimism was justified. "When it went the wrong way, I don't think it was unexpected," remembered Jane Livingston. "The night they were counting the votes I was sitting on the telephone. Andy the bookmobile driver, he was from Kewaunee, he was down there in the courthouse, and every once in a while you'd get a call from Andy, and it wasn't good. It meant that Andy was going to lose his job." The following day the newspapers reported the results. "Only three Kewaunee county units favored the library—Algoma, Casco village and Luxemburg village," the *Algoma Record-Herald* told its readers. "Each of the ten towns gave it a resounding slap in the face and Kewaunee City rejected it 652 to 653—just one vote difference."[13] Indeed, the majority of negative votes were cast in rural areas—the very areas served by the bookmobiles. In Montpelier the library had its poorest showing, with 505 votes cast against, and only 64 (11 percent) in favor. In Door County, too, the referendum followed the geography of reading. The southern communities of Brussels, Clay Banks, Forestville, Gardner, and Nasewaupee all rejected the library. Only Union and the township of Sturgeon Bay voted to keep it. From the city of Sturgeon Bay north, majorities all favored the library. Farthest north, the most ringing endorsement came from Washington Island, where 330 voted "yes" and 85 (just over one-fifth) voted to turn it down.[14]

Their fears realized, the Commission staff tried to find solace in a rise in circulation figures that indicated, they argued, overall success for the Demonstration. But they perceived as a persistent problem that the project's main users consisted of rural children—individuals who could not themselves vote, and whose parents lacked resources to counter the orga-

---

13 Ibid.

14 "Referendum Vote on Door-Kewaunee Regional Library," typescript, 4 November 1952, Community File, Series 1976 WHS Archives.

nized opposition. "I'm sure that parents were voting. Parents in Kewaunee County," said Livingston. "The people who had children in school were really supporting it." In Montpelier and other southern Kewaunee townships, however, library supporters found themselves heavily outvoted. Even in Door County, not all the townships voted for the library, as community pressures came into play. Recalled a former librarian, "One particular parochial school that we served—that community did not go for the bookmobile. The priest didn't like us. It was a Catholic school—I suppose it was probably mostly Belgians." The priest's opposition was a matter of principle, rather than arising from personal experience, she went on. "He never set foot on the bookmobile. I never saw him when we stopped at the school. But it was very clear to everybody that he preached about it that he did not want the library to continue."

Library supporters were also up against some formidable political opposition as anticommunist rhetoric and the Korean War dominated the national agenda. In an open letter to the Kewaunee County supervisors, a Kewaunee resident wrote in the *Algoma Record-Herald*; "I heartily agree with the stand you have taken in voting negatively on the Door-Kewaunee Regional Library. Why? Because the cost of it was born by so many people and the benefits realized by so few." To this voter, the need to respond to the threat of international Communism took precedence over domestic calls on the public purse. "The past decade did not . . . in view of the present and future world conditions, warrant such an enormous cash outlay . . . Due to the instability of international relationships we may be called upon to defend our freedoms more vigorously than ever before, against an indomitable foe." For the time being, this voter felt, the priority for national military spending far outweighed local initiatives. "If we fail, all our Bookmobiles and our entire educational system may be of little consequence. If God will that we survive this crisis . . . then, and only then we shall return to Traveling Libraries and improvements in our educational program. If we are called upon to reimburse a military commensurate with an all out war effort, the tax burden will be great enough without also having to pay for a bookmobile service."[15]

---

15 Open letter dated 19 March 1953 to Mr. Ray P. Fulwiler, Supervisor, Fourth Ward, Algoma, Wis., from Frank Wessely, *Algoma Record-Herald*, 30 March 1953.

Republican rhetoric that called for reductions in government social spending probably also played a part. And yet simple party politics cannot be held responsible for the final referendum result. In the general election, a higher percentage of Door County residents voted Republican than of Kewaunee County, and those living in the north shared many of the same politically conservative beliefs as those living further south. Despite the national Republican Party's record of opposition to government funding for libraries, librarians were convinced that it was cultural and ethnic differences that were principally responsible for the project's failure. The voting disparity reflected, they felt, an ethnically based geography of reading that made southern residents less open to new ideas. "All those ideas in children's heads. Afraid of ideas," said Shirley J. "And that's not uncommon. It was more common then." Outside influences were severely curtailed by lack of access to print. "There were many, *many* children in Kewaunee County who took no daily paper, no books, no magazines . . . It was not unusual in rural Wisconsin at that time," she went on. "In Door County because there was a mix of outsiders who had moved in, that had a little different background, but there were a lot of homesteads that still today don't have a daily paper."

Had they been asked, the children might have judged the project differently from the adult voters. In December 1952, as the Kewaunee bookmobile made its final rounds, there were "a lot of tears among the children because it was the last time the bookmobile was coming," Shirley J. reminisced. "There were teachers who were in tears the last couple of rounds of the bookmobile because . . . this was the first time they had been able to get materials that supported the textbooks." As children and even teachers wept, mothers expressed distress at this loss to their offspring, and even anger at those who had voted against the service. "Mothers—some mothers I remember talking to Andy and to me about how disappointed they were because this was an opportunity for their children that they had not had," said Shirley. "And they were unhappy with the neighbors who voted against, and because that's the way it works they had to accept it." Some Door County parents, by contrast, were relieved at their own county's positive response. "I remember my parents talking about that . . . that they were glad that the bookmobile was not going to be discontinued, because we loved it,"

said former school student Eileen R. Among library supporters, resentment at those who had fought and won against the Regional Library
lingered for decades. They were seen as an old guard, hindering progress. In the years that followed, Livingston admitted, "I'd watch the
obituary columns in that area, and I'd think, 'Well, another one has
gone down. Eventually we'll get rid of them,' which is an awful way to
feel." Over time, though, a feeling of accomplishment overlaid bitter-
ness. "I think we started something . . . the fact that in much of the area
there's been a movement in the last few years towards establishing a
library is maybe a seed that we planted long ago."

In accordance with their belief in the importance of information as
providing the basis for informed citizenship, the library staff together
with state officials and local newspapers had worked hard to produce
statistical and other forms of evidence that would buttress a rational
decision on the part of voters to continue the project. In the final vote,
however, the appeal to economic rationality failed in face of cultural
forces that saw reading as a waste of time and money, and even as
potentially dangerous. Ethnic and religious variation played a part in
this outcome; it was the descendants of immigrants from Eastern
Europe as well as the mostly Catholic Belgians who mounted the
staunchest opposition to the library and prevented its continuation as a
regional organization. These citizens made astute use of democratic
institutions that included the local press and government to coalesce
and mount an ultimately successful challenge to what they saw as an
unwarranted interference in their communities and an unjustified call
on their resources. Gender and age, too, played a major role. As circulation statistics revealed, state officials' fears that the library project
would be dominated by children had come true. Thus the library service that enjoyed the lowest status (and was dominated by women)
actually absorbed the bulk of the public resources. On the other hand,
men—more influential in the political system that would decide the
library's future—failed to make substantial use of the library either for
purposes of civic engagement (as desired by state officials) or for cultural uplift and recreation. In the patriarchal world of the rural Door
Peninsula, this failure had devastating results for the library.

Rolling On: The Door County Bookmobile

Over the decades that followed Door County's approval of the library, the bookmobile became a regular feature of country life in the northern part of the Peninsula. For a while, Eileen R. and her husband moved to Sturgeon Bay, where they and their children enjoyed the services of the city library. "There was a big—I don't know if it was a oak or a maple—tree . . . and a librarian would meet there with the kids and they'd sit under the tree with the kids and read books in the summertime. Our kids loved it. They just couldn't wait for that day." But then in 1965, they moved back out into the country near Jacksonport. There, she said, "the bookmobile came out in the summertime . . . We would come home with armfuls of books . . . Whatever you wanted to take you could take—there was no limit on the number of books that you could take." The bookmobile's visit was a social event. "They met their friends, and we met our friends down there, because in the country you didn't see your friends like you do nowadays . . . yeah, it was a social gathering." Still, visits to the library entailed some surveillance responsibility. "I know that we would come home with lots of books, and I was always nervous. Oh gosh, we've got to hang on to these books and know who's got what book so they can get back to the bookmobile."

Door County women like Eileen R. appreciated the bookmobile for its value to their children, and also for themselves. On the other hand, after 1952, Kewaunee County women experienced a retraction of reading opportunities. The Kewaunee bookmobile librarian took a temporary job at the county headquarters before leaving the district for a post elsewhere in Wisconsin.[16] Librarians from Algoma and Kewaunee continued their interactions with those at the former headquarters on an informal basis, but the formal cooperative arrangements that expanded collections and services as well as saving labor on technical processing were over. The rural schoolteachers went back to their old teaching routines, at least until consolidation finally reached the Door Peninsula and the rural schools closed.

---

16 Interview with Shirley J., Sturgeon Bay, 14 March 2001.

Before the Demonstration, the Sturgeon Bay Public Library had charged a modest fee of fifty cents to rural users, but library use in Algoma and Kewaunee had been free. In the weeks before the referendum, perhaps in an effort to persuade rural areas to finance the library, the three city governments threatened to introduce or raise fees for rural residents' use of the city libraries. "If the Regional Library Service is discontinued, the cities of Algoma, Kewaunee and Sturgeon Bay will continue to operate city libraries," announced the three mayors in local newspapers. "But in fairness to the local taxpayers supporting those libraries, it may be necessary to ask non-resident users to pay a share of the cost of the service."[17] When the Regional Library failed in Kewaunee County, the two Kewaunee County cities moved to make good on their threats, to the dismay of some rural residents. Noted the *Algoma Record-Herald* in January 1953, "The Algoma Public Library set up a fee system for non-residents after Kewaunee County withdrew from the Regional library leaving the city on its own. It was decided to require $3 rural fee cards by non-residents who wish to use the facilities of the Algoma Public Library. Similar action was taken by the Kewaunee Public Library." An exception was made for high school students from rural areas who attended the city school, many of whom lived in the school dormitory and were considered residents.[18]

Three dollars in 1953 was a not insignificant sum, and far from a token amount. Perhaps library supporters derived some grim satisfaction from the protests that resulted. "The question that this action brings to mind is what is the purpose of such actions?" wrote one outraged "Rural Neighbor." "Is it to be discriminatory between the rural and city folks? Is it to cause the Librarian more work? Is it to increase the funds of the city library or city treasury? Is it intended to be a slap in the face for those who formerly used the Bookmobile and now are denied its use? . . . If any reasons for the above seem valid, would it seem just to deny the right to city dwellers to come to the rural areas to enjoy the privileges of private lands of hunting, fishing, picking flowers, field trips by school children and gathering wild fruit, or any other

---

17 *Kewaunee Enterprise*, 20 October 1952.

18 *Algoma Record-Herald*, 22 January 1953.

reason to pay a 'nominal use sum.'"[19] Despite the outcry, however, over subsequent decades efforts to start a library in one of the larger Kewaunee County villages repeatedly failed.

In Door County the county system flourished, although the nature of the bookmobile service changed. Employing both a librarian and a driver seemed a luxury the community could not afford, and since the (male) driver already carried out the clerical functions of checking books in and out, dispensing with the (female) librarian as readers' adviser seemed to be the logical next step. That the librarian might have been prepared to drive the van seems not to have been taken into consideration. Carrying out the job of driver-cum-librarian provided the drivers with new opportunities. Kathy G. related that her father, Ralph Arnold, drove the Door County van during the 1950s and 1960s. Ralph, a shy, retiring person who possessed a chemistry degree and at one time worked for Dow Chemical, joined the Door County Library as bookmobile driver in 1953. He heard about the job through his wife, Helen, who had already started to work part-time in the library by 1950. Helen liked the flexible hours, working with people—especially children—and working with books. Helen was a prolific writer—her hobby was writing to congressmen, Kathy recollected with a laugh. After she retired she took writing classes and joined the League of Women Voters. Ralph and Helen both enjoyed reading, and passed on their enthusiasm for books to their three children. Helen liked reading self-help literature and books about politics. Ralph was fond of mysteries, a taste he shared with Kathy. Both he and Helen subscribed to a number of periodicals. Along with the local newspapers, the *Sturgeon Bay Advocate* and the *Green Bay Gazette*, Ralph took *Field and Stream* (which Kathy also enjoyed) and *Outdoor Life*. Helen took *Saturday Review*, *Better Homes and Gardens*, *Life*, and *Horticulture*. For birthdays, they gave their children books and subscriptions to *Jack and Jill*, the *Mickey Mouse Club Magazine*, and *American Girl*.

Through their jobs, Ralph and Helen found themselves extending their family's literacy practices to a wider clientele. Ralph set aside his retiring self as he found new fulfillment in storytelling, picking out

---

19 *Algoma Record-Herald*, 15 January 1953.

tales to read to the children, and selecting the books to circulate from the van. He was very friendly, Kathy told me, and people all over the county came to recognize him. In the summer when she was about twelve or thirteen, Kathy drove around with her father on the bookmobile. At Rowley's Bay they would stop in the park while campers borrowed books. Outside the store that sold ice cream in Ellison Bay, library patrons—mostly women and children—would be waiting for the bookmobile. For these Door County residents, waiting for the van and browsing its contents provided social opportunities. Some boarded and struck up a conversation, while others simply picked their books and moved on. Ralph never seemed in a rush and was happy to chat to people as much as they wanted. Kathy's job was to help fill out the circulation slips and date-stamp them, while Ralph answered questions and filled out requests for books.

As bookmobile driver, Ralph became a significant local figure. Like Andy Kroeger, he made friends with readers and their families, and at least in part because people liked him, some were willing to support the service. But when Ralph retired in 1967, the Door County supervisors saw an opportunity to retire the bookmobile too. Their proposal met great resistance, however. "The first time they wanted to take it off the road, what a big protest there was," said Gayle G. "I mean it was huge. The radio—it was all you saw . . . in the paper so many people got behind it . . . Big fight that was." Gayle's family discussed the controversy with interest. "I remember them turning the radio on and hearing all these people on talk shows talking about why we had to keep it . . . People wanted so much to keep it after they got used to it, you know." Passions ran so high, Gayle remembered that her uncle commented, "I haven't seen a rebellion like this for a long time."

Once the supervisors capitulated to public opinion and decided to buy a new van, they also had to hire a new driver. Ralph would be hard to replace, the librarians no doubt thought. But by chance the classified ad came to the attention of Bob H., a Wisconsin native who had just moved back to Door County after spending twenty-one years on the West Coast as parts manager for a car dealership. "Well, why not try it?" Bob said to himself. "I like books and I've always been an avid reader. I can remember walking five miles when I was a little kid to get to a place where I could get books." Although he had never worked in a library before, his experience in the car dealership seemed relevant. After all, both involved classifying and retrieving. "I had a parts department, and a book department, it was similar to it as far as putting things in different places," he pointed out. Bob seemed like a good fit to the library staff, too. "We were looking, we had advertised for a driver," said Jane Livingston, "and he came in and stood there and talked a few minutes . . . There were several [library staff] around the room, and when he left we all said, 'That's the one!'" A strong factor was Bob's own love of reading. "Bob was a reader to start with," Livingston explained. Bob, too, saw the bookmobile as an ideal environment. "I fell right into it like a kid in a candy car with all [those] books," he said. "Which one am I going to read [next]?" But Bob also had a way with people, especially children. "He thoroughly enjoyed the kids," commented Livingston, "and he was very accommodating, you know, was willing to go out of his way."

Bob's new bookmobile held 2,700 volumes, arrayed on shelves. "All the sides [were] organized just like in the library, fiction, nonfiction, biography, children's section, and even the children's section were kind of sectioned off," he told me. As in the previous van, the children's area was arranged by grade level. "I had like kindergarten and first graders, . . . second and third graders then the . . . fourth and fifth graders. 'Course some of them, by the time they got to that, could read almost anything, which was fine. They could go to the bigger section. Then the young adult section, I had a young adult section for the high schools." Wives often had the task of picking out books for their husbands, and learned to rely on Bob to help make the selection. "I had some wives come in and say, 'Well my husband (or John or whatever his name is) likes westerns or likes mysteries—can you pick some out for him?' I'd start picking them out, and then first thing you know, they'd say, 'I can't pick them out anymore—you've got to pick them out!'" To avoid repetition Bob would keep little notes for himself about what patrons had already checked out. He also learned to plan ahead. "Mr. A. in Jacksonport, [his wife] would come over and get the books and I'd always pick a pretty good sized book for him . . . When I first started I'd give her four, and then it got to be six, and then eight, and finally I picked some out before I left the library in the morning if I knew I was going to that particular stop during the day sometime. I'd just take a box full of about twelve of them—[that would] usually last him till I'd come back the next time."

Schoolchildren, too, were expected to choose books for their parents. "One of the first times I ran across it was the old Garnet school, out there—little Barbara B.," said Bob. "She was looking up in the mystery section, and she was only in the second grade, and I told her, 'Barb,' I says, 'I don't think you could read these.' But, 'Oh I want some for my mother .'. . So I picked out three or four and she'd take them to her mother. So then it got to where Barbara would come to me, 'Mr. H., can you pick some books out for my mother?—she wants you to pick them out.'" Southern Door resident Gayle G. also remembered choosing books for her mother with the help of the bookmobile driver. "He kind of knew what she liked. Kind of the thing where . . . he'd pick 'em out, she'd read them, or I'd pick 'em out, she'd read them, and if she didn't like them I suppose she didn't finish them. She never complained because she worked 'out' so she couldn't get there." As a child, Gayle thought of the bookmobile's visit as a high point in her life. "I can remember when I was young, sitting on the corner waiting for the bookmobile to come. It was a big event," she said. "I mean, we just loved to see him come."

Eileen R. remembered checking books out from the bookmobile during summers in the 1950s. She and her brother rode their bikes from their farm to the village of Jacksonport where a small group of mostly women and children waited for the bookmobile to arrive. Sometimes she checked out books for her mother, too. "She wasn't a real big reader either, although she did enjoy it, but working on the farm, you know, they didn't really have a whole lot of time for that. But they were always excited . . . to know what books we were reading and what the books were about and we would tell them about it. But my dad was not a reader. Again I think it was just because they were so busy and then at night they were tired . . . but we were always encouraged to read." Although not great readers themselves, Eileen's parents passed on a value for reading; "My mother would always say there are so many treasures in those books and so many things to learn like experiences that you may never have. But by reading a book . . . we were always encouraged to read and we always had books at home."

Although women patrons predominated, Bob encountered "quite a

few" men who came to the bookmobile to pick out their own reading—
"Regulars—you bet!" He noticed that men had different reading tastes.
"Women loved the love stories," he said, "and men, they kind of kept
away from them. Westerns, I would say, the men were more into westerns, and mysteries, and historicals . . . Biographies I had to carry a
few of those along . . . [I]f I'd get a new biography in, why, they'd scarf
it up, you know." Fiction was most popular, but, Bob said, "The main
nonfiction moved, well I won't say as much as the novels, but I was for-
ever changing it." Women checked out "a lot of cookbooks," as well as
books about crafts and sewing. The van also carried reference books,
"just like a regular library." Bob drew the line at magazines, however.
"I never carried magazines—I just didn't have the room for them," he
explained. Paperbacks, too, presented a problem for which Bob found
his own solution. "People were donating so many of [those] paperbacks,
I'd go through and pick out a lot of fiction out of them . . . Well I had
some of the ladies that liked [those] romances, then I'd have a box of
those and they could just take them and . . . I'd write on the slips five
or six paperbacks. If they brought them back, okay. If they didn't it
was okay [too] because they were donated to start with."

Aside from these unorthodox practices, Bob followed professional
procedures, especially when selecting the books. He considered his
bookmobile just like a branch library. "That's exactly what I was, only
I was traveling." Bob ordered all his own books, mostly based on reading reviews. He was a particular fan of *Kirkus Reviews*, a publication
founded in 1933 by Virginia Kirkus, formerly head of the children's
book department at Harper & Brothers, which provided reviews of
books in advance of publication. At first Kirkus made her bimonthly
bulletin available only to subscribing bookstores, but two years later
libraries were also able to subscribe. Bob found *Kirkus Reviews* depend-
able. "I liked those . . . and I very seldom got stung with them. *Kirkus*
was a high priced review source, but you have to pay for that service
. . . If she said it was bad it's bad, and if it wasn't, or mediocre or whatever . . . I went with her pretty well, even with the children's books."
Bob also read reviews in magazines and newspapers. "Of course you
picked up magazines that came through the library—they always had
reviews in them. In fact I've gotten the *Chicago Tribune* all my life, the
Sunday paper, and their book section in the *Chicago Tribune* is pretty

good. I used to get quite a few out of that, you know. Okay: this book—might read the review, and I've got customers that might read this, so I'd order it." Once a month the Door County Library held a staff meeting, at which staff came in from the branch libraries to discuss book selection. Sometimes Bob was challenged to defend his choices, but he kept an eye on what kinds of books his customers preferred, and that usually provided sufficient justification. Still, his own tastes sometimes intervened. "I like history books—fiction, and nonfiction, historical novels . . . I probably leaned a little bit that way on some of those, but I never had any trouble getting them moved so I figured, well, okay."

Bob noticed different reading preferences in different parts of the county. "It's amazing [how] people down this [southern] end of the county read [differently] than people at the north end of the county," he commented. He was hard put to specify what that difference consisted of, but he responded to the patterns he perceived. "Certain novels would seem to move better in this area than they would in that area, so that way I could kind of—well, I'm going south so we'll take some of these. Or I'm going north—I'll take some of those." Sometimes the differences emerged from patterns of sociability on the van. Patrons recommended books to each other, Bob recalled. "We had a lot of the women do that. 'I just had this, can you give that to her this time?' You know it worked that way then. Actually the children were that way too. A lot of them were good readers. 'My girlfriend wants to read this, this time. Can she have it—can we have it back, or renew it?' Sure—sure, no problem."

Bob put much effort into loading his van with appropriate materials that he picked up from the main library in Sturgeon Bay. After visiting a large school "where four or five hundred books went out," he felt he had to replenish his stocks, because "I always felt when I went to a new school they had as much right to a full load as the last school." His designated space in the library was small, he said, so he organized the books in advance, setting them out in cartons and boxes that he marked according to content. "This was novels and these were young adults, this was fiction, or nonfiction, and this was fairy tales . . . you know, on down the line. I'd have to just get them out where I could work on them, and go through them—pick out a few, put them back on the bookmobile. There were lots of times I didn't get home at night until nine o'clock. A long day."

Over the next twenty-two years, until he retired in 1989, Bob H. became a familiar and well-loved figure, as generations of schoolchildren experienced his unique brand of librarianship. "One of the first grader girls I used to read to—I used to read to the first grade girls up at Peter and Paul . . . Before I left, she was teaching the first grade class at Corpus Christi, and [she said,] 'Mr. H. you've got to come in and read to my first graders!' Isn't that something? . . . I read to her when she was in first grade and now I'm reading to her first graders." From southern Door County to Washington Island, the bookmobile traveled the Peninsula in all weathers. "The bookmobile tried get up [to the Island] twice a year," Bob recounted. "About twice a year if the weather was right, we'd take the ferry and go to the school on Washington Island." Initially, he visited mostly rural schools during the nine months when they were in session, and made community stops mainly in the summer. "They consolidated the schools I think in '73 or '74 . . . I started making more community stops because the schools were all in one place. I would make the school stop twice a month for the lower or the middle grades, and then one time for the high school . . . [Then] we decided we'd go out on Saturday and . . . the kids could get to the bookmobile on Saturday too."

Because the northern Door County communities already had libraries, Bob—himself a southerner—concentrated his bookmobile stops in the southern part. "This whole southern area especially was farming— almost all farming," he said. It was hard for (male) farmers to catch the bookmobile on weekday stops, and consequently most of his "customers," as he described them, were women—except on Saturdays. "A lot of times on Saturdays if mom went shopping some place [father would] bring the kids." In the mid-century years, most women were full-time homemakers, although things changed as time went on, Bob said. "I had one case I can remember [in the] late seventies, I think it was or early eighties. She got on one day—she didn't seem right, she was always so bubbly—and she had three kids. She always brought her kids with her . . . but she read herself and the kids read, and she says, 'Bob, you know, I'm going to have to go to work—I may not show up as much,' and she was really down . . . on the fact that in order to keep the family going, she was going to have to go get a job along with her husband. And she says, 'I hate it. I hate it.' That's our society."

Things were changing in other ways, too. "[When] I first started, you'd go to these little country schools—if they had one shelf with books on it, that was unusual, really, except for their schoolbooks. You know, the textbooks. But just for reading, they didn't have it—they just didn't have it—so it was an excellent service." Later, however, schoolchildren came to rely less on the bookmobile, because the much larger consolidated schools themselves had better libraries. "We'd have to spend every day of the week down there at the big schools in order for them all to get through. So we decided that . . . once they got the new school they had a better library system . . . that helped them as far as their books were concerned." On the other hand, the weekend run brought children to the bookmobile in larger numbers. "A lot of the kids would come in, especially once I started on the Saturday run. Then the kids starting coming back to the bookmobile and getting books."

Patterns of use were also shifting. "There was a place up at Garret Bay just out of Ellison Bay that I went out into in the summertime," Bob recalled. "There were cabins there that people would come back to every [year] . . . I would go back in there and it'd be the same ones come back every year . . . One family was always up—it got to where mom and dad said, 'Well, the kids won't be up, they're too old. They got their jobs, they [won't] be here this summer.'" As time went on, however, the "old summer people" who came back "summer after summer" gave way to "Tourists—really tourists. Weekend or just seven days, maybe, won't come back for another three years . . . even if they [ever] come back." Then there was television—and the Internet. When Bob started his rounds in the late 1960s, he said, people used the library because they read for recreation, and they could not afford to buy books. In those days, although television existed, "it wasn't the cable system and satellite and all that. So it was just local stations, network channels, and they didn't have that many programs that the children would watch." But as the years went on, he added, "television became more popular and computers started coming in. [People were doing] less and less reading—you could tell it . . . Now if they can't see it on TV they pick it up on the computer, Internet."

By the late 1980s, the bookmobile itself was beginning to show its age. "Some days . . . especially in the winter time, you get way up north, or some days way south, you begin to wonder if you're going to get back with it . . . Well it was using a quart of oil every couple of hundred miles . . . It was on its last legs." Not only was the bookmobile unreliable, it was beginning to affect Bob's health. "Especially in the winter when it's all cold, and you sit way over the motor, and the cracks and everything were coming in. I'd be half sick by the time I got home from the fumes." Bob checked out the price of a new van. "We could have got a real decent bookmobile for around fifty-five to fifty-eight thousand . . . Milwaukee had just bought one for $150,000 down there. I went down to see it—just to see it, but we didn't need that." However, the county board—a new generation of skeptics—found even the lower estimate hard to swallow. "That county board—a lot of them (I probably shouldn't say this)—they didn't think it ever got used . . . [They'd say,] 'You never see anybody there, nobody uses it.'" Reluctantly, Bob made the decision to retire. "I think if they'd have bought [a new vehicle] I would have stayed on a couple [or] three more years." After he left, the library experimented with, he said dubiously, "a van-type thing . . . that went about two years or three, and that was actually more work." The driver had to "load up these book trucks, and put them in and tie them down, and then he'd go to a place where he could take them off and put them out" in places where people could come and choose books. It only lasted a few years, though. "It finally practically broke his back . . . so they just didn't hire [anybody to run] the bookmobile, which is a shame, because they could still use one."

Bob missed his job—the best job he ever had, he asserted. "It was a good experience for me. I really enjoyed it. I wouldn't take a million dollars for it. Nope, I wouldn't. I loved the people and I loved the kids. In fact I loved the kids when I quit more than anybody." Door County readers missed him, too. Everywhere he went people recognized him. "My customers . . . they come up to me, 'Hi Bob . . . I sure wish you were on that bookmobile again!' You know, I got a lot of that . . . [W]hen I'd go into town, or see somebody, why it was, 'Oh you've got to get back on that bookmobile, you've got to get it together, we can't find no books, you know.'" As the years passed this happened less often, he said, "Because those kids are getting older and they got their families, they got their own things going." But even recently, he said, it still happened occasionally. "About a year or so ago this young man come up to me. I was in the post office, and he says, 'Weren't you the bookmobile man?' I says, 'Yes, I was.' He says, 'I can remember you,' he says, 'you used to read stories to us when we was in kindergarten. He remembered that—stuck with him all these years . . . Made me kind of feel good."

A Library for Southern Door

Although the bookmobile service ceased its rounds in the 1990s, readers in Door County found other ways to boost library service. In the 1970s, Olivia Traven, now retired as librarian of Bailey's Harbor, spearheaded the drive to build a new county headquarters in Sturgeon Bay, to replace the old Carnegie building. Along with expanded library facilities, the building also housed the Miller Art Center, with a permanent collection of works by twentieth-century Wisconsin artists. And in 1981, eighteen women of the Homemakers' Club of the southern Door County village of Forestville (population around four hundred), tired of the fact that while northern Door County had several library branches, southern Door had none, took matters into their own hands and founded the first Door County branch library south of Sturgeon Bay. "When I first started on the library [board] I was always complaining about, you know, we have nothing, in southern Door," said Gayle G. "At one of the meetings [the Door County library director] said to me, 'Instead of complaining why don't you do something?'" Forestville township had been one of the southern Door communities that had turned down the Regional Library, by a vote of 253 to 302 (46 percent to 54 percent), and at first it seemed like an impossible task. "I thought, well, yeah right, but how am I going to do this?" Gayle said skeptically. "You know, you don't just go start a library by yourself."

But as Gayle continued to ponder the issue, a strategy occurred to her. A longtime member of the Forestville Homemakers' Club, she recognized in her fellow members a dynamic community force. "Those girls are pretty active—I betcha we could talk them into that." Although women's clubs, with their typically more urban and affluent membership, had a long history of sponsoring small public libraries, rural homemakers had no such venerable tradition to draw upon. But Gayle was right—the Homemakers' response was instant. "It didn't take a meeting. Just when I told them, everybody was for it. It was just like—there was no convincing." Rather than appeal to lofty principles of cultural uplift, the club members saw the issues mainly in practical, utilitarian terms. Many of the Homemakers were library users themselves, Gayle said. "If they weren't themselves, I think they liked their children to have ability to go to get some reference books without them running them around all the time . . . You work all day, and then you got to come home, and drive back to Sturgeon Bay to get reference books, and it gets late and . . . you get tired and pretty soon it's like, 'Oh we're not going to do that tonight,' and here they could just go and get one."

With help from librarians in next-door Brown County, the Homemakers inherited a collection that was about to be discarded. But space was a major concern. There was a room over the fire station, but the fire fighters resisted this suggestion, for fear, they said, that the women library patrons would park in front and block the fire truck. So they found space in the old one-room school. "We spent a lot of nights here scrubbing up books and getting ready," Gayle remembered. As they strove to turn the room into a library, the project gathered momentum. "Once it took off, everybody had their expertise . . . We had retired teachers . . . everybody, you know, they just all worked at it." Not everyone could come every night, but with whatever help was available, the group "washed books and stamped and scrubbed . . . to get the library going."

Working together on the library project gave the Homemakers an enormous sense of achievement, solidarity, and above all, pleasure. "They were great, I tell you," said Gayle proudly. "And it was fun. I think that's the part that has so many good memories. Everybody has good memories of it—there was no conflict . . . Just everybody worked together." Food played an important part. "We would bring rolls, somebody would bring dessert—we ate our way through the library process." There was always an element of the unexpected, however. "We never knew what was going to happen. It was . . . like the time when they had a potluck and everybody could bring what they wanted, and it was when angel food cakes were the thing—with the icing, I think. Thirteen ladies came with thirteen angel food cakes—that was all they had to eat. Isn't that funny? I mean—oh, how they talked about that . . . the year of the thirteen angel food cakes!"

Eventually the village constructed a purpose-built facility that now provides a community focus and that is free and is open to all. A few years after its opening, however, the "new" library was in need of some renovation, and Gayle found herself in the forefront of a fresh community effort, even though by this time the Homemakers' Club had disbanded. "I went and one day I said, 'I just can't stand this carpeting anymore—we need to do something.'" Gayle appealed to the village board for funds for some interior decorating. "I said, you know, 'I'm almost ashamed.' . . . Well, once we got going with it—as long as they didn't have to do any of the work—you know." Gayle and a group of volunteers added to the money that the village board provided with cash that they had raised themselves. "We bought the paint and painted and bought [the librarian] a new desk." They also had some help from the women who ran the Miller Art Center in Sturgeon Bay. "One of the gals . . . came one night and she said, 'Gayle you don't have any pictures!' and I said, 'No,' so then they gave us the pictures." Patrons noticed the difference and appreciated it. "We've had a lot of compliments from what it looked like before to what it does now." Like the old bookmobile, the Forestville library provides a space for social encounters. "It's almost like a social center in the winter when there's not much population," Gayle said. "People meet there, you know, go to the mail, stop at the library." The children especially love to use the library. "We have a nice children's area—they like to play in there, the kids." And the women continue to foster their reading. "I know my grandchildren—their other grandma takes them to the library," Gayle commented. "Their mother takes them to the library, we go—they love the library!" Yet the children "just don't know what an opportunity that is," she went on. "I just feel so bad I didn't have this when I was growing up because I would have been there all the time too."

After the referendum, Jane Livingston continued as director of the Door County Public Library. In 1954 she married Mayor Stanley Greene in the "wedding of the century," recalled a library employee. Together the Greenes continued to work and advocate for literacy and the library, Jane as library director and Stanley as politician, library board member, and regular broadcaster on local radio. Eventually

Jane decided to retire. Changes were taking place in the library world too fast for her, she said. "It's been a real good life. It's been fun. A challenge. And what's more, I think I have lived and worked in the best of times. People who work in libraries now wouldn't say that. I was between the one-lady libraries—I could take it from there up to the regional libraries—eight county libraries. I could help it along, but I didn't have to deal with computers. I don't even touch 'em. I just go and ask the girls."

Over subsequent decades, Door County libraries continued their mutual cooperation under Livingston's leadership, and the Door County bookmobile continued to roll into the 1990s. Statewide, the era of library cooperation was by no means finished, either. Strongly influenced by the Wisconsin-Wide Library Idea and experience with the "Idea in Action," Wisconsin librarians and WFLC officials continued to plan for regional libraries and to push for state and federal aid. By the 1970s patterns of collaboration were forming that would revolutionize the distribution of books and other materials through public libraries. Underpinned by levels of federal support inconceivable at mid-century, the future of public libraries seemed rosy indeed. Yet only a decade or so later, they were facing unforeseen challenges, as electronic technology offered up both fresh possibilities and new sources of threat.

9
Epilogue

The Wisconsin-Wide Library Idea . . . recognizes the State's
responsibility for initiating and subsidizing public libraries, a
responsibility directly related to a basic constitutional principle
of the United States—equal educational opportunity for all.

*"State Plan for Further Extension of Public Library Services to
Rural Areas," 1957*

With the election of Dwight D. Eisenhower as president in 1952, many
conservatives hoped to see Roosevelt's New Deal rolled back. In fact,
Eisenhower largely maintained the status quo with respect to government programs, neither retreating, nor pressing for new initiatives. In
the case of libraries, though, he presided over an expansion of government when, in 1956, with passage of the Library Services Act (LSA),
federal assistance to libraries at last became a reality. The LSA was
designed to improve library access specifically in rural areas. In 1956
the U.S. Office of Education had conducted a study that showed that
twenty-six million rural residents lacked any kind of public library service, and that an additional fifty million had only inadequate service.[1]
The bill provided for an annual appropriation of $7.5 million, to be
allotted to states according to the size of their rural population, and to
be matched by the states on the basis of their per capita income. Funds
could be used for salaries, books and other materials, library equipment, and operating expenses, but not for buildings or land. Over the
next five years, state library extension agencies added over five million

---

1 James W. Fry, "LSA and LCSA, 1956–1973: A Legislative History," *Library Trends* 24, no. 1
(1975): 9.

books and other materials, and over two hundred bookmobiles, to the nation's stock of library resources. Still, some resisted federal help. Arguments for and against federal involvement in library funding ranged on either side of a long-standing divide. Some legislators like Laurence Curtis (Republican, Massachusetts) envisaged the federal government's role as stepping forward only when states were unable to fill citizens' needs. Other opponents were particularly anxious to reverse what they saw as New Deal weakening of individual incentive and self-reliance. Yet others opposed the raising of taxes. Many combined these strands into defense of a conservative view of democracy that accorded only a minor role to federal government.[2] In the end, however, Indiana was the only state to refuse LSA funds. Indiana's Republican governor, Harold Handley, was reported as fearing that Hoosiers would be "brain-washed with books handpicked by Washington bureaucrats," and turned down $700,000 of funding in the first four years after the act passed.[3]

In Wisconsin, by contrast, the WFLC eagerly prepared a "State Plan" to support its claim to a share of federal bounty. This document reiterated many of the principles and practical suggestions first articulated in *The Wisconsin-Wide Library Idea*, declaring that its "guiding principles" were "as valid and applicable in 1956 as they were in 1948."[4] In particular, it urged local libraries to put forward plans for cooperative county or multicounty systems. Another impetus toward regional collaboration and away from local independence came in the same year from the American Library Association, when it issued a new set of standards for public libraries. Calling for "librarians, library boards, government officials and interested citizens" to assess "the adequacy of their present library services" and formulate "plans for improvement," the standards urged them to adopt a "cooperative approach," arguing that this was "the most important single recommendation" of the document.[5] Despite these official promptings, Wisconsin counties were slow

---

2 Douglas Raber, "Ideological Opposition to Federal Library Legislation: The Case of the Library Services Act of 1956," *Public Libraries* 34, no. 3 (1995): 162–69.

3 Fry, "LSA and LCSA," 11, 12.

4 "State Plan for Further Extension of Public Library Services to Rural Areas," *Wisconsin Library Bulletin* 53, no. 1 (1957): 296–97.

5 *Public Library Service: A Guide to Evaluation with Minimum Standards* (Chicago: American Library Association, 1956), 7.

to respond. By 1959, WFLC secretary Janice S. Kee reported that eleven counties were working on setting up county or multicounty libraries, but so far all were still at the planning stage.[6] Greater impetus occurred only after another decade of work by the library commission and the Wisconsin Library Association that resulted in passage of legislation authorizing cooperation among all types of libraries, especially school and public libraries, and providing for state aid for library systems. Senate Bill 47, hailed as landmark library legislation, passed into law late in 1971.[7] The following years saw a rush of new library systems, and by the beginning of 1973 four had been set up. In 1976, both Door and Kewaunee counties joined the Nicolet Federated System, along with five other neighboring counties. By 1987 all of Wisconsin's libraries were participating in systems, making free public library services finally available across the state.[8]

Public Libraries as Community Space

In the second half of the twentieth century, reliance on federal aid to public libraries became normalized, as gradually librarians and politicians dropped their opposition. In 1960 President John F. Kennedy authorized an extension to the LSA, and in 1963 encouraged the development of legislation to include urban areas and buildings in library funding. Carnegie libraries were aging, the bill's sponsors pointed out, and yet no latter-day Carnegie was on hand to finance their replacements. Kennedy was assassinated four days before the Senate passed the Library Services and Construction Act (LSCA) with only one dissenting voice—that of John Tower (Republican, Texas), who feared that government would exercise undue influence over what books would be provided. In January 1964, the House passed the LSCA by 254 votes to 107, and President Lyndon Johnson signed the bill on February 11. The matching grant authorization rose to $25 million, a

---

6 "The District Library Meetings, 1959," *Wisconsin Library Bulletin* 55, no. 4 (1959): 292.

7 "The Story So Far: Library Law Revision and State Aids for Public Library Systems," *Wisconsin Library Bulletin* 68, no. 4 (1972): 194.

8 Charles Seavey, "Public Library Systems in Wisconsin, 1970–1980: An Evaluation" (Ph.D. Diss., University of Wisconsin–Madison, 1987).

$20 million construction title was added, and coverage was extended to all counties (not just those in rural areas).[9]

Passage of the LSCA fitted well with Johnson's Great Society vision, which, with the Civil Rights movements of the 1960s, helped cement a rights-based understanding of citizenship resting on a foundation of federally supported individual claims to constitutional entitlements. In 1966, the U.S. Senate Appropriations Committee surveyed federal facilities for American Indians in the western states to determine the adequacy of state and library services and whether or not they were benefiting from state libraries, and found that thirteen tribes had small community libraries, most of them consisting of donated materials largely irrelevant to their needs and interests. In Wisconsin, though, the Menominee Tribe (previously residing on the Menominee Indian Reservation) formed itself into a county, declaring its independence of the Bureau of Indian Affairs. With the help of LSCA, in 1966 the county received a grant of $8,000 to develop a reference library collection and services, which the county librarian (granddaughter of a former tribal chief) targeted especially at children and young adults, since the county at that time contained few adult readers.[10]

Other communities used federal money to support bookmobile "outreach" services. In 1950 the number of bookmobiles totaled six hundred, increasing to nine hundred by 1956. By the early 1970s, swelled by LSA and LSCA funds, this number had risen to over two thousand.[11] In Fresno County, California, the public library used an LSCA grant in 1968 to buy a bookmobile to serve mostly Mexican American farm workers in the San Joaquin Valley. Called "La Biblioteca Ambulante," and staffed with Spanish-speaking librarians, the bookmobile carried materials in Spanish and English to remote rural areas. In the late 1970s and 1980s, with passage in 1978 of California's tax-cutting Proposition 13, the program fell victim to a series of cuts in service hours, routes, and personnel, such that by 1989 the bookmobile

---

9 Fry, "LSA and LCSA," 15–16.

10 Plummer Alston Jones Jr., *Still Struggling for Equality: American Public Library Services with Minorities* (Westport, Conn.: Libraries Unlimited, 2004), 71.

11 Barb VanBrimmer, "History of Mobile Services," in *The Book Stops Here: New Directions in Bookmobile Service*, ed. Catherine Suyak Alloway (Metuchen, N.J.: Scarecrow Press, 1990), 27.

department consisted of only two part-time library assistants. One of these, Owen Smith, who worked half-time with the bookmobile and half-time with the Fresno Corrections Department, described the result: "It's . . . very hard to get at the shelves when there are 30 to 40 kids inside the vehicle, all intent on getting their books before we have to move on." Smith's dual employment gave him a unique perspective. "What I see in the jail is, of course," he said, "the result of migrants not being able to acquire the information they need to learn English, to learn to read, and to cope with the system adequately . . . A lot of library work can be done for what it costs to keep someone in jail for a year."[12] Over a hundred years after Dewey first articulated it in the pages of the *American Library Journal*, the library faith continued as a powerful justification for library workers.

Rising oil prices and the high cost of vehicles deterred other communities from starting or continuing their bookmobile services, and, with passage of the LSCA, the federal government stressed the desirability of constructing permanent rather than mobile libraries. However, by the 1980s and 1990s, such building efforts had become the subject of great debate. Even before the widespread adoption of wireless digital technology a 1996 report titled *Buildings, Books, and Bytes: Libraries and Communities in the Digital Age* highlighted a discussion that librarians and information scientists were already engaging in: what should be the role of the library in the digital age? Based on focus group interviews and surveys with library leaders and citizens, the report found that although survey participants valued libraries for their book collections and children's services, nonusers of libraries were unwilling to pay taxes in their support, and libraries were felt to lag in adopting new digital technologies.[13] In 1996, the conversion of books into bytes was symbolized when federal funding for public libraries was renewed in the Library Services and Technology Act (LSTA). Further federal aid came in the form of E-Rate (or Universal Service) legislation, also passed in 1996, which helped provide network connections to libraries and schools at a discounted rate. In 1995 the Bill and Melinda Gates Foundation gave a

---

12 Rachael Naismith, "Library Service to Migrant Workers," *Library Journal* 114, no. 4 (1989): 54.

13 *Buildings, Books and Bytes: Libraries and Communities in the Digital Age.* www.benton.org/publibrary/kellogg/buildings.html.

philanthropic boost to the provision of computers in disadvantaged public libraries, and extended this program in 1997 to all state-library certified public libraries that served low-income communities.[14]

However, in 2000, President Bill Clinton signed into law the Children's Internet Protection Act (CIPA). This legislation required that libraries that received federal funding to support Internet access (through E-Rate or through the LSTA) should implement protections that would restrict young people's access to harmful or inappropriate materials (to be defined locally), and mandated the use of filtering devices on computers to limit young people's access to images that were obscene, child pornography, or harmful to minors.[15] Since the law did not distinguish between computers used by children, adults, or staff, it raised major questions about intellectual freedom and privacy among librarians and civil liberty advocates. The American Library Association mounted a legal challenge that ultimately failed in 2003 when the Supreme Court upheld the law. Between 1999 and 2003, public libraries had made 68,320 applications for E-rate funding, while many other public libraries received LSTA funds as part of a library system or consortium.[16] In effect, these libraries now had to decide between accepting government funding and at the same time ceding some control over the kinds of information materials they made available, or asserting their independence and forgoing federal aid. To some librarians, the warnings of those of previous eras who feared government encroachment upon local autonomy no longer seemed so quaintly paranoid.

Although the 1970s saw a flurry of library building in the wake of the LSCA, in the late twentieth and early twenty-first centuries developments in digital technology gave rise to a new rhetoric: the library without walls. Commentators speculated about the possible demise of

14 John Carlo Bertot, Charles R. McClure, and Joe Ryan, "Impact of External Technology Funding Programs for Public Libraries: A Study of LSTA, E-rate, Gates, and Others," *Public Libraries* 41, no. 3 (2002): 166–71.

15 Joyce Latham, "Positioning the Public Library in the Modern State: The Opportunity of the Children's Internet Protection Act (CIPA)," *First Monday (Online)* 6, no. 7 (2001). The act also covered schools receiving funding through the Elementary and Secondary Education Act.

16 John Carlo Bertot, Paul T. Jaeger, and Charles R. McClure, "CIPA: Decisions, Implementation, and Impacts," *Public Libraries* 44, no. 2 (2005): 105–9.

the "traditional" library, made obsolete (they claimed) by new methods of delivering information straight into citizens' homes via personal computers and other devices. Access to books and information became increasingly privatized, while an increasingly elaborate array of information technologies, from television to the Internet, accelerated the conversion of information from a character-shaping process to a consumer commodity, the product of a so-called information economy.[17] Several large-scale digitization projects ambitiously aimed to capture whole library collections of public domain and other out-of-copyright works electronically. Competing projects included Google Book Search and Open Content Alliance, originally supported by Yahoo! and Microsoft, among others.[18] The widespread availability of personal information devices scattered throughout a household, available in cars, on planes, and even when walking down the street, called into question the need and the viability of community-supported information spaces, like public libraries.

Nevertheless, cities large and small continued to build libraries. Sometimes the process was contentious. As we have seen, in the little village of Forestville, Wisconsin, a homemakers' club had to struggle for library space in the face of opposition from the firefighters. At the other end of the scale, when the city of San Francisco proposed to replace its central library (known as Old Main) with a new building, the library's move to its new quarters in 1996 was also highly disputed. Critics complained that the new building, though architecturally splendid, lacked space for the book collection, although providing ample room for computer terminals. A large number of books were unceremoniously dumped; just how many was not clear. Nicholson Baker, whose *New Yorker* article "The Author vs. the Library" ignited a blazing row, alleged that thousands of books had been sent in secret to the city landfill.[19] Library director Kenneth Dowlin dissented from this estimate, but admitted in an interview, "'I don't know, okay? Because I

---

17 Jorge Reina Schement and Terry Curtis, *Tendencies and Tensions of the Information Age: The Production and Distribution of Information in the United States* (New Brunswick, N.J.: Transaction, 1997). See especially 104–17.

18 Barbara Quint, "Who the Heck Is Tristram Shandy? Or What's Not Wrong with Google Book Search?" *Information Today* 24, no. 9 (2007): 7–8.

19 Nicholson Baker, "The Author vs. the Library," *New Yorker*, 14 October 1996: 50–62.

didn't count the books, and there are no records of what was discarded.'"[20] Participants in the San Francisco altercation lined up along a "books vs. technology" axis and the controversy itself came to symbolize an ongoing battle in the 1990s that pitted bibliophiles against technophiles. Underlying the ostensible clash about space and technology was a debate about reading and information. On the one side were those who argued for the importance of a sustained, reflective, literary mode of reading—the kind of reading that would help shape thoughtful, committed citizens. On the other side were those who saw in digital technology the means to organize and gain access to an overwhelming quantity of information. In the latter discourse, sustained reading was less vital than speed and availability of information access, in providing citizens with comprehensive knowledge about policy issues.

Librarians claim, though, that the digitization of books only whets readers' appetites to get their hands on the real object, and thus lures them into the library's physical space. Despite prophecies about the death of the library, at the turn of the twenty-first century commentators were moving away from the hyperbole of the virtual library to recover the sense of library as place. Chicago built a new downtown library in 1991 and saw its investment rewarded in higher circulation as well as higher in-library use. In *Better Together: Restoring the American Community*, Robert D. Putnam (also author of *Bowling Alone*, a lament for the loss of community in American life) commented, "No longer a passive repository of books and information or an outpost of culture, quiet, and decorum in a noisy world, the new library is an active and responsive part of the community and an agent of change. In addition, the Internet, which seemed to threaten its reason for being, turns out to be one of the things that bring people to the library."[21] The Chicago Public Library also built new branches. Putnam described the new Near North branch (located on the border between the mostly white, affluent Gold Coast, and the mostly African American and poor

---

20 Nicholas A. Basbanes, *Patience and Fortitude: Wherein a Colorful Cast of Determined Book Collectors, Dealers, and Librarians Go About the Quixotic Task of Preserving a Legacy* (New York: HarperCollins, 2003), 401.

21 Robert D. Putnam, *Better Together: Restoring the American Community* (New York: Simon and Schuster, 2003), 35.

Cabrini Green neighborhood) as a vibrant space where residents of all ages would come to use the Internet, hold book club meetings, take job skill classes, do their homework, display artwork, and borrow books. Both downtown and in Cabrini Green, the new libraries have been at the forefront of neighborhood renewals, Putnam points out.[22]

In 2008, the New York Public Library announced plans for a one billion dollar expansion of its famous 1911 building on Fifth Avenue. Leading the fund-raising effort with a $100 million donation, businessman Stephen A. Schwarzman explained the reasons for his generosity. "The library helps lower- and middle-income people—immigrants—get their shot at the American dream," he told a *New York Times* reporter. Library research had revealed that 60 percent of the system's patrons were members of minority groups, and 60 percent were from families with annual incomes of less than $50,000. One of the plan's main intents was to make the Fifth Avenue library more attractive to such users, by including rooms for children and teenagers, computer workstations, and a café. Drawing on language that would have resonated with library supporters a hundred years earlier, the reporter assured readers that books would be moved from a branch that is closing, and other branches would be refurbished, using as a model the Bronx Library Center which had become "a magnet for young people in the neighborhood, most of whom are African-American, Caribbean or Latino."[23] No debacle on the lines of the San Francisco Public Library was likely to occur here, the article implied, and *New York Times* readers could be confident that the library would still be fulfilling its role as providing a safe place where young people (and especially immigrants) could participate in worthy pursuits that included reading and writing.

Organizations as Sites of Reading and Writing

Throughout most of the twentieth century, reading and writing frequently took place in an organizational context. Government-spon-

---

22 Ibid., 36–37, 41–42.

23 Robin Pogrebin, "A $100 Million Donation to the N.Y. Public Library," *New York Times*, 11 March 2008.

sored community organizations like the agricultural extension agency, the rural school system, and the public library routinely provided access to standard forms of print that included informational genres like newspapers, pamphlets, textbooks, and other reference books, as well as literary genres like poetry, plays, and novels. Schools and libraries provided students and adults with opportunities to read for pleasure and cultural self-development, as well as pragmatically to fill gaps in their knowledge. These official sites of reading were also sites of writing. Extension-sponsored homemakers' clubs channeled reading materials to rural women and provided related cultural opportunities in the form of writing and performing plays and keeping journals. At school, students and teachers worked on writing assignments that grew more complex as students advanced through the system.

On the Door Peninsula, the public library was a resource for readers, and also for writers like Door County's Helen Arnold, who as a citizen and library worker made a project of writing to her elected representatives, as well as contributing pieces to the local newspapers. To garner community support for the Door-Kewaunee Regional Library, librarians often found themselves writing not only official reports, but also persuasive articles, and designing leaflets that sought to influence as well as inform the public about the library's services and the value of reading. Official organizations had close links with non-governmental but quasi-official institutions such as women's clubs, settlement houses, the Scouting movement, and the YMCA/YWCA. These voluntary organizations developed separately from but in close connection with those that received tax support. Women's clubs, for example, were independent associations that maintained close ties with tax-supported groups as well as with the political structures of their local, state, and national communities. Community organizations also intersected with the world of commercial print publishing and distribution in important ways. As major purchasers of text and trade books, schools and libraries had the potential to exercise considerable market power, especially through the agency of intermediaries like state and county superintendents of education and the H. W. Wilson Company.

Positions in community organizations included those that paid a salary, like teacher, librarian, home economist, and extension worker and those that did not—book club participant, Scout leader, women's club member, library patron. The extent to which individuals could take advantage of the opportunities offered by organizations varied according to factors of class, gender, race, and ethnicity. For middle-class white women from the Progressive Era onward, many organizations (especially those supported by taxes) offered employment or, in the case of voluntary groups, scope for the exercise of organizational skills and abilities, at least at lower managerial levels. For African Americans, Native Americans, Asians, and even white Americans of eastern and southern European descent, however, the range of organizations on offer was far more restricted. Native Americans found themselves excluded by law, custom, and distance, segregated as they often were on remote reservations that lacked amenities considered basic elsewhere. Asian immigrants, forbidden citizenship until the 1940s and 1950s, were not only subject to many of the same legal and cultural constraints, but were also neglected by public sector workers like librarians. Federal and state laws as well as local customs systematically excluded black Americans from full participation even in tax-supported organizations like the public schools, universities, and public libraries. In parts of the country where Jim Crow laws mandated segregated accommodations, schools, libraries, and extension facilities for blacks were always vastly inferior to those on offer to whites. In the north, too, access to technically unsegregated organizations was patchy and uncertain. Voluntary organizations, including colleges and universities as well as churches and self-help groups were organized by African Americans themselves, often very successfully, but tended to lack financial and other resources on the same scale as their white counterparts.

Immigrants and their descendants from northern Europe fitted more easily into the prevailing Anglophone and Protestant print culture than those from eastern and southern Europe, as religion, language, family structure, and work patterns influenced the place of print in peoples' lives. Some ethnic and religious groups created a parallel publishing structure that provided them with an alternative to that of the dominant culture, but the legitimacy of these was challenged by ideas of what counted as patriotism during two World Wars, and as successive generations learned through school and work that fluency in English was essential to meaningful participation in American society.[24]

The cultures of print established and sustained by most of the organizations described in this book operated in an inescapably racist world—one in which the significance of culturally constructed racial difference was so taken for granted that it went unremarked, at least by the white majority. The popular novels that public library patrons of all ages found on the shelves would have done little to shake acceptance of the belief that the racial and ethnic ordering of American society was anything but natural and appropriate. In this respect, the print culture fostered by governmental organizations like the extension service meshed well with that of the commercial publishers of best-selling novels to sustain a general acceptance of white superiority. Print culture organizations helped define what it meant to be an American, to run an American home, and to raise an American family. Over time, these organizations, their publications, and programs acted as homogenizing agencies, attempting to smooth out the effects of ethnic and racial difference.

Even after official Americanization programs had morphed into adult education, through print, European immigrants and their descendants on the Door Peninsula found their gendered domestic traditions confirmed or challenged in ways that had implications for what counted as appropriate roles and activities for men and women, girls and boys. For those white women whose class, religious, and ethnic background matched the ideals espoused by extension workers, teachers, and librarians, participation in a non-domestic cultural sphere provided possibilities for economic gain and cultural fulfillment. Even women born too early to take advantage of expanded educational opportunities could influence the development of their communities by joining voluntary

---

24 It would be a mistake, however, to conclude that the non-English press experienced a uniformly steady decline over the twentieth century. Although by 1960 non-English weeklies dropped overall by 76 percent relative to 1910, this fall was largely accounted for by a decline in the German and Scandinavian weeklies; weeklies in many other languages increased their circulation during this period. See Joshua A. Fishman, Robert G. Hayden, and Mary E. Warsauer, "The Non-English and the Ethnic Group Press, 1910–1960," in *Language Loyalty in the United States: The Maintenance and Perpetuation of Non-English Mother Tongues by American Ethnic and Religious Groups*, ed. Joshua A. Fishman (The Hague: Mouton, 1966), 54.

women's clubs. For poorer women or those with an ethnic heritage that resisted official values for literacy, their family's domestic expectations were more likely to clash with those of the extension and school officials. Extension homemakers' clubs gave rural women a chance for social and cultural interaction and for expanded reading and writing outside the tightly controlled world of family and church. Even in the late twentieth century, however, such modest ventures outside the home were still sometimes subject to a steady drip of criticism. Only determined resistance against such constraints, including attending and organizing meetings, discussing, reading, and writing, enabled these women to enlarge their geographic and cultural space.

By the early twenty-first century, struggles over ethnicity, language, and print had not disappeared. Indeed, they may have intensified in an information economy where, in the words of Jorge Reina Schement and Terry Curtis, "language becomes a strategic resource far beyond its importance in the old industrial era."[25] Latinos, Schement and Curtis point out, in pushing for more information resources in Spanish, might trigger old resentments about the place of languages other than English in American public life. Evidently ignorant of the history of Wisconsin's libraries in providing materials in many languages, in 2007 a Monroe, Wisconsin, resident sent "a barb" to the Monroe Public Library "for offering materials and a special night of celebration for the Spanish-speaking members of the community." "Will you be offering this also in Italian, German or perhaps Chinese?" expostulated this correspondent. "It is appalling that this country caters to the Spanish-speaking, but I never expected it to happen here. This is America . . . we speak ENGLISH."[26] The debate also played out in the pages of ALA's official journal, *American Libraries*, in November 2007.[27] Advocating in favor of collecting Spanish-language fiction, Todd Douglas Quesada argued that restricting such materials would affect at least sixteen million legal residents or citizens, and would alienate them from free and open information access. Opposing this view, Julia Stephens complained that by creating bilingual collections, librarians were "contributing to

---

25 Schement and Curtis, *Tendencies and Tensions of the Information Age*, 218.

26 *Monroe Times*, 9 November 2007.

27 Todd Douglas Quesada, "Spanish Spoken Here," *American Libraries* 38, no. 10 (2007): 42.

a divided America" and "undermining the American democracy that has created one nation for all." Librarians should focus their efforts on helping immigrants to learn English and "join the American culture," Stephens asserted, while recognizing their "duty to uphold the American way of life and save their English book and journal collections for Americans in the future."[28]

The "Right" Reading

Public library activities made visible complex beliefs and attitudes about reading that sometimes clashed with each other. Tensions persisted over the value of literature as opposed to mere literacy, over the value of useful information as opposed to stories, over who should be encouraged and indeed allowed to read what, and who should pay. Should libraries focus their efforts on adults rather than children? Should librarians accept a primarily consumerist (give them what they want) or educative (give them what they need) role? Libraries frequently appealed to values of informed citizenship in justifying their existence, but what did that actually mean by the middle of the twentieth century?

In the case of the Door-Kewaunee Regional Library Demonstration, ideas about literacy were contested from the very outset. To some extent, by encouraging the active participation of Door and Kewaunee residents in the implementation of the project, the officials of the WFLC made this diversity inevitable, and even welcomed it. Some library supporters saw the project as a valuable form of adult education, as well as a way to increase adult access to useful information. The library, these supporters believed, could help combat dangers to democracy presented by mass communication and increasingly sophisticated forms of propaganda. Other library supporters saw the project principally as a way of raising children to value books and reading. Local residents made selective use of the library collection in ways that expressed their

---

28 Julia Stephens, "English Spoken Here," *American Libraries* 38, no. 10 (2007): 44.

own values for reading and for information. Many adult women used the library to explore and extend their activities as consumers of goods and services for the home. Women also read stories with domestic settings, but few adults used the library to check out books on urgent political issues of the day. Opponents also appealed to a variety of arguments. Nervous about government encroachment on their independence, some opposed state or federal funding for what they felt was a matter for purely local control. Some librarians came into this category, along with others who had no interest in libraries. Into the latter category fell residents who saw spending money on reading as an extravagance that the community could ill afford. Some of these were not opposed to the funding of libraries in principle but felt that in the early 1950s military spending should take precedence. Yet others took issue with the kinds of materials that the library funneled into their children's hands.

In the past, as today, interlocking organizations like the public schools, libraries, and the extension service shared a value for the "right" reading as well as for scientific, rationalized information. But sometimes these categories of print presented separate and competing justifications for claims on community resources, as officials stressed a value of information in contrast to that of stories. At the same time, these distinctions were not necessarily clear to all participants. When a schoolchild or a homemaker read a historical novel, was she reading for pleasure or information? Did readers draw a line between reading for self-improvement and reading for fun, and if so, where? In the minds of individual readers, as well as of those who helped shape their reading, the boundaries between "literature," "stories," "information," and "trash" blurred and shifted, depending on circumstances of time and space.

Although it is probably true that all print cultures construct hierarchies of good and bad reading, the specific boundaries set around the literary field and the nature of the groups who attempt to set those boundaries vary over time. An extensive literature describes the stratification of reading during the nineteenth and early twentieth century, and explains this at least in part as an attempt to control the "chaos" resulting from the publishing explosion that accompanied the industrialization of print production and distribution, as well as the spread of mass literacy.[29] As scholars Joan Shelley Rubin, Janice A. Radway, and Jay Satterfield have shown, in the 1920s and 1930s commercial book clubs and publishing ventures like the Modern Library played upon the fears and aspirations of the upwardly mobile, who sought to shore up their economic prosperity with cultural capital (though not without opposition). Cultural authorities contended over who would establish and maintain a hierarchy of reading that left no doubt as to who and what were on the top and at the bottom. In a telling passage, Radway comments, "Many of the Book-of the-Month Club's critics took up an oppositional stance toward capitalism and the culture industry it funded, but they did so as members of an aristocracy of taste."[30]

Libraries played a part in this cultural contest. While the Book-of-the-Month Club and the Modern Library helped construct the "middle-brow" reader by distributing "expert" advice on a commercial basis, by the mid-1920s some public libraries also employed professional readers' advisers to help patrons develop their own reading programs along approved lines at no charge. The fashion for carrying out "scientific" surveys of the "reading public" also gathered momentum in the 1920s, '30s, and '40s. Bernard Berelson's contribution to the Public Library Inquiry drew on the results of a 1947 national survey of public library users along with a summary of all studies of library book use and users published since 1930.[31] Although these indicated that the "public" was overwhelmingly interested in reading fiction, Berelson condemned such reading of stories in terms that would have struck a chord with the profession's founders a hundred years earlier. In the middle of the twentieth century, library leaders continued to express reading values that they had inherited from their predecessors, and that they also continued to absorb from contemporary "aristocrats of taste."

---

29 For an overview, see Carl F. Kaestle, "The History of Readers," in *Literacy in the United States*, ed. Kaestle et al. (New Haven: Yale University Press, 1991), 33–72. See also Lawrence W. Levine, *Highbrow/Lowbrow: The Emergence of Cultural Hierarchy in America* (Cambridge: Harvard University Press, 1988).

30 Janice A. Radway, *A Feeling for Books: The Book-of-the-Month Club, Literary Taste, and Middle Class Desire* (Chapel Hill: University of North Carolina Press, 1997), 257.

31 Bernard Berelson, *The Library's Public* (New York: Columbia University Press, 1949), 137.

How were these values translating into practice in real libraries? The policies of Wisconsin's Door-Kewaunee Regional Library, along with the reminiscences of its participants, show that at least at this time and in this region of the United States, local librarians turned something of a blind eye to the strictures of cultural authorities, while many library patrons seemed unaware of them. Interviewees maintained that reading was neither common nor popular in the region at that time, and linked reading most strongly with ethnicity, rather than class or gender. While Scandinavians were credited with being "readers," other ethnic groups—especially Belgians—were not. Books and reading did not play an important role in the Belgian community, respondents believed, at least in part because little print material was available in Walloon. The presence of Belgians in the locality even stood in their minds as a rough index of an absence of books and reading.

Other residents remembered growing up in families that encouraged reading, and that contributed to their own love of it. For these teachers, librarians, and library patrons, what made their families "readers" was their preference for reading as a pastime, rather than the content of their reading. To these mid-century rural and small-town residents—even those professionally employed by print culture organizations—a reader was one who simply enjoyed reading a lot. Clearly they had failed to absorb the culturally authoritative message that devalued popular materials. A "reader" was one who read many books, including fiction, and who made little distinction between those reading materials sanctioned by the library and those that were not. At the same time, these readers did understand that there was a hierarchy of value in reading. "My English teacher asked me one day about my reading list," former teacher Emily H. recounted, "where I obtained those good books and I said, well, I had a card from the Sturgeon Bay library." Yet the act of reading itself had a value which transcended this hierarchy—what one read was less important than the fact of reading.

So does it make sense to describe these readers of popular materials as resistant—even as poachers? In some ways, far from showing resistance, the readers in this study had thoroughly absorbed a value for reading in general, a value that the library elite would surely have approved—in general. When proclaiming their fathers to be the "real readers" in the family, Jane and Kathy were applauding their accomplishment. They made no apology for the fact that the content of their fathers' reading failed to reach the approved standards of the day. In fact they seemed not to recognize that reading mysteries or westerns would have offended against the official canon. Thus they exercised far more autonomy than those claiming membership in the aristocracy of taste might, perhaps, have imagined. Far from defining their reading in terms of its difference from culturally approved reading, the further away from the seats of cultural authority that readers were situated, the less attention they paid to them. For most of the readers at the organizational sites described in this study, the aristocracy of taste was simply irrelevant.

Perhaps reading resistance and conformity are less diametrically opposed than print culture scholars sometimes assume. The rural women readers of Door and Kewaunee counties conformed to the cultural expectations promoted by major commercial publishers by choosing books and magazines that featured domestic consumerism. At the same time, in so doing, they were turning away from the traditions of their mothers and grandmothers. The women who joined homemakers' clubs eagerly followed the rationalized, scientific curricula laid out for them by extension agents, lessons that taught them "better" ways of cooking, cleaning, raising their children, and organizing their homes. But mere attendance at such club meetings did constitute resistance for those women, some of whom endured years of ridicule and disapprobation in their patriarchal communities. Librarians exercised local autonomy in knowingly rejecting the judgment of library leaders like Bernard Berelson by selecting books based on "popular" criteria, but at the same time they adhered to a long-standing civilizationist view of the value of reading that cast themselves as missionaries, with the task of converting members of the community to the library faith. When Marlene and Delores borrowed comics from their friends, they knew that their teachers and librarians disapproved, but they did it anyway because the comics were fun. As children they understood very well the hierarchy of reading that these professionals imparted to them, but were willing to take a risk in the pursuit of pleasure. In the long run, though, they came to believe that the comics were at least harmless, and in some ways might actually be beneficial after all. In the contexts of these organizations, resistance and conformity went hand in hand, and perhaps inevitably so.[32] In most organizational settings individuals have at least some choice about the ways in which they carry out their tasks and interact with each other.

We cannot assume, then, that simply because mid-twentieth-century cultural authorities condemned romances, mysteries, and westerns, actual readers of such literature were exercising resistance. Academic, professional readers like print culture researchers might recognize, too, that to define an act as "poaching" represents an attempt to delegitimize it. The naturalization of fish and game poaching testifies to the success of those who stood to benefit in legitimizing their claim to ownership of, and authority over, the use of these resources. In the analogous case of the poaching of literary texts by readers, we must ask, who stands to benefit from the establishment of a claim to authority over texts? The answer, it seems clear, is those who seek control over the stratification of reading—including academic, professional readers. Print culture researchers need to work hard at uncovering the reading values of real, historically situated readers. Otherwise, professional readers, members of a self-styled academic elite, are in danger of seeing themselves, like latter-day gentry or colonial administrators, try to expropriate the act of reading from nonacademic populist readers, and in the process produce and reproduce an aristocracy of taste.[33]

Scrutinizing the public library's history reveals that while library leaders demonstrated how they construed the ideal reader through their professional rhetoric, organizational structures, buildings, and collecting policies, these were not simply imposed on a passive reading public. Research into historical readers in specific localities can provide an important corrective to "top-down" analysis that over-privileges a monolithic interpretation of cultural authority. Such studies foreground readers' own choices and influences on local library practice—influences that

---

32 Perhaps only in the setting of what Erving Goffman called total institutions (such as maximum security prisons, quarantine hospitals, the military, and closed religious orders—organizations that aim above all for obedience to a strictly policed set of practices) would total resistance or total conformity on the part of individuals be possible. See Erving Goffman, *Asylums: Essays on the Social Situation of Mental Patients and Other Inmates* (Garden City, N.Y.: Doubleday Anchor, 1961).

33 See Christine Pawley, "Beyond Market Models and Resistance: Organizations as a Middle Layer in the History of Reading," *Library Quarterly* 79, no. 1 (2009): 73–93.

sometimes reinforced and at other times subverted official policies and goals. Local librarians, too, might diverge widely from authoritative recommendations; authoritative articles published in professional journals may not necessarily be interpreted as an accurate guide to actual practice. And official policy itself is never unified or uniform. Even in the nineteenth century, the rhetoric on reading in public libraries was divided as library leaders attempted to balance competing ideologies while promoting the health of this always financially challenged institution. In its own small way, the Door County bookmobile itself represented contested terrain. In selecting reading materials, driver Bob relied on the one hand on the stalwarts of standard professional collection development, including *Kirkus Reviews, Booklist,* and the *Chicago Tribune.* On the other hand, he was happy to "dilute" the collection with donated romances, mysteries, and westerns—paperbacks that patrons often returned, but sometimes did not. By investigating both the library profession's rhetoric and the experiences of specific reading communities, historians can show that reading as a cultural practice, and the associated identity of "reader," emerge in diverse forms from a complex set of environments. At any time and place, multiple literacies are in operation, sometimes in conflict with each other.

To bring to light the overlap among the various organizations of reading in this study—not only the library, but also extension service, the homemakers' clubs, and the rural schools—it was necessary to cast the net widely: to take account of institutional documents (including circulation records), to talk to rural residents, and to delve through secondary literature as well as primary sources into aspects of the women's lives that might initially seem irrelevant to their reading. Yet reading cannot be incised from the rest of people's experiences. To understand the meaning of reading in common readers' lives, researchers need to describe as many layers in the "sandwich" as they can. Only then can we get beyond the concept that reading consists of a series of discrete acts performed by individuals, to see it rather as an ongoing cultural practice deeply enmeshed in organizations and communities. A thorough-going attempt at thick description, then, can suggest entirely different kinds of answers to these tricky "how" and "why" questions. For example, the question "How did farmwomen read in the

1930s?" can be answered, "After dinner, while stretched out on the sofa," or "while mending clothes by the light of the kerosene lamp." Similarly, the question "how did children read?" might meet a variety of replies, including "by borrowing from cousins," or "by visiting the public library on their way home from school," or "by borrowing from the bookmobile at its stop outside the ice cream store." Such responses may appear inconsequential compared with the possible range of individual interpretive answers, but for the farmwomen themselves, the meaning of reading while lying on the sofa as opposed to reading while multi-tasking might be far from trivial. Similarly, to a school student, visiting the library on the homeward journey could signify unusual independence and autonomy. It is rather the researcher's own interpretation that has the capacity to intrude and perhaps mislead. Only by interrogating the social, material, and cultural circumstances that surround various practices of reading can the fear of misinterpretation be allayed and the truly diverse nature of people's print experiences brought to light.

Recognizing the role of organizations in providing opportunities for reading helps us discern the activities of those millions of ordinary readers and writers for whom the technologies and practices of literacy were and are an indispensable part of everyday life. Such a focus lets us build thick description by bringing to the fore primary sources that individual analysis might overlook. Collections of institutional records, including minutes, memos, correspondence, work diaries, publication lists, and accessions and circulation records, are rich repositories of primary source materials on print culture that require close scrutiny. It is clear from interviewing residents and perusing institutional texts that, over the course of a long career, librarians like Lutie Stearns and Jane Livingston had an extraordinary influence on the shape of library services in Wisconsin, and yet no record of their individual achievements explicitly appears in the catalog of Wisconsin Historical Society archives. This is often the way with women's history and the history of minority racial and ethnic groups, for whom reading and print provided one of the few available avenues for public engagement and personal fulfillment.

Public Library Records: A Endangered Species

For print culture historians, the records of organizations such as public libraries constitute vital primary sources—enduring evidence of the engagement with print of millions of ordinary Americans. Yet the survival of such records cannot be taken for granted. In the spring of 2006 I went back to the Wisconsin Historical Society to revisit the Door-Kewaunee Regional Library Demonstration records. I wanted to take a look at two photographs that my notes reminded me were rolled up in the third of the unprocessed cartons. Searching through the online catalog ahead of my visit, however, I encountered a difficulty. The entry for the Demonstration had changed call numbers, and now there seemed to be only one box, not three. Moreover, the catalog description made no mention of photographs. Not seriously concerned, and in no particular hurry, I waited until I was in Madison and could visit the archives in person. In the reading room I talked to a reference archivist and explained my problem. With his help, I reran my catalog search, and then together we looked through the recently reorganized files of images. The Door-Kewaunee photos were too big, I recalled, to fit in these file drawers—could they be somewhere else? It appeared that the only alternative was that they were still in a single archival box, so I filled out the usual form and requested it to be brought to my table. By this time I was beginning to feel a little concerned, but it was not until I saw the box itself that I realized that something was seriously wrong. The box was too small, I immediately realized, not only for the photographs but also for the thousands of circulation slips that the three cartons had previously held. Indeed, the only records left in this small box were librarian time sheets from the project—records that I had not found useful for my research. What could have happened to the circulation records and the photographs, I asked the helpful reference archivist?

He promised to pass my question on to the head of reference, and I left, hoping that the mystery would soon be sorted out and my anxieties allayed. But two weeks later, the head of reference e-mailed me with a sad story. Five years earlier, it seems, a public records archivist (no longer employed at the WHS), had appraised the WFLC records, including the three cartons of Door-Kewaunee records. This person's conclusion was "that the activity reports should be retained and the balance of the material destroyed because it lacked significant research value. Our records show," the head of reference went on, "that the material deemed unworthy of continued preservation was discarded in May 2002, leaving just the one box." The archives staff had reviewed this decision internally, he said, and also sought approval from relevant users, including university faculty members.

How could this happen, I asked myself in a state of shock, and was I myself in some way to blame? Obviously none of the archives staff or university faculty would have proceeded with this decision had they known that a researcher was still actively working with these records. What could I have done differently? If I had not been living and working in faraway Iowa, perhaps I might have heard of the appraisal project in time to prevent this destruction. Maybe it could have been avoided if I had not taken so long to complete my research, and if I had at least published some papers with more explicit titles. I had actually tried to present two papers in 2001 that had the words "Door-Kewaunee" in the title, but one of these conferences (scheduled to start on September 14) had been canceled following the terrorist attacks on New York. And even if it had taken place, would any of the key players have noticed? Given a perennial shortage of money, space, and other resources due to repeated budget cutbacks at the Wisconsin Historical Society, and a similar shortage of faculty at the University of Wisconsin at that time, the answer was probably no. [34] When systems are under the sort of constant financial stress that many cultural institutions face in the political climate of the early twenty-first century, it was hardly surprising that the decision to destroy these records had slipped through unchallenged.

All in all, I concluded, the destruction was a symptom of a fundamental weakness: the institutional frailty of the Wisconsin Free Library Commission. As institutions that many regard as non-essential (unlike the police or fire departments) libraries are at permanent risk—it is simply a fact of their existence. Merged with the Department of Public Instruction in 1965, the Commission no longer enjoys name recogni-

---

34 See, for instance, "Safeguarding a Public Legacy," Report of the Library-Archives Study Committee, January 2003. www.wisconsinhistory.org/libarch_study/report.asp.

tion or political standing. And library records, as library historians are only too aware, have rarely been valued by either historians or librarians. Given these circumstances, the amazing thing is that the records survived for so long. Ironically, it was probably a lack of financial resources that prevented their being processed much earlier—an act that in all probability would have resulted in the same outcome, but before I had had a chance to carry out my research.

The most helpful reading of this cautionary tale is as a spur to devising strategies for avoiding a repeat. Historians of reading need to work closely with archivists not only on their personal projects but also to further the interests of the field as a whole. Bringing to archivists' attention the importance of institutional, as well as personal, records in the history of reading is an important step. But perhaps even more, historians need to advocate for the public institutions that preserve the history of the public. If, against all the political odds of the day, librarians and officials of the Wisconsin Free Library Commission could persuade the state legislature of Wisconsin to fund a library experiment in the early years of the Cold War, surely print culture historians can do no less for public archives fifty years later.

Appendix 1
Wisconsin Free Library Commission Statistics

Tables in Appendix 1 are drawn from statistics collected by the Wisconsin Free Library Commission and published in *The Idea in Action*.

Table 1. Total Circulation, 1949–1952

Year	Circulation	% increase over 1949
1949	85,366	
1950	156,877	83
1951	205,907	141
1952	222,151	160

Table 2. Circulation: Library Units and Bookmobiles, Sample Periods

WFLC SAMPLE PERIOD 1: MARCH 15 TO JUNE 1, 1951

	Total Circulation	% of total
Adults (15 years old and over)	16,451	29
Juveniles (5–14 years old)	39,940	71
Total	**56,391**	**100**

WFLC SAMPLE PERIOD 1: MARCH 15 TO MAY 31, 1952

	Total Circulation	% of total
Adults (15 years old and over)	18,299	30
Juveniles (5–14 years old)	43,029	70
Total	**61,328**	**100**

Table 3. Circulation: Bookmobile Only, Sample Periods

WFLC SAMPLE PERIOD 1: MARCH 15 TO JUNE 1, 1951

	Total Circulation	% of total
Adults (15 years old and over)	3,642	12
Juveniles (5–14 years old)	27,986	88
Total	31,628	100

WFLC SAMPLE PERIOD 1: MARCH 15 TO MAY 31, 1952

	Total Circulation	% of total
Adults (15 years old and over)	2,758	9
Juveniles (5–14 years old)	26,886	91
Total	29,644	100

Source: *The Idea in Action*, 31

Table 4. Juvenile Circulation and per Capita Borrowing at Schools Served by Bookmobiles in Door and Kewaunee Counties, by Governmental Unit, 1951

Town or Village	School Enrollment	Books per Child
Door County		
Bailey's Harbor	39	26.4
Brussels	239	13.4
Clay Banks	55	24.8
Egg Harbor	171	20.4
Forestville	223	19.2
Gardner	130	22.7
Gibraltar	111	21.7
Jacksonport	132	19.3
Liberty Grove	177	19.4
Nasewaupee	131	24.5
Sevastopol	302	21.0
Sturgeon Bay	61	19.9
Union	80	26.6
Town totals	**1,851**	**20.3**
Ephraim Village	27	16.9
Sister Bay Village	53	20.5
Village totals	**80**	**19.3**
Door County totals	**1,931**	**20.3**
Kewaunee County		
Ahnapee	112	22.8
Carlton	148	30.6
Casco	86	23.2
Franklin	149	40.2
Lincoln	179	27.4
Luxemburg	93	29.1
Montpelier	156	22.4
Pierce	47	26.6
Red River	183	29.3
West Kewaunee	119	27.4
Town totals	**1,272**	**28.3**
Casco Village	118	19.7
Kewaunee County totals	**1,390**	**27.6**
Grand total	**3,321**	**23.3**

Source: *The Idea in Action*, 45.

Appendix 2
The D-K Database

The tables in Appendix 2 are drawn from the D–K Database of surviving circulation records. This consists of a single file showing data taken directly from the yellow slips themselves: patron name, book title, date, and so on. The total number of individual users was 1,816. But because it was not possible to determine whether all these individuals were male or female, young or old, the total number of usable names was reduced to 1,770, or 97 percent. The judgment of age is based on several factors. First, these early 1950s adults conventionally signed themselves Mr., Mrs., or Miss. This is the most important criterion. It is further validated by handwriting evidence (patrons filled out the slips themselves). If a mother of small children filled out their slips for them (in those days before daycare), the mother often also charged out a book of her own. A third and related factor is that patrons from the same family seemed to visit the bookmobile together, so that several siblings might charge out books at the same time. I feel confident of the general age groupings that result. I am less sure of the exact boundary of the "child" category. Older teenagers might well be counted in the "child" category. Overall findings support the project's official findings with respect to age, however.

Table 1. Gender of Adult and Young Borrowers (%)

	Adult	Young	All
Female	95	62	67
Male	5	38	33
Total	**100**	**100**	**100**

Table 2. Age Groupings of Male and Female Borrowers (%)

	Female	Male	All
Adult	21	2	14
Young	79	98	86
Total	**100**	**100**	**100**

Table 3. Girls' and Boys' Charges

	Charges	Percentage of total	Percentage of those whose sex is known
Girls	2353	46.5	62.3
Boys	1425	28.2	37.7
Total known	3778	74.7	100
Not known	1281	25.3	
Total children's charges	5059	100	

Table 4. Most Popular Titles

Author	Title	Pub. date	Charges	*Children's* Catalog 1951 Grade level
Ariane (Pseud. Georges Duplaix)	*Lively Little Rabbit*	1943	15	1–3
Tresselt, Alvin R., ill. by Roger Duvoisin	*White Snow, Bright Snow*** (Caldecott Medal 1948)	1948	12	k–3
Clark, Margery	*Poppy Seed Cakes***	1924	11	1–3
Bannerman, Helen	*Little Black Sambo***	1923	10	1–3
Grey, Katherine	*Rolling Wheels*	1937	10	7–9
Knight, Eric	*Lassie Come Home***	1940	10	6–9
Henry, Marguerite	*Misty of Chincoteague*** (Newbery Honor, 1948)	1947	9	4–7
Lenski, Lois	*Strawberry Girl*** (Newbery Medal, 1946)	1945	9	4–6
Alcott, Louisa May	*Little Women***	1869	8	5–8
Austin, Margot	*Peter Churchmouse*	1941	8	k–1
Cavanna, Betty	*Going on Sixteen* *	1946	8	7–9
d'Aulaire, Ingri, & Edgar Parin	*Nils*	1948	8	1–3
Emerson, Caroline D.	*Mickey Sees the U.S.A*	1944	8	Not included
Hader, Berta & Elmer	*Cock-a-Doodle-Doo* (Caldecott Honor, 1940)	1944	8	k–3
Kohler, Julilly	*Football Trees*	1947	8	Not included
Lippincott, Joseph Wharton	*Wilderness Champion: The Story of a Great Hound* *	1944	8	5–8
McCloskey, Robert	*Homer Price***	1943	8	4–7

* and ** *Children's Catalog* star and double star system

Table 5. Charges of Caldecott and Newbery Books.

Award	Girls	Boys	"Child"	Total children	Adults	Total charges
Caldecott Medal	13	14	13	40	1	41
Caldecott Honor	19	19	26	64	6	70
Total Caldecott	32	33	39	104	7	111
Newbery Medal	29	5	11	45	2	47
Newbery Honor	28	9	34	71	3	74
Total Newbery	57	14	45	116	5	121
Total Awards	**89**	**47**	**84**	**220**	**12**	**232**

Table 6. Most Popular Authors.

Author	Genre	Charges
Lenski, Lois (Newbery Medal & Honor)	fiction	85
Huber, Miriam Blanton	reader	49
Lindman, Maj	fiction	44
Bough, Glenn Orlando (4 with Bertha Morris Parker)	science	41
Gates, Arthur	reader	42
O'Donnell, Mabel	reader	34
Meader, Stephen W. (Newbery Honor)	fiction	33
Brown, Margaret Wise (Caldecott Honor)	fiction	32
Haywood, Carolyn	fiction	29
Tousey, Sanford	fiction	29
Mitchell, Lucy Sprague	fiction	28
Quinlan, Myrtle Banks	reader	28
Smith, Nila Banton	reader	28
Beals, Frank Lee	fiction	27
Parker, Bertha Morris	science	26
Mason, Miriam Evangeline	fiction	26
Potter, Beatrix	fiction	25
Buckley, Horace Mann	reader	24
Flack, Marjorie	picture books	24
Petersham, Maud & Miska (Caldecott Medal & Honor)	picture books, some religious	23
Tresselt, Alvin R. (Caldecott Medal)	fiction	23
Grey, Zane	fiction, westerns	22
Johnson, Margaret S. (some with Helen Lossing Johnson)	fiction	22
Lattimore, Eleanor Frances	fiction	22
Garst, [Doris] Shannon	fiction	21
Hader, Berta (& Elmer) (Caldecott Medal & Honor)	fiction	21
Hildreth, Gertrude	reader	21
Disney titles	fiction/picture	50

Table 7. Girls' Favorite Authors

Author	Genre	Girls' charges	Boys' charges
Lenski, Lois	fiction	44	22
Huber, Miriam Blanton	reader	20	12
Gates, Arthur	reader	19	9
Haywood, Carolyn	fiction	18	3
Mitchell, Lucy Sprague	reader	16	3
Hunt, Mabel Leigh	fiction	15	1
Buckley, Horace Mann	reader	14	3
Horn, Ernest	reader	14	3
Alcott, Louisa May	fiction	13	0
Lindman, Maj	fiction	12	12
Lattimore, Eleanor Frances	fiction	11	4
Mason, Miriam Evangeline	fiction	11	9
O'Donnell, Mabel	reader	11	10
Quinlan, Myrtle Banks	reader	11	7
Blough, Glenn Orlando	science	10	16
Brown, Margaret Wise	picture books	10	9
Grey, Zane	western	10	12
Hildreth, Gertrude	reader	10	6
Jones, Elizabeth Orton	fiction	10	0
Potter, Beatrix	picture books	10	9
Smith, Nila Banton	reader	10	5
Thomas, Eleanor	reader	10	1
Tresselt, Alvin R.	picture books	10	5
De Leeuw, Adèle	fiction	9	3
Jackson, Kathryn & Byron	picture books	9	6
Sondergaard, Arensa	various genres	9	3
Wilder, Laura Ingalls	fiction	9	3
Baldwin, Faith	romance	8	1
Evers, Helen & Alf	picture books	8	3
Garst, Shannon	fiction	8	7
Norris, Kathleen	romance	6	2
Disney	fiction/picture books	30	12
WPA Writers' Project	nonfiction	17	12

Table 8: Girls' Favorite Titles

Author	Title	Pub date	Genre	Charges	*Children's Catalog* 1951 Grade level
McDevitt, Jean	Mr. Apple's Family	1950	fiction	7	not included
Tresselt, Alvin R.	*White Snow, Bright Snow* ** (Caldecott Medal 1948)	1947	picture book	7	k–3
Alcott, Louisa May	*Little Women* **	1869	fiction	6	5–8
Emerson, Caroline D. (Disney)	*Mickey Sees the U.S.A.*	1944	picture book	6	not included
Gay, Romney	*Home for Sandy*	1942	reader	6	not included
Huber, Miriam Blanton	*I Know a Story*	1938	reader	6	not included
Hunt, Mabel Leigh	*Matilda's Buttons*	1948	fiction	6	not included, but other titles
Lenski, Lois	*Strawberry Girl* ** (Newbery Medal, 1946)	1945	fiction	6	4–6
Disney, Walt	*Dumbo of the Circus*	1941	picture book	5	not included
Jones, Elizabeth Orton	*Little Red Riding Hood*	1948	picture book	6	not included, but other titles
Reely, Mary Katherine	*Seat Mates*	1949	fiction	6	3–5
Buckley, Horace Mann	*In Storm and Sunshine*	1938	reader	5	not included
Buckley, Horace Mann	*In Town and Country*	1938	reader	5	not included
Cavanna, Betty	*Going On Sixteen* *	1946	fiction	5	7–9
Hunt, Mabel Leigh	*Double Birthday Present*	1947	fiction	5	1–3
Horn, Ernest, & Grace M. Shields	*Making New Friends*	1940	reader	5	not included
Lenski, Lois	*Little Auto*	1934	picture book	5	not included, but other "Little" titles
Gray, William S.	*We Look and See*	1946	reader	5	not included
Quinlan, Myrtle Banks	*To and Fro*	1939	reader	5	not included
Voight, Virginia Frances	*Apple Tree Cottage*	1949	fiction	5	4–6
Periodical	*Women's Home Companion*			5	—

* and ** *Children's Catalog* star and double star system

Table 9. Boys' Favorite Authors

Author	Genre	Boys' charges	Girls' charges
Lenski, Lois	fiction	22	44
Blough, Glenn Orlando (4 with Bertha Morris Parker)	science	16	10
Tousey, Sanford	fiction	16	4
Beals, Frank Lee	western	13	7
Grey, Zane	western	12	10
Huber, Miriam Blanton	reader	12	20
Lindman, Maj	picture books	12	12
Meader, Stephen W.	fiction	11	6
Parker, Bertha Morris	science	11	5
O'Donnell, Mabel	reader	10	11
Petersham, Maud & Miska	picture books	10	6
Williamson, Hamilton	picture books	10	2
Brown, Margaret Wise	picture books	9	10
Burton, Virginia Lee	picture books	9	2
Flack, Marjorie	picture books	9	5
Gates, Arthur	reader	9	19
Hader, Berta	picture books	9	3
Lippincott, Joseph Wharton	fiction	9	1
Mason, Miriam Evangeline	various genres	9	11
Osswald, Edith, & Mary Maud Reed	reader	9	5
Potter, Beatrix	picture books	9	10
Farley, Walter	fiction	8	3
Gramatky, Hardie	picture books	8	1
Disney	fiction	12	30
WPA Writer's Project	nonfiction	12	17

Table 10. Boys' Favorite Titles

Author	Title	Pub. date	Genre	Charges	*Children's Catalog/* 1951 Grade level
Ariane (Pseud. Georges Duplaix)	*Lively Little Rabbit*	1943	picture book	7	1–3
Lippincott, Joseph Wharton	*Wilderness Champion: The Story of a Great Hound* *	1944	fiction	7	5–8
Beals, Frank Lee	Buffalo Bill	1943		5	not included
Bond, Guy Loraine	*Three of Us*	1949	reader	5	not included
Burton, Virginia Lee	*Katy and the Big Snow* **	1943	picture book	5	1–3
Gramatky, Hardie	*Little Toot* **	1939	picture book	5	1–3
Osswald, Edith, & Mary Maud Reed	*My Dog Laddie*	1941	reader	5	not included
Austin, Margot	*Peter Churchmouse*	1941	picture book	4	k–1
Bannerman, Helen	*Little Black Sambo* **	1923	picture book	4	1–3
Battle, Florence	*Jerry Goes Fishing*	1942	picture book	4	not included
Blough, Glenn Orlando, & Bertha Morris Parker	*Animals and Their Young*	1945	science	4	1–3
Bontemps, Arna, & Jack Conroy	*Fast Sooner Hound* **	1942	fiction	4	1–4
Brown, Margaret Wise	*Little Farmer*	1948	picture book	4	not included, though other titles
Brown, Vinson	*John Paul Jones*	1949	history	4	not included
Crampton, Gertrude	*Tootle*	1945	picture book	4	CC '46 1–3
Farley, Walter	*Son of the Black Stallion*	1947	fiction	4	whole series, 7–9
Hader, Berta & Elmer	*Cock-a-Doodle-Doo* * (Caldecott Honor, 1940)	1939	picture book	4	k–3

(Table 10 continued)

Author	Title	Pub. date	Genre	Charges	*Children's Catalog*/ 1951 Grade level
Johnson, Margaret S., & Helen Lossing Johnson	*Dixie Dobie, a Sable Island Pony*	1945	fiction	4	*CC '46* 3–5
Johnson, Margaret S., & Helen Lossing Johnson	*Smallest Puppy*	1940	fiction	4	2–4
Lenski, Lois	*Little Sail Boat*	1937	fiction	4	no, but other books
Meader, Stephen W.	*River of the Wolves*	1948		4	7–9
Petersham, Maud Fuller & Miska	*American ABC* * Caldecott Honor	1941	biography	4	3–6
Stong, Phil	*Honk the Moose* **	1935	fiction	4	4–5
Tousey, Sanford	*Jerry and the Pony Express* *	1936	fiction	4	3–5
Williamson, Hamilton, & Elmer Hader	*Baby Bear*	1930	picture book	4	not included
Periodical	*Boys Life*			7	--
Periodical	*National Geographic*			5	--
Periodical	*Saturday Evening Post*			5	--
Periodical	*Sports Afield*			5	--
Periodical	*Time*			5	--

* and ** *Children's Catalog* star and double star system

Index

Christine Pawley is professor and director at the School of Library and Information Studies and director of the Center for the History of Print Culture at the University of Wisconsin–Madison. Her book *Reading on the Middle Border: The Culture of Print in Late-Nineteenth-Century Osage, Iowa* was published by the University of Massachusetts Press in 2001 and was co-winner of the 2002 Benjamin Shambaugh Award from the State Historical Society of Iowa for the best book on Iowa history.